SO MANY STARS

* * * * * * * * * * * * *

SO MANY STARS

* * * * * * * * * * * * * *

AN ORAL HISTORY OF TRANS, NONBINARY, GENDERQUEER, AND TWO-SPIRIT PEOPLE OF COLOR

* * * * * * * * * * * * * *

CARO DE ROBERTIS

ALGONQUIN BOOKS OF CHAPEL HILL
LITTLE, BROWN AND COMPANY

Algonquin Books of Chapel Hill / Little, Brown and Company
Hachette Book Group
1290 Avenue of the Americas, New York, NY 10104
algonquinbooks.com

First Edition: May 2025.
Algonquin Books of Chapel Hill is an imprint of Little, Brown and Company, a division of Hachette Book Group, Inc. The Algonquin Books name and logo are trademarks of Hachette Book Group, Inc.

The publisher is not responsible for websites (or their content) that are not owned by the publisher.

The Hachette Speakers Bureau provides a wide range of authors for speaking events. To find out more, go to hachettespeakersbureau.com or email hachettespeakers@hbgusa.com.

Little, Brown and Company books may be purchased in bulk for business, educational, or promotional use. For information, please contact your local bookseller or the Hachette Book Group Special Markets Department at special.markets@hbgusa.com.

Design by Steve Godwin.

ISBN 9781643756875 (hardcover)
ISBN 9781643756905 (ebook)
LCCN 2025931858

Printing 1, 2025
LSC-C
Printed in the United States of America

For queer and trans people of color everywhere

CONTENTS

* * * * * * * * *

SO MANY STARS

* * * * * * * * * * * * * * *

INTRODUCTION

* * * * * * * * * * * *

SAN FRANCISCO, CALIFORNIA, 2022. Adela Vázquez opens her door impeccably dressed, the picture of elegance at sixty-four years old. She leads me through her brightly decorated Victorian flat to the kitchen, where she's prepared a feast for my visit: finger sandwiches and a cake baked from scratch. I'm here to interview her about her life as a trailblazing activist, drag performer, trans Latina refugee, and mentor to younger trans generations. I feel incredibly lucky to be in her presence, given access to her stories and her voice. The fact that she also stayed up late baking a cake for me—for us, for this encounter—is so moving that I fight the urge to weep.

There is so much I long to say, that aches in my throat, unspoken. About what every one of these interviews means to me personally, as a Latinx immigrant who's had their own long journey to claiming the many gender terms that personally resonate: genderqueer, gender fluid, nonbinary, transmasculine, butch, and woman. About what it would mean for kids of my children's generation—the youths I've met at their middle school Queer and Sexuality Alliance—to meet someone like Adela, to know their identities have roots, a precedent, a heritage. About the overwhelming love and awe I feel after each conversation that contributed to this oral history, along with a hunger to share what I've heard with the world.

I hold these thoughts in, because this afternoon is not about me. My hostess and I chat in Spanish as we eat the delicious refreshments and sip tea. Afternoon light pours over us, gilding the porcelain cups. We laugh and talk until it's time to set up the recording equipment, and begin.

A GENDER REVOLUTION is happening in our culture. It is not without roots; it is not new. Today's trans and gender-expansive movements are part of a deep, rich story. Gender variance beyond the binary has existed throughout history, in every society, as natural as any other part of human existence. And yet, even in an era of increasing visibility for trans and gender-nonconforming people, legislative attacks on our rights have also risen sharply. Meanwhile, mainstream portrayals of trans and nonbinary lives rarely feature elder generations, let alone elders of color. A myth persists that transness is an invention of the young, a "fad" that can be easily dismissed.

But the truth is that those of us who are trans, nonbinary, genderqueer, two-spirit, or otherwise gender variant have a lineage; we have an inheritance; we are part of radiant cultures and histories. As for elder trans and gender-nonconforming folks of color, they are right here among us with plenty to say. Their lives are testaments to our true histories, and to the intersectionality at the heart of real freedom. Their voices are essential to a full picture of who we are as a society, and who we might become.

This book gathers the voices of twenty such elders. Among them are trans, genderqueer, nonbinary, genderfluid, butch, two-spirit, transfeminine, and transmasculine people. They are Black, Latinx, Indigenous, and Asian/Pacific Islander; they hail from Mexico and the Philippines, Panama and China, Chicago and Texas and throughout the United States. At the time of interview—in 2022 and 2023—they were in their fifties, sixties, and seventies. Some of them spoke to me in Spanish, or in a mix of Spanish and English. Sharyn Grayson and Tina Valentín Aguirre, among others, spoke passionately about their past and present roles as trailblazing community leaders, while Tupili Lea Arellano, C. Njoube Dugas, and others described the everyday activism they contributed to social movements. Artists—from drag icons Landa Lakes and Donna Personna to punk musician KB Boyce and queer tango leader Andrés Ozzuna—spoke to the intersection of creativity and gender liberation. Nicky Calma and Bamby Salcedo each traced their journeys from immigrant sex worker to groundbreaking leader for trans rights. From Chino Scott-Chung and Joan Benoit's journeys into queer parenthood to Yoseñio Lewis and StormMiguel Florez's forays into liberation through kink, from early memories of awareness of one's true gender to the milestones of transition, everyone I interviewed had a unique, potent story to tell. (More details on each elder can be found in the About the Narrators section.)

Collecting these stories, and weaving them together, has been one of the greatest honors of my life.

The work began as a fellowship with the *I See My Light Shining* oral history project, helmed by the visionary writer and MacArthur Fellow Jacqueline Woodson. This project brought together ten writers from across the country to record interviews with elders of color. My particular focus was BIPOC queer and trans elders. I developed a list of narrators through a combination of my own community networks, extensive research, and word of mouth. I traveled to the kitchens, living rooms, and offices of these extraordinary people with my microphone, recorder, and open ears.

I heard treasures. I heard riveting anecdotes, rare intimacies, keen beauty. I heard behind-the-scenes tales of what it meant—and still means—to forge an authentic path through the world against the odds. What is it like to experience your gender in childhood, in a culture where absolutely no mirrors or language exist that reflect who you are? What was it like for people of color to come out—and to defy gender norms— in the seventies, eighties, and nineties? How do BIPOC queer and trans people seek and weave community and chosen family in the world? How have dramatic historical tides such as the AIDS epidemic, early drag scenes, and queer-led social justice movements transformed people's personal lives?

The more listening I did, the more I was inspired by what I was hearing, and its potential to delight, entrance, and heal. As a novelist, I sensed the narrative power pulsing through their testimonies. And the more I listened, the more I felt the makings of a great tapestry, a collective story of how trans and gender-variant people of color defied society's notions of gender and race to innovate cultural spaces where they—and future generations—could more fully exist.

It's a vast, exhilarating story. And a true one. Each individual voice weaves through it, a luminous thread.

I wrote this book to offer readers that intricate tapestry, that collective history, as well as views of the particular threads that glimmer within it. In these pages, I hope to capture some of the lived experiences that have gone unrecognized by official histories for far too long, yet have made our current reality possible. I also hope to pay tribute to these remarkable people who broke ground with their social actions and everyday lives, and to convey some of the beauty and power of their journeys.

THIS BOOK DRAWS ITS TITLE from the words of one of its narrators, Crystal Mason, who, in the chapter "What Is Gender to You?," describes a sky full of stars as a metaphor for the evolving lexicon of gender terms and pronouns. "You look up and you see a million stars. You know some of those stars are what's possible for your life. . . . We create possibilities when we create new words, and new understandings." Mason's words speak to a vision of expansiveness, not only for the language of gender, but for the very way we approach the human experience. We can be enriched by recognition of difference, of nuance, of vast possibility. In that spirit, each of these narrators has had an utterly unique trajectory, yet at the same time is an essential part of the broader landscape of queer and trans BIPOC history, that is to say, all our history; history itself.

I've divided the book into four parts: "Emergence"; "Forging Lives"; "Being the Change"; and "Horizons." If you wish to read from cover to cover, you'll find a narrative arc to carry you. However, if you're compelled by particular themes or topics, there is room here for nonlinear reading as well.

For example, a trans youth hungry to hear of how previous generations fostered community in the face of familial transphobia might begin with chapter 7: "Chosen Family," then turn to chapter 14: "Thoughts for Younger Generations" for insight, encouragement, and expressions of love. A queer artist seeking inspiration in past creative endeavors might open chapter 10: "Art and Expression" and chapter 11: "The Art and Power of Drag." A cis parent wondering what gender nonconformity can look and feel like in childhood might start with chapter 1: "Glimmers in Childhood" and chapter 2: "Family Matters," while a student of resistance movements and activism will find riches in chapter 8: "Activism," and chapter 9: "The AIDS Crisis."

Whichever approach you take, whatever your connection to these stories may be, I hope they speak to you. These stories shed light on our collective past, and our possible futures. I hope they offer you insights, mirrors, wonder, joy, a depth of understanding. I hope they offer you a chance to see the world anew.

con mucho amor,
Caro

PART ONE

* * * * * * *

EMERGENCE

* *

ONE

Glimmers in Childhood

ADELA VÁZQUEZ: I knew from the very beginning. From the age of four.

TUPILI LEA ARELLANO: I knew very early. I didn't have the verbal cognition, but I knew I was different. I never said I wanted to be a boy, but I didn't want to be a girl. I didn't want to be either/or, you know what I'm saying?

YOSEÑIO LEWIS: I knew from Day One, the moment of consciousness, that I was different. I was aware that I was a problem for some people. In my world, I was a boy. I played with boys, I was a boy, and that's all there was to it.

STORMMIGUEL FLOREZ: Everybody thought I wanted to be a boy. That just felt foreign to me, to want to be another gender. It felt wrong and embarrassing in some way, and I don't even remember secretly feeling like I wanted to be a boy. I just felt like I wanted to be who I am.

JOAN BENOIT: Oh my god, I've always been read as queer. From a young age. I distinctly remember a day, when I was seven years old: my great-grandmother was in from the reservation. At that point, great-grandma must have been in her eighties, early nineties. She was from the Chippewas of the Thames First Nation. She was in Michigan as a young person, born and raised with traditional ways. When the French came, she and her family went to Canada to try to avoid being put on a reservation and she didn't get put on a reserve until she was in her twenties. She was my mom's grandma. She was cool. Grandma Rose. I have a picture of her somewhere. We were visiting, and she said to my mom—I was sitting on my mom's lap—she said, "I thought you had three boys and two girls."

And my mom said, "I do."

And she said, "Oh this one, this one here's a special one. You need to pay attention." Like she knew who I was.

She said it and looked me right in the eye.

She knew me.

My mom spent her life ignoring the traditional teachings. She was trying to assimilate. Out of all of my siblings, I think I'm the most Native-identified. I'm Anishinaabek, from Michigan, an Ojibwe woman. It's always gone back to the traditional ways. And not the colonizers' ways. The way I build community and the way I try to carry myself, it's an understanding that I'm going to be an ancestor just like them. That's a lot of the work around identifying as two-spirit. There are teachings that we need to bring back.

My parents didn't get me. I felt misunderstood my whole life by them. And then my great-grandmother understood who I was.

I've carried that moment with me my whole life.

LANDA LAKES: I grew up in South Central Oklahoma. We didn't live in town, but in a little space between Stonewall and Tupelo. We were right in the middle.

We lived on Indian land, we were extremely poor, so we didn't really have neighbors. We lived in this really old house, my mom, my dad, my sister, and myself. We didn't have regular running water, we had water that came from a well. That was pretty much my youth. Sometimes we had electricity, and sometimes we didn't, because my father found it very difficult to get work in Oklahoma as a full-blood person. It was hard for him to find work and keep it. A lot of people didn't want to hire Native people back then, so he often would work further away, near Oklahoma City or down in Texas.

I was my grandfather's favorite grandchild. I was always with my grandpa. I would spend the night over with my grandpa, and in the mornings, when dawn came, he would get up and sing these prayers in Chickasaw, or Choctaw. And it influenced me enough that throughout my life, it's the first thing that goes through my mind when I wake up in the morning: I do a prayer. I do a prayer every morning. I think that's really helped me a lot.

It's helped me to retain a lot of the Chickasaw language. It isn't spoken out here, because nobody knows it. My grandpa always warned me that if you didn't speak Chickasaw every day, you're going to lose it, it just fades. I don't think I would have retained it if I didn't pray every morning.

I thought it was unfair that my sister got to be a girl, but somehow I didn't get to be one. I was disappointed about that a lot. At the same time, there were many moments of delight that I had, when people would sometimes think that I was my sister's sister. I had long hair. I always thought, "Oh look, I'm pretty!" I always thought girls were pretty.

ADELA VÁZQUEZ: I was born in a little town in Cuba. In the carnivals, I would dress like a girl. You were not supposed to do this, but I was always a girl. Always. Since I remember. From very young. I was a fat kid. I was a fat, loud, queeny little kid.

In a way, everybody knew that I was a girl.

MS BILLIE COOPER: I was born in Philadelphia, Pennsylvania, in 1958. We weren't poor; I wouldn't say we were poor. My family had the basic needs. My mother and father worked two or three jobs each. We were just on a daily trajectory of living, surviving.

Then I started noticing the world. Other things around me. Around five or six years old, I started noticing that I was different. When I was eight to ten, I was like the mother of the neighborhood. Instead of playing hockey or football, or you know, riding mountain bikes and all that, I was playing with Susie-Bake ovens.

I was called homosexual, you faggot, you sissy. You dick-sucker, you cum-catcher. As Black people, at least for me, I wasn't called queer.

I would say something smart to them, and have other people laugh with me at them.

I was always a jokester; I always had people laughing. Sometimes at me, but most of the time with me. That was the way I got through life without having to fight.

It came from other Black people, that need to tear me down. Back then, growing up, there was no booklet on how to treat people that were different from you. My mother and father didn't have a booklet on raising children. No booklet on how to raise this Black child, how to keep this Black child safe. It was a hit-and-miss, for everything.

When I was just beginning to find myself, I would hear all the negative stuff. I would be compared to so many negative institutionalized words about myself, and meanings about myself, and what people thought about me. I was real vulnerable back then. I wasn't hurting nobody. But so many people told me I was an abomination, I would die, I didn't mean anything to nobody, you know, my life had no meaning. And it was just, that's the way of the world; that's the way of the world. And being Black back then, I didn't really have a whole lot of outlets to voice my opinion, and to voice how I felt I should live my life.

DONNA PERSONNA: I was born in Texas, a place called Pharr, and it's far away, yes, Pharr, Texas. In 1946, to a large Mexican family. My father was born in Nuevo León, Monterrey, Mexico. He turned Baptist to be with my mother, and he became a Baptist minister. In 1947, his church sent him to San Jose, California, to found a Spanish-speaking Baptist church. But this is the funny part. I say all these years later, thank God that they got me the hell out of Texas, and brought me to a wonderland, California. I really believe in magical things, and that's the truth. I do not believe I would be alive today if I'd stayed in Texas.

I am a Texan in my soul. I'm Mexicana, and I'm Tejana. But when I go there, I hear all kinds of things that tell me that my survival would not have been viable there.

One time when we were visiting, I said to one of my cousins, "Well, why aren't you in school?"

He said, "Oh, they caught me speaking Spanish."

He was sent home because he was speaking Spanish. They call it assimilation, but I don't go for that. Hell, no.

I've been like this since I was seven years old. That's why I'm saying I would have been killed.

I just wanted to be me. Me, all along. I understood that I wasn't like my brothers. In my family, I always did everything with the girls, and the girls wanted me there. I helped them fix their hair, I gave them tips on beauty, and the boys went off and did boxing and football and roughed it up and stuff, and they never invited me.

I didn't have a gender, it was just who I am, from the inside. That's what I knew.

SHARYN GRAYSON: I was born in Dallas, Texas, in 1949. In my early childhood experiences, I felt that I was always the same person. I didn't care for anything that boys were doing. Nothing. None of that. It just did not excite me. I had my girlfriend, a cisgender girlfriend. We had a very close relationship. I was always just being myself. It was like this innate feeling that I knew who I was, but I just didn't have the proper tools yet.

And because I had no words to define it, I didn't know. I mean, it's strange, now that I think back on it. I've always been me, and that's another fortunate and blessed thing, that I was allowed to be me. I didn't feel constricted or constrained.

Even my teachers at school. Let me say this. I think I was naturally always more feminine than the guys that I knew. But even they were protective, and I was just allowed to be who I want. I think everybody just accepted that. "Oh, that's who they are." And that was it.

NELSON D'ALERTA PÉREZ: I was born in Isla de Pinos, Cuba, in 1954. My childhood was wonderful even though I was abused many times. I was a very cute little boy, but very effeminate, very gay. Once I was abused on a boat, and I'm still terrified of the sea. Because the man told me, "If you don't do this, I'll throw you in the water." That's a very heavy thing.

My parents were photographers. They worked really hard, really hard, and we weren't rich, but we were middle class, well-off, in a part of Cuba that's a separate island with a high standard of living.

School was awful because I was so feminine throughout my childhood, and still am. Studying was really hard because they'd throw things at me. I was afraid to go to recess. I went out for recess, and they pushed me, they threw me around. And the whole school laughed, yelling at me. "Sissy! Little faggot! Girly face!" That followed me until my last years of school. Until high school when I said, "I can't do this anymore. I'm going to work." I loved school because I was fascinated with learning, but I couldn't do it, because of the machismo problem. I think that's a terrible thing.

The principal called the police on me once. She accused me of having brought all the gays, all the homosexuals to the school.

I said to her, "I wish I had that power! But I don't."

She was stunned.

Once she told me, "You have to wash your hair and get rid of that dye."

I said, "What kind of woman doesn't know that hair dye doesn't come out with shampoo?"

And so she and I had a war. But she won, because I had to leave. The kids wouldn't leave me alone, the students were very cruel.

I suffered from horrible anxiety because of that, something I still have to deal with. My parents, they were amazing and everything, but they had to work so much and had so much to do. I think I must have told them. I think I complained to my mom about the bullying at school. But nothing happened; now that I'm older, I can't remember them helping me to deal with that.

And it's sad.

I adore my parents. I don't know their reasons, I don't blame them, but in that regard, they failed me.

BAMBY SALCEDO: I was born in the beautiful city of Guadalajara, in the state of Jalisco, in Mexico, in 1969. My childhood was very difficult. I didn't have a family that had the necessary resources, the education needed to understand a person like me. My mother and father were very young. They came from extreme poverty and always stayed in survival mode. So, unfortunately, I couldn't receive the attention, the affection, the love I was looking for. My mother was never around. She was in a relationship with a very abusive person. My escape was to seek refuge on the streets, to seek refuge in drugs, where I could find that relief, that healing. I was a street child. I would sell chewing gum, I would shine shoes whenever I had the chance. I would commit crime. I would sell my body. I exploited my body for money. I had to do those kinds of things, as a way of surviving. I always wanted to help my mother, because I knew about her suffering and her sacrifice and what she was trying to do, all her determination to provide for us.

In my childhood, I was always intelligent. But I didn't know it. And neither did other people. Maybe they did know; they didn't want to admit it. That's why I didn't believe in myself.

I couldn't see reflections of me anywhere.

Mostly, what I saw was violence, a lot of things a child should not see.

I was also—or am—a child sexual abuse survivor. The world took advantage of my queerness or my transness, in some ways, even though then, there was no language to say that.

I felt and was a certain way from a very early age. It's as if people knew it, too. In fact, even my mother knew, but she was in denial. She didn't want to admit it for several reasons. My family had such great expectations for me, and so did society. My mother was very religious. I was the son she had, who supposedly would be the man of the house.

But the world knew. They could see it in me.

A very specific incident stays with me, that marked me for life. I was maybe six, seven years old, I don't know. I was walking down the street, feeling as if I was the last Coca-Cola in the desert. I felt like I was in my power, like I was just beautiful, and like I was just telling the world, "Here I am." Right? Just in my own thing. Walking with this beautiful feeling.

And all of a sudden, a car honked at me. I felt like the person who was in the car—who was a man—knew what I was feeling, or what I was trying to project. And I got scared. My light got dim. I just kept on walking and that was that.

It was about experiencing myself as female. I felt like I was me in that very moment. Like I was just walking in my truth, in who I truly was. I was walking, just feeling amazing, and I felt like I was just beautiful, but I couldn't even describe what that was, because, obviously, I didn't have language. And then, it was this moment: "You're not supposed to be that. You're not."

FRESH "LEV" WHITE: I was born in a hamlet called Valhalla, New York. Probably forty miles out of the city. I was released shortly after, separated. I was a child of the system for around six months. I was fostered by the family that found me at six months. They ended up adopting me ten years later.

Going through school, I was teased by girls a lot. I remember having girls literally follow me the ten blocks, whatever it was, home from school, three or four of them taunting me. I was kind of masculine. But what I remember was that no matter what they did, boys don't hit girls. And so, I might get pushed or whatever. And then, what I did back then is, I would take it out on the boys because there was always an opportunity to fight a boy. So, there was a lot of fighting boys. This is like third grade, fourth grade, fifth grade. That's how I worked it out.

I wanted to do the things that boys did. I felt masculine. I don't know that I felt like a boy because I can't claim to know what that feels like. But I felt like those were my people. Like that's where I'm supposed to be hanging out.

KB BOYCE: I was born in 1963 in Brooklyn, New York. And I knew I was queer, but I didn't have the words to explain even to myself that I was transmasculine.

When I was a little kid, I assumed I was a boy. I saw myself as a little boy. All my friends were boys. I was very much of the run around, fall down, get cuts. I had a lot of energy. And in those days, I was just like, "Yeah. I'm a boy. I'm a boy." Really I was just a rambunctious little curious kid. I didn't feel gender, I just felt like I was me. And that was what was important: just being myself.

C. NJOUBE DUGAS: I grew up in a really large family in San Francisco, California. My parents were both part of the Great Migration coming from the South. Most of the people in our neighborhood were hippies. They had this really "just let them be free" kind of attitude. Like, so long as you're not hurting each other, right? So that's what we believed. That we could just go be free.

I don't think I really experienced gender as it's known. I just assumed it was okay for me to love girls. I even told my mom, "When I grow up, I'm going to get married, and me and my wife, we're going to move to the country." This was around 1969, and I already knew that.

CRYSTAL MASON: I grew up in Richmond, Virginia. When I was five, we moved to a part of town called Northside. It was a working-class neighborhood. It had just been desegregated, maybe five years before we moved there. Almost all of the white people had moved out by that time.

MS. BILLIE COOPER: My neighborhood was Black; my whole life was Black. That was my life. I didn't meet my first Spanish person or white person until I got into eighth and ninth grade. I mean, I saw white people and Spanish people, but we didn't connect; we didn't interact with each other.

TINA VALENTÍN AGUIRRE: I was born in San Diego. I grew up in Logan Heights, Barrio Logan it's sometimes called. In the seventies, and it was almost exclusively brown and Black. I only knew white people from television. I didn't really understand that white people were like us. The first time that a white person farted around me, I was like, "What?" I didn't know that white people could fart. I just thought that's us, and how we live. I didn't assume that we were the same.

The truth is, although we are all humans, how we are treated—there really are big differences. I carry that with me in all of my work.

FRESH "LEV" WHITE: We were living in the Bronx, in a neighborhood that was just a rainbow of people. I'm saying this because I think it's unusual for some folks.

CRYSTAL MASON: I used to spend a good amount of time alone. At that time on television, there were a lot of those cop shows. Private detectives. I remember imagining myself being that private detective, and there was always some woman I was saving. In that time, I didn't change the roles. I just inhabited the male role.

This was when I was probably five, six, seven, for a long time.

I don't remember actually ever seeing myself in the role of the woman—or the person to be saved. Which later in life would come back to bite me.

CHINO SCOTT-CHUNG: Growing up in Denver, my dad—as many immigrants do—wanted his kids to be successful and to assimilate. My dad would move us to the whitest, most middle-class places he could. Those are the schools we went to, and that's where I grew up. When I was a kid, I wanted to be blonde, blue-eyed. A blonde, blue-eyed girl. That's who I wanted to be. That was my idea of the most successful, best person that I could become. And of course, that's who was all around me and in the media and everything else.

It's weird. In some ways, fighting against those stereotypes, having to fight against them my whole life from the moment I was born, really pushed me into wanting to be as masculine as possible.

STORMMIGUEL FLOREZ: I grew up in a big, extended family, near the Northeast Heights of Albuquerque. The high school I went to was very mixed. We lived in a neighborhood with a lot of families. As kids, we all played together all the time. It was back in the seventies, when you let your kids play in the streets until eleven o'clock at night playing kick the can or whatever. I was always around cousins; we were all taking care of each other.

When I was really little, I was a tomboy. I played with both boys and girls on my street but really there was a difference between me and the other kids. I knew they could stand to pee and I couldn't. I tried and made a mess. Like, I got it. I never felt like, "Oh, because I can't pee standing up, I'm not good enough or I'm not boy enough." It was just like, "Oh, I see that difference, and I'm still like one of the boys."

The little boy next door was having a birthday party, and his mom was like, "Well, who do you want to invite?" and he's like, "No girls, no girls." She said, "Okay, well, who?" and I was the first person that he said.

So I really was seen that way as a kid. As one of the boys.

I just got to be me, and that was great.

It never really felt like a problem until I started getting told to act a different way.

VIVIAN VARELA: I was raised in Corona, California. That's just where life was, in Corona. At the time, it was just a little town.

When I was growing up, I was always very curious about things. I was kind of tomboy-ish. I really did not like to wear dresses. I liked to run around in the yard and play in the water, things like that. I wasn't much for dolls. I had a dancing doll, which was my favorite. I loved that doll because I would dance with her. You connect her to your feet, and then, with music, you just hold the doll and dance. That was my favorite doll. So, gender: there you go. I was the boy. I identified as the boy, in the dance.

When I was a kid at church, I followed around and tried to chase down the preacher's son. He was very cute. Always clean-cut, the way he dressed. I loved that.

Maybe I wanted to be that.

I felt male.

YOSEÑIO LEWIS: I was born in 1959, in Rhode Island. I grew up learning Spanish from my Panamanian family. I knew that I was a first-generation US-er, but I was also drawn to ways and thoughts and foods and smells and tasks and holidays of a whole other world. And I belonged to that world as much as I belonged to the world I was born into.

I had my best buddy, Bobby. He lived across the street from my grandmother, and we just played in the street all day. I had a great time with him.

We had one day that cemented for me who I was in the world, and how I was going to walk.

I was three years old. We both had to go to the bathroom. We went in, and he just pulled his zipper down, did what he had to do. I pulled my pants down and was going to sit down. I thought, wait a minute, why am I sitting down and he's not? I had no awareness of bodily differences. It just didn't occur to me until then.

I set on the notion that I must be sick, that whatever I was supposed to have that he did have, mine must have fallen off and I must be bleeding to death. So we have to go to the hospital so the doctor can fix whatever happened.

I proceeded to have a panic attack and say to him, "We have to go to the hospital! Hurry up and finish."

And he said, "What? What's wrong?"

I said, "I'm dying, something happened. Look at you and look at me, we're different, something's wrong! Let's go to the hospital. They'll take care of me. They'll make me whole."

Bobby was a couple of months older, so of course he was much more sophisticated than I ever could be. He said to me, "Listen, I take showers with my dad, and I notice that his thing is way bigger than mine. I got nervous, and I said, 'Daddy, why is my thing so small? Yours is so huge! It's like you can't even see mine.' And he said to me, 'You're young. When you get older, it'll start to get bigger and bigger.' It's okay, you're not sick. There's nothing wrong with you. It will grow."

And that was enough. He was my best friend. He would never lie to me. He just told me, "You're going to be fine," and that was good enough for me. And then we pulled our pants up and went out and played some more, and that was that.

I got the validation that I needed: I am a boy. Even though I look different, I am a boy, and so it's okay for me to think the things that I think. It's okay for me to wear the clothes that I wear. It's okay for me to want the things I want, and to do the things I do.

ANDRÉS OZZUNA: Growing up, everything we did, we did at home. This was in Argentina, during the dictatorship: everybody stayed inside. I mean, I'd go to school and come back. My mom would go to work and come directly home. But our whole lives stayed in our neighborhood. It's not like we went out. It wasn't safe. And also, we didn't have enough money to go anywhere. So all the entertainment was indoors, or on the patio. We lived with my grandfather, my grandmother, my uncle, my aunt, father, mother, and sister. There were a lot of us.

I always wanted to be with the boys. But my mom wouldn't let me. She didn't let me do tomboy things. I couldn't play with the boys, I couldn't play with balls, I couldn't play with race cars, nothing. "No, you can't do that. You can't play rough. You can't."

I remember when my period came. I was about eleven. It was tragic for me. I wanted to kill myself. I saw how my cousins were developing into men, and I couldn't understand why. What had I done to deserve this? How come they were growing facial hair, and not me? It was horrible. I had no way of understanding it as part of my identity. I just hated what was happening, and felt all this anger. Sometimes, I fought with my cousins, because I was jealous of what I couldn't have.

I didn't understand that I wasn't a woman, that I was trans, until I was in my forties.

C. NJOUBE DUGAS: I didn't really experience what it was like to be a female until I started my period, and then I was pissed. From the time my body started changing, whenever that age was—ten, eleven—I did not feel comfortable with it. I did not want breasts. I was like, "What? I don't want a bra, what are you talking about?" A part of me was shutting down.

It just changed everything. I wanted to continue to ride my bike with my shirt off in the summertime. I didn't like energy from men or boys, I didn't even understand why they were attracted to me, like, "Don't you see I'm a dude?" I even asked this guy, "How could you be attracted to me? Don't you see me like, as your little bro?" It was so baffling.

KB BOYCE: I ran around with no shirt on until I had no choice and had
to start wearing shirts because, you know, early puberty set in. That
meant that I suddenly started sprouting breasts and menstruating at a
very young age. And ooh, that freaked me out. Because I really, really
felt like I was a boy.

I didn't really understand what was going on and why, suddenly, I
couldn't grow up to be a boy. I didn't understand gender. I didn't have
words for any of the stuff.

FRESH "LEV" WHITE: I had a nice-sized backyard, and sometimes my dad
would let the grass grow a little high. That would be where football
happened. Just like, going out there and playing rough, playing stick-
ball, feeling my full self in the ways that I played, really feeling like I
got to be the full expression of me. I would come home, and I would
always have something ripped. My mom would be like, "What are
you doing out there?"

It was when I had the freedom to just be in my full self, which
usually happened around games and sports.

I can just feel it now, the excitement, the butterflies—not fear, but
more like freedom. And so, yeah. I felt big. I'm just opening my arms
to say, I felt big, and open, and fully available to be me. Yeah.

I pushed that line a lot. Even inside, even playing with my younger
sister. It's who I was. And I have to say, some of it, I believe—I've had
some therapy over the years—was this childhood trauma that happens to babies when they're separated at birth. There's this way that
I've never been able to be caged. There are times that I have been, but
mostly, it was just like, I can't help but be myself.

YOSEÑIO LEWIS: When I was out in public with family members, and
somebody said, "Oh, what a cute little boy," my face would light up.
For that brief moment, I was being seen. And I was alive. That kept
validating me.

At Easter, I have to dress up, I have to wear stockings, it made me uncomfortable as all get-out. But I would do it. I learned how to play the game, to be the boy that I was, but not too much. I learned very quickly: don't ever talk to anyone about it.

STORMMIGUEL FLOREZ: There were those moments of being told I was in the wrong bathroom, even in elementary school. I remember trying to go in the bathrooms only during class, because if somebody saw me walk into the girls' bathroom, oftentimes, they thought I was in the wrong bathroom. It's like, "Okay, I have to be careful about how I enter the space. I know I'm supposed to be here, but other people don't."

I never really thought about being read as male until those bathroom spaces. In my world, I was just being me and getting to wear my brothers' hand-me-downs. I didn't feel like I was doing something wrong, but I was definitely embarrassed. I stressed out about it enough to start planning around it at a very early age.

Then I started getting it from other people. From my peers. I had another friend who was a little tomboy. One teacher in particular used to call us out in front of the class and tell us we weren't acting ladylike. A male teacher, probably gay looking back. I think about him and I think about his mannerisms. Definitely feminine. Maybe he just didn't have a place to put that and so he took it out on me.

TUPILI LEA ARELLANO: When I was in junior high, in eighth grade, they were making us sew a dress. They wouldn't let me be in shop. They said, "¡estás loca!"

I go, "No, no, I want to be in shop, I don't want to sew things."

My mom ended up sewing my dress. It was apricot satin. Oh my God, we were going to have to model them in front of the student body.

That's the first time I had suicidal ideation.

I said, "I can't do this, I cannot do this."

I have a blackout from modeling that dress. I don't remember the day, or day after.

Okay?

That's what an insult it was to my sacred gender.

DONNA PERSONNA: We had a library in our home, and sometimes I would go and just pick up a book. I was bored, I didn't have anything to do. So I picked up this book. It was a big, red book, a medical book. I turned the page, and there were stories about homosexuality.

I'm ten years old, something like that. Some of the things I remember: it's an anomaly, it's not normal, and some of the solutions for it are separating that child from the family, from siblings especially because it could influence them. In some cases, they should be institutionalized and taken away from the parents.

And I thought, what? So I can't.

No, I've got to be a boy. I've got to be a boy.

I felt this weight on my shoulders. I could ruin my family. That kept me from ever speaking of it, I never would talk about that, because I didn't want the consequences.

I want you to understand, I want everyone to understand. Why did I have to be thinking things like that?

That was like sixty-seven years ago, and it's always been with me.

FRESH "LEV" WHITE: There were no models of same-gender, same-sex relationships. None. It was all down-low.

NICKY CALMA: I was born in Manila, Philippines, in 1967. I went to an all-boys disciplinarian Catholic boys' school. Of course, religion was always in the picture. Everything was based on that. The Philippines is ninety-five percent Catholic, so that influenced a lot in our household. We'd go to church every Sunday. My dad would make us read the Bible.

When I was maybe eight or nine years old, we went on vacation in the "Summer Capital of the Philippines," called Baguio City. It's up in the mountains. And it's cold there. It's a vacation spot for a lot of Filipinos, especially during summertime, and we stayed at this popular hotel. That was the first time I saw someone who was transgender. She was playing this musical organ in the lobby, entertaining people, providing music. I was watching her, I was looking at her, and I was like, this woman is too beautiful, perfect. She was gorgeous, she had beautiful hair. The way she played the organ, she was very graceful. The music was connecting with her movement. She was wearing this beautiful halter top, a jumpsuit, and it had sequins on it. Rhinestones and sequins. And that excited me. That excited me a lot.

She started staring back at me. And she was like, "What can I do for you? Do you have a request?"

I said, "No, no, no." I was a little shy. "I was just watching you."

My mom was also observing me, watching her.

Her name was Lady Valerie, I found out, and she was the entertainment at the lobby of the hotel. This organist, this humungous monster of an instrument. I mean, you really need to know how to operate this thing, with two hands and two feet. That was my first exposure. The impact! There were a lot of questions. How did she get those beautiful breasts? What did she go through in the transition? It stayed in my mind. I kind of picked up on her scent.

I couldn't put my finger on it, because I didn't know what transgender was at that time. In the Philippines, trans folks are categorized as gay. Let's say you were assigned male at birth: suddenly you became this flaming gay person. And then, when you're assigned female at birth, you become this big bull dyke, or you start to think that maybe I'm a man? You're lesbian. Transgender did not really exist. You don't talk about transsexuals, you don't talk about transvestites. Having that Catholic influence, those were the unspoken words. *Trans* was just not there.

But that piqued my curiosity. That was the catalyst.

KB BOYCE: It wasn't exactly called transgender back then, but there were women in my neighborhood, Puerto Rican women, trans women, who were the fiercest. I had so much admiration for them. They were so brave and—don't mess with them. They would hurt you. Anyway, it was seeing them living their lives, when I was really young, and just seeing the stuff they had to put up with. I mean, yeah, I was getting bullied for being androgynous, but these were trans women out there, oh my God, who were so brave!

That was my first experience with transness. And I super admired them. I mean, I was super impressed. It didn't really speak to my experience because I'm transmasculine, but just watching them navigate really stayed with me. To this day, when I think of them, I still feel chills.

TINA VALENTÍN AGUIRRE: There was a trans Black woman who would walk around my elementary school. It was fourth grade, and at that point I had met two friends who are gay Chicanos. Chemy and Ruben. Chemy and I always stood out as super effeminate, queer kids. We hung out together, and we would see this Black trans woman walk by. I would walk up to the fence and she would wave and I would wave. Eventually she would start to talk to us.

The teachers would say, "Don't do that, don't talk to adults."

That made sense, but for me, it was that moment of, "Oh, there's somebody who's different like me, and she's just living her life!"

Also I think she started to see, "Oh there's this baby queer trans person, I'm just going to say hi and talk if they want to talk."

That was a first time I thought: Oh, yes. I had a euphoria, a joy, about gender.

CHINO SCOTT-CHUNG: In that time, it was really hard to come out. There was a lot of homophobia, a lot of hatred against gay and queer people, and I knew that and I saw that and I lived that. It was all around me, the hatred, the gay bashing, even as far as killing queer people, murders of queer people. It was everywhere.

DONNA PERSONNA: I saw how they treated other little faggots. A redheaded boy, I clocked him as gay, but I heard whispers that other boys made him do sexual things, in the gym and stuff. They made him do things. What does that lead to? Like first, they want that and then they want to beat the fuck out of me or put me out in the street? I didn't know. It was not being in control. It was bullying. I heard that, and said, no, no, I'm not going to be objectified.

MS BILLIE COOPER: In junior high school, I loved it, because I noticed the boys. We were seated alphabetically, and this guy named James Carr, we always sat next to each other. I was flirting with him, but I don't think he knew. Oh, I fell in love with him. And one day I told him I loved him, and he hated me ever since then. I felt crushed. I found myself walking by his house and just headed across the street, just said, "Oh I love you, James Carr, I love you." I loved him so much. He was so handsome; he was so hot. But he could care less for me.

And in high school, I really noticed boys. I got on the wrestling team so they could pin me down on the mat.

I wanted to be pinned down, honey, by those boys.

KB BOYCE: I had a very strong sense of self. For some reason I was just like, "All right, I'm different."

I felt that I had to find a way to navigate this world without losing myself.

* *

TWO

Family Matters

FRESH "LEV" WHITE: There were things that my family saw in me, but wanted to reject at the same time.

CRYSTAL MASON: My family always saw me as a bit of a curiosity, who was loved but a little bit like, "Hmm, she's a little strange."

KB BOYCE: It didn't make sense that my mom wanted me to wear dresses. We fought constantly.

ANDRÉS OZZUNA: I think my mom knew a lot earlier than me.

KB BOYCE: There are moments when families sit around and talk with the kids. "What do you want to be when you grow up? What are you going to be?"

And everyone's like, "Oh, I'm going to be a doctor. I'm going to be a fireman. I'm going to be this and that and the other."

And when it was my turn—out of the thirteen kids that were all hanging around—they said, "Well, what are you going to be when you grow up?"

I said, "I'm going to be a dude."

And they laughed and laughed.

That hurt my feelings. I didn't understand. Because it made sense to me: I was going to grow up to be a dude, you know? What's so funny about that?

CRYSTAL MASON: I used to like to whistle. My grandmother, who was always one of my biggest supporters, used to say to me, "Stop whistling. People are going to think you're a man." So there were small attempts when I was younger to put me in a box.

But not a lot, really. I didn't have a lot of pressure to conform.

There weren't many role models. I didn't have words or names or understandings.

JOAN BENOIT: I hated dresses. I played sports. My parents always attributed it to the fact that I was surrounded by three brothers. I wanted to wear their suits. I wanted to do the things that they were doing. I thought, why can't I drive the tractor and mow the lawn? That's so much more fun than doing the dishes, are you kidding? I don't want to learn how to sew. If I have to iron another one of dad's hankies, I'm going to scream.

My chores were all domestic. I was trained to be a homemaker my whole life. That was my training.

I knew who I was. I've always known who I was.

My mom said, "You always wanted to be a boy."

And I said, "It wasn't that I always wanted to be a boy. I knew that I liked girls and I didn't know that there was an alternative."

To be with girls, you had to be a boy. That's all I saw. That's all there was to see. There was nothing else to see.

VIVIAN VARELA: From a very young age, my mother wanted me to be more feminine. She would comment, "Why can't you walk like Aurelia? Do you see how Aurelia walks?"

And I was like, "Yes, but that's not me. I walk the way I walk."

My mom would try. She would say, "Look at this dress." And I would feel like I wanted to throw up. I tried; I did wear dresses. It didn't work. It was unpleasant, uncomfortable. I didn't like it.

Since I didn't have much adult supervision, I pretty much wore what I wanted to wear. I was working at twelve years old, cleaning someone's house, so I had money to buy cords. My brothers, they were impressed, they wanted to have that, too. So, I was more into male clothes. I didn't realize what I was doing. But that's what I was doing.

I was only about ten when my parents divorced. After that, my mother would leave us with babysitters. That was very difficult for me to navigate, because I'm the oldest of six. I always felt a responsibility toward my siblings. I had to make sure that there was food in the house. There were points where we did not have anything to eat.

My grandmother went to the Mexican Baptist Church. She would scare the living daylights out of me. "You'd better go to bed, you'd better do this, you'd better do that, because Jesus is coming." That was her threat. We never got spanked. It would be in a stern voice: "Jesus is coming." That was her way of getting us to fear God.

I took it seriously. I thought, I'd better behave.

I think negative connotations of God started there.

There was something inside of me that wanted to follow my own path. Even as a child, I was looking to maintain my own integrity. I don't know how else to explain it. If something didn't seem right, I wouldn't do it. If I was curious about something, I wanted to try. The word is *tenacity*.

DONNA PERSONNA: I question everything, and I've done that all my life. Being a Baptist or a Christian, my parents were going to baptize me, and my mother says, "You were born a sinner."

I say, "Wait, Mom, wait until I do something bad."

She says, "No, no, you were born, you have a stain."

I say, "I don't like that, I don't like that."

I mean I was seven, eight years old, talking like that to my parents.

Another time, in San Jose, my father kicked me out of my own church. "You don't know Spanish well, so we're sending you to an English-speaking church."

"Oh, okay."

Well, they just didn't want me in there because I was too much of an activist, questioning things.

CRYSTAL MASON: I was the youngest. I got a choice about whether I wanted to go to church or not, and I was like, "No, thank you."

My mom was like, "Why?"

"Well, they're all hypocrites."

And she said, "Yeah."

Then we didn't really speak about it in depth. There was no big pronouncement; I was just allowed to stop going. My brothers and sister, I don't know how they felt about it, but it was always a little funny because they were getting dressed to go to church and I was basically always in my pajamas.

LANDA LAKES: I was constantly in my sister's dresses. I ripped or busted out my sister's dresses so often that it became a problem! Any time my parents were away, that was the first thing I would do.

I vividly remember one time when I put on my sister's dress and my parents had left, but then they remembered something, so they came back. My grandpa was supposed to be watching us, and most of the time that really meant that my grandpa was on a cot outside, asleep, so we would do whatever we wanted. My parents came back way, way fast, and I didn't have time to get out of the dress, so I jumped under the bed to hide, and when I did that, it tore the dress. As soon as my sister heard it tear, she stormed out of the house to tell my parents that I was under the bed, wearing her dress.

That's the story my family tells about me, with the dress on. I'm pretty sure I got in trouble. I don't know how much. My parents were not above spanking, that was just what you did with your kids back in the early seventies.

There were many other instances where I do plainly remember getting into trouble for things like that.

NELSON D'ALERTA PÉREZ: When my mom would go out or she was working, I would put on all of her clothes and I felt an incredible satisfaction because for me, it was a dream. Very private moments. I was fascinated by women's clothing and shoes and all of that.

I played by myself a lot because my sister didn't want to play with me. She had a lot of problems with me being so feminine and taking her things. She didn't understand.

TUPILI LEA ARELLANO: I was born in 1952 in Silver City, New Mexico. We lived there two years and then we moved to Tucson, Arizona.

My father was a miner. He was a foreman, a very well-paying job. Really hard, but that's what paid working-class, Indigenous, Mexican men. He used to go down underground, in the mines. There was hardship in my family. There was the alcoholism, which is very hard to navigate. I grew up in a dancing family. My mother and I would sing together. We had a Mexican songbook. She'd be in the kitchen cooking, and I'd be leading the songs with her.

My parents were resourceful; they could figure out anything. They planted the seeds in me that creativity was necessary, and community was sharing, staying alive by sharing.

I would sometimes sneak my brother's clothes and put them on. I had a neighbor, Cathy, a German girl, my best friend. She had two brothers too. She used to get their clothes, and I used to get some of my brothers', and we'd dress in them.

I said to Cathy, "Let's ask two girls and take them to the Dairy Queen and buy them ice creams." Five cents for an ice cream cone then. We stole those shiny jackets that my brothers had, we dressed up, and we had these two friends, we went and got them. We walked to the Dairy Queen, and we bought them ice cream cones.

Cathy and I were pretending they were our girlfriends.

I was eight.

LANDA LAKES: Here's something that is really bizarre. When I was very young, I used to do little strip shows for my cousins. They were boys. I would set up chairs on our back porch, and then I would do a show and everything. But there's one time I remember doing it, and then my cousin, she wanted to dance next, and strip, and I was like, "No, that's not right for you to do it." It was immoral. Somehow I felt like it was okay for me, because I guess taking off my top didn't mean anything, but if she was to take it off, that would be something different.

We were very young, probably five. I've always wondered where I got the idea to do a strip show. Maybe *Gilligan's Island* or something. But for some reason, I was fascinated with the idea. I thought I was a showgirl, when I did it. I even had a name for myself at the time, I called myself Juanita Yakatubi.

When I look back at it, I just think that, in many ways, my spirit was shining, my spirit said, this is who I am. Even from a young age. I think when you're younger, sometimes your spirit is freer. And it may not necessarily mean anything for some people. But sometimes, what you do then has serious notes that you carry throughout your life.

ADELA VÁZQUEZ: I never had any problems at home with being who I was, thank God. When I was born, my grandmother immediately adopted me as her child because my mother had fallen in love with a man and gone off to live with him. My grandmother took responsibility for me and raised me from the day I was born.

I was given a lot of love. I got to do whatever I wanted.

When I wanted a doll, my grandmother bought me one. She'd say, "You can't take it out on the street, but it's your doll."

Inside the house, I played with paper dolls. I played with girls, and like them I had my own little kitchen, my own dolls. I was a girl. I've been female all my life. I was raised as a girl, and I was very feminine. I'd go to the beach with my grandparents, and I remember one time a lady said to my grandfather, "What's up with that boy with the body of a woman?" And my grandfather told her, "That's my grandchild."

When I was nine, I sent a letter to the Three Kings and told them

I didn't want them to bring me any more presents for boys, because I was a girl.

TINA VALENTÍN AGUIRRE: I know I ruined at least one Christmas because I didn't want a goddamn G.I. Joe doll. I did not accept it, I was like, "That's not my gift, Santa needs to do better."

NELSON D'ALERTA PÉREZ: I wanted to play with dolls, I wanted to have paper dolls.

ADELA VÁZQUEZ: When I sent that letter, my family took me to see a psychiatrist.

"This is a normal child. Homosexual, but normal," they said.

My grandparents had an education. My grandmother was the first rural teacher in our area. My grandfather was an agricultural engineer in the sugar industry. And beyond that, there were many gay people in my family, I wasn't the first.

So they knew. They knew what I was.

This acceptance means a great deal, because it's given me tremendous confidence. Confidence in what I'm doing with my life.

TINA VALENTÍN AGUIRRE: My family was really different from others in Logan Heights. My mom had dwarfism, so she was a little person and was really short. I think shorter than four feet tall. She stood out. My two brothers were also little people, and then me and my dad were not. Before going to school I didn't really know that we were different. Once I was in school, I started to see how people treated us. In the case of traditional Mexican families, people with dwarfism were given stereotypes that they might be a demon, or a bruja, or really bad.

There was a time we went to Tijuana, Mexico. The border is just right there. We went shopping in downtown Tijuana, and somebody— a woman who was on the street, selling wares—got her broom and started to hit my mother and called her a bruja because she was little. We didn't get that extreme form of treatment in Logan Heights.

I did learn very early on that people can be really mean around differences. I also learned that people don't expect us to stand up for ourselves when we're bullied. And so, there were times, say when me and my mom would be on the bus, and people would look at my mom or say things to my mom, almost like we didn't understand them. A lot of times, people thought maybe we didn't speak English, and of course, we did. My mom was really polite. I was not. At five or six I started to learn, oh, you shouldn't talk to my mother that way, you're not better than her, and you're just being really mean. I learned the power of, when people say "Stay in your place, be quiet," sometimes it's good to let them know, "Nope! That's not acceptable. You need to stop." The fact that I was a little kid saying that, and people thought that was inappropriate? I could care less.

I just knew really young that if you're going to do that to my mom, who's an extremely positive, loving person, that means that you're going to treat anybody who's different that way. It really instilled in me that it doesn't have to be me that you're bullying. If you're making somebody else feel bad because they're different, the likelihood is that eventually you're going to try to do the same thing with me. I need to say something. I learned there's a fine line between civility and complicit behavior. I did learn really quickly to do these things in public, with witnesses. To say out loud, "If you do this, you want to hit me or push me, I have tons of witnesses and I will make sure you are punished for it."

It's not mine to hold that you're afraid of me and you think I'm wrong because I exist. I have a right, me and my family and my chosen family, my friends, we have a right to live happy lives.

SHARYN GRAYSON: My mom and I had a conversation when I was about fourteen. The idea of transitioning at that time wasn't something that I really had in my mind. I didn't understand that until later. But she knew. I remember the conversation being that she wanted me to be happy, but she was afraid. Of course, the world is a very mean place, and she was afraid that they would hurt me. But my mom knew who I was at heart, and she never, ever tried to stifle that. She was always very supportive. She was my very best friend, and after I had transitioned and we would go places together, they would say, "Oh, are you two sisters?" And I'd say, "No, that's my mom!" She always got a big kick out of that.

I can say that I was one of the very few fortunate people in having that relationship with my mom.

ANDRÉS OZZUNA: I had a masculine aunt, and my mom wouldn't let me get close to her. I'd go with my mom to her work, and there was a masculine woman there. I remember it perfectly. I had a kind of radar or something when I'd see someone, a masculine person, I'd want to be friends with them. I'd want to talk to that person. I felt a kind of attraction. But my mom caught on right away and she'd say, "No. Sit here and stay and don't move." And if I moved, she'd beat me. My mom hit me a lot. Back then, she was very violent. It was like, either I get close to them, or she kills me.

So I stayed where I was.

JOAN BENOIT: I got a long history of lesbianism in my dad's side of the family. I have an aunt, my father's older sister, she's going to be eighty-eight this year. She joined the nunnery. She knew who I was early on, too, because she tried to recruit me for the convent for most of my childhood, well into my teens.

When I came out, she said to me, "I understand," as she'd been living with a woman, Kay, for the last twenty-five years. "You come live with Kay and I, and we'll show you the right way to be." We'll take away your phone, and you won't get any mail, and we're going to brainwash you, basically. "Because you're sinning, even if you don't think you're doing anything wrong, because Hitler thought he was right"—just horrible, horrible letters I got from her. Because of the Catholic Church.

CRYSTAL MASON: My mother had a sister who was a serious bull dyke and who came to all the family functions with her partner. They lived in an apartment with my aunt's kids. She was part of our family, so I was always a little curious about that arrangement. I remember once when I was at their house, I realized that there was one bedroom for my cousins, and then my aunt's bedroom, and that was it, right? In my head, it was like, "Well, where does she sleep?" About the partner. But nobody ever talked about it.

The relationship looked like marriage to me. I don't know if she was really a role model because we never really talked. She was a visual point of reference, because I also came out as butch, and used to like to think of myself as a bulldagger because I loved that word, and that's pretty much what she was.

She loved me. She would always say that I was her favorite niece, and she was so proud of me for leaving Richmond and doing my own thing, but I feel like she was also a little distant, and maybe—I wonder sometimes if my extreme outness butted up against her old-time feelings about being out. To me, it felt like at some point she went back into the closet. I don't even know if that's the right term. She changed. She changed the way she lived her life and what she looked like. I don't know how that happened because I had been living away for so long. I don't recall her ever having any more girlfriends.

But one thing I remember: she had some sort of illness and was in the hospital—this was when I was in my early twenties and first coming out—and I went to visit her. There was a woman in her room who was pretty, now I would say femme, but then I thought just a lady, right? She actually started flirting with me. At that moment, I wasn't sure what was going on, but I knew it was making me feel some kind of way. I remember my aunt saying to her friend that she should leave me alone, which told me that my aunt also knew even then that I was a dyke. Because she knew her friend was chicken-hawking. Her friend was probably late forties or something. She was a nice cougar.

KB BOYCE: I began to understand my sexuality very young because I had crushes on all the girls. Oh God, I want to say from the age of five, six. My sisters were much older, so they were teenagers when I was that age. I would see their friends, their teenage friends, and I just thought they were gorgeous. I just loved my sisters' friends. Whenever they would hang out at my mom's place, I would sit there at their feet and listen to everything they said, and play with the hairs on their legs, just in heaven.

Just in little queer heaven.

TUPILI LEA ARELLANO: When I was eight, I came out, I really came out.

My abuela, she was a foster mom. We used to go visit. One of the times, there was this new girl, her name was Yolanda. I was eight and she was ten. The second time I went, Yolanda and I were already swooning for each other. She was feminine, and strong.

She asked me, did I want to play house when we went to bed. Okay. She slept in a rollaway bed with a younger girl. She invited me into the bed, and she says, "Okay, I'm going to be the mother, you're going to be the dad." She was the choreographer for all of it.

There was kissing and holding. You know what? I don't ever remember up until then, feeling like I belonged in the world. I'd a sense from very early on that I don't belong here. I still have that sense. But then, I belonged here and it was going to be fine. My gender, my queerness. What a gift Yolanda gave me, it was such a good experience. Just like, oh my God, finally.

Next time we went to my grandmother's, all the foster kids were gone. My stepgrandfather who lived there had been molesting the kids, so they had to take all the kids, and Yolanda went, too. We didn't know where she was.

They took my grandmother's license away because this cabrón, he molested everybody. I'm pretty sure he molested me. I don't have access to memory of that, but I have access to going in his pickup truck, just him and I, and him giving me an apple and money. Something was off about that, and I never wanted to go with him again.

I grieved and I was heartbroken.

After that, I was more bold.

MS BILLIE COOPER: When I graduated elementary school, my brother and sister started chasing me around the house with knives and bats and sticks, calling me faggot and homosexual. One time, my brother stabbed me in the corner of my eye right above my nose. I thought I had lost my eye, because I saw blood, but thank god I didn't.

I had to watch out, not only being Black, but being gay—you know, effeminate. Because that turned a whole lot of people off. It was always there; they saw it. "That little queen. That little faggot, Billie Cooper." But some people used to call me Miss Billy back then, and I loved it.

Some people genuinely liked me, and some people despised me because of, you know, you're Black; you're not supposed to be living your life like that. You're not supposed to be doing that, and yadda yadda yadda. But it wasn't no game; it wasn't no pretense.

I stayed; I held fast and I was true to who I was.

NELSON D'ALERTA PÉREZ: My mother knew I was homosexual since I was a boy. I never had a closet because my mother told me, "You're gay. You're homosexual." I was five or six years old. I was kind of shocked because I didn't know what she was talking about. My mother had a lot of problems with homosexuality, and I imagine she had psychological problems too, but I never asked her.

She encouraged me to commit suicide. She'd say, "I have a problem with you." And then she'd say, "Let's commit suicide." I was a child.

This went on until I was forty. Her saying "Let's kill ourselves." When I was forty, I finally said, "No. That's a one-way ticket. You want to go? You go. I've got no problem here. I'm happy and content the way I am. And if I were to be born again, I'd want to be exactly this way. Maybe even a little more."

NICKY CALMA: When my mom would have her manicurist come to service her, I would ask, "Put color on my nails, too." I wanted that.

"Just put it on," my mother would say. And then she would tell me, "Make sure you take it off when your dad comes home."

And one time, I made a decision, a bold decision, not to take them off. We were eating, and my dad saw it. He went in a rage. He was like, "What is this? What's going on here?"

And I said, "Oh, just playing."

My mom looked at me, and was turning red already. In her eyes, I could see, "What did I tell you? You need to take these things off."

My dad's final statement was, "Take them off after dinner."

So, that was it.

I love my dad, but I don't love him.

The role I was going to play was a gay man, and my dad caught on to it. He said, "No. You need to move out if you're going to play that role. I don't want queers here, I don't want gays here in this house." He always told me, "If you're going to be living under my roof, and you're going to be eating the food that I buy with the money I earned, then you have to follow my rules."

That was the catalyst for me to really think, "I've got to get out of here."

ANDRÉS OZZUNA: I had a best friend. You know when you're with someone all day? I must have been eight, nine, ten years old. Now I see it as having been in love. If we fought, I would cry, it was terrible. And sometimes we'd walk holding hands. Very innocent. The possibility of homosexuality didn't exist even remotely in my mind. This was in the late seventies and early eighties, in Argentina. I mean, I didn't have that concept. Not at all. I didn't know it existed.

When I was fifteen, I came out. Because that same girl, when I was twelve, she went to go live in the capital. I lived in the province. We didn't see each other. When I was fifteen, she calls me on the phone. "Why don't you come here?" I had to take the bus, it was like an hour-and-a-half bus ride to where she lived. I went on a Saturday. And I got there, and she says, "This is my girlfriend." And that's when I understood everything. In that moment, I realized I was gay. I had never realized before, but when she said that, I understood everything.

I discovered myself. "Of course, this is my problem. I like girls."

I always felt like I didn't fit in socially. I was always so awkward, I was incredibly shy, I never talked, I hid all the time.

I told a girl at school. She told her mother, who called my mother. The news flew fast. My mother basically beat the crap out of me. Obviously, I denied it, what else was I supposed to do when she was trying to hit me? I mean, she was hitting me—what am I going to say, "Yes"? I saw no choice between saying yes or saying no.

Because if I said no: "Don't lie to me!" Bum, bum, bum.

If I said yes: bum, bum, bum.

So I felt like I had no choice. I felt extremely depressed. I wanted to leave, but I had nowhere to go, no money, I had nothing.

My mom didn't want to give me any money. My sister had a little boyfriend, and she could bring him over, spend the whole day hanging around the house with him, but I couldn't do anything.

Depression. But I couldn't do anything about it. If you have no money, it's that or the street. I got a job, so I'd have some money, and I finished high school by night. I went to the night school for adults. I hadn't done well in school, I'd had to repeat a grade, I had too much low self-esteem, I didn't feel like I was a person who could get an education. I wanted to work and make money. I wanted to eventually leave, rent an apartment or something. I never made enough money. I stayed in the house until I was twenty-three.

KB BOYCE: In the seventies in Bed-Stuy, there were Puerto Rican folks, there were Black folks. That was about it. You didn't see anything out of the norm, hardly ever. People knew me. They knew my family. We were kind of the freaks of the neighborhood. Black nationalists. We wore dashikis, dreadlocks back before that was a thing. We kind of stood out. Sometimes that felt unsafe, because it upset people that we were just so free.

I'm very lucky to have come up in a kind of matriarchy. My mom and my three sisters ruling. You know, there were very few male figures in our life. It was the women holding it down, and teaching us how to do whatever we needed to do.

I'm very blessed in that my family was supportive around being freakish, you know? It was normal for me. My mind being open, I got that from my family, you know? I got a lot of bravery from that, and it's obviously carried through the rest of my life.

My biggest issue was having to wear dashikis when I was a kid. My mom would put me in a dashiki, a dress. And that was what I had to walk around wearing. I wasn't really very into that.

I did not want to be in a dress, ever.

The fights. It was a lot. I was a boy, in my mind. Nothing else made sense.

It was getting to the point where I felt unsafe in my own neighborhood walking around, because of homophobia. So for punk rock to come along, suddenly I had this feeling of freedom, like, "These folks are not messing with me anymore, I can just be myself." I was completely androgynous, and all of my clothes were black.

I was also very, very good at hiding the growths, the mammary glands. I was not binding. It was just clothing choices and terrible posture.

That got me out of a lot of sticky situations, folks not wanting to mess with me anymore. It was super helpful.

The band itself started out as a cover band of junior high school kids, where we would play parties for other kids. That's when punk rock happened in the world. It was not hard to write punk songs. So we got into that, and wound up getting club gigs, and that began my life as a working musician.

I was a painfully shy child because I felt so awkward, I felt so unseen, and yet I found myself as the front person in a punk rock band playing in nightclubs, having to get up onstage and sing songs that I wrote. I had to just walk headfirst into that, in New York, in crowded nightclubs. And I would get offstage and be so shy I could barely speak. I also had a little bit of a stutter, and that would come up when I was nervous, you know? But onstage, I suddenly was able to just do the thing. That brought me joy.

I moved out at seventeen, and then I was able to just relax and be myself, as much as I could as an African American queer person in the early eighties in New York.

NELSON D'ALERTA PÉREZ: My grandfather really championed my education. He was like my mentor. He taught me how to fence, and to paint, he was a painter, he taught me a little. He took me to see opera and he told me, "You're going to come back here your whole life." And I did, I became an opera and ballet fanatic. In Cuba, with communism, the arts were very accessible. I have to say, that was a part of it I liked.

Every time I would complain because I'd been called a faggot, my grandfather would say, "You're an artist. You're an artist."

It was a great gift.

My grandfather created a strength in me, the strength to develop myself. To be brazen. He told me: "You can do it. Anything you want."

CRYSTAL MASON: When I was a kid—especially the younger years of my life—I was not suicidal, but I was not all that interested in being alive.

One of the best things my mom ever did for me was to feed my curiosity for books, and through the books, I realized that there were other lives out there and there were other things beyond what I knew, and that the things that I was dreaming of maybe weren't that far out.

That's the thing that made me start to be curious about life, and being part of life.

This idea that there were possibilities, even for a fat Black girl, to make a life that, in my imagination, fit me better.

TINA VALENTÍN AGUIRRE: Being assigned male at birth meant that there were lots of expectations. I was expected to play with boys. As a kid, I didn't have to wear makeup or anything to confuse people in terms of gender. It just kind of happened. Not only did I feel different, people saw me as different. Sometimes people would think I had lipstick on when I didn't, or mascara, and what I learned pretty early on was that they were reading something that was actually part of me.

It was tough for my dad. Pretty early on, my mom shared with me that she was okay with me being feminine, because before me, she and my dad had decided they would only have one more kid, and so she got pregnant, and they had a car accident, she had a miscarriage, and the child was a little girl. I think she was like six months pregnant. They were horribly disappointed. For her it was really dangerous to have kids as a little person. They told her each time that she could easily die and they did not recommend her to have kids. In those days, the medical industry was really bad in terms of how they acknowledged little people and how they should be able to live and thrive and have kids if they wanted. But they decided to try again. She really wanted a girl. She had me. And when she realized that I was feminine, she said, "Well, this is kind of what I always wanted anyway." So, she was accepting.

She started to teach me her recipes and started to have me around when she was with my tías, her comadres, and then I learned how women really support each other. I grew up helping my mom and my tías put on dresses, zip up dresses, put on their shoes. I'd help them with their makeup and hair. I learned really quickly, in my early teens, how to do liquid eyeliner, how to do hair, how to put together looks. Really young I would start to help my mom pick her outfits, because I was always with her.

I think she understood that my version of femininity was strong and beautiful.

For me, from a young age, femininity meant you should still be kick-ass. Obviously. Because the women in my family were all kick-ass.

So I just led with that.

THREE

* *

First Ventures

TUPILI LEA ARELLANO: I was seventeen when I started going to a gay bar, in Tucson, Arizona, drinking and dancing and building community. Sir James, it was called. It was out on a road that didn't have a lot of traffic at night or on the weekends. It was secluded. The outside was nondescript, and it had to be that way. But inside, there were signs: the rainbow, little rainbow flags, rainbow this and rainbow that.

I was already working, earning my money, and going to community college. The first night, oh, my God! I remember. It was a feeling like the world had opened up to me, like there was a place for me in the world. There were people there that looked queerer than me!

Drag queens, for one. Drag queens all over the place loving us up, and some of them felt very nurturing, like moms, talking so sweet to us. I could really relate to the drag queens because they were playing so deeply with gender. I used to watch them perform, and I learned a lot of my moves there. I used to love watching them. And there were super gay men—*super* gay, honey—the way they walked and talked and danced and everything. I loved that. And there were butch dykes. The two women who ran the bar, they were a couple: Judy and Judy. They called themselves diesel dykes, and they were both so butch, oh my God. I was fascinated by them: "Oh, look, at those two diesel dykes, they love each other so much."

They would also threaten us. They said, "If anyone's in here underage, we could lose our liquor license, they've been harassing us, and you know what? Both of us are going to get together and beat the hell out of you." Oh, my God! That scared the shit out of me. I was not a stranger to domestic violence. One night, the liquor control did come in. I ran in the bathroom, and I stood on the toilet and locked the door. They never came in. They never busted me.

I was a regular, and I'd go every weekend. For some of us, that was our home. We were very tight with each other. Once in a while, Judy and Judy would invite somebody to breakfast, to come home with them after we had been drinking. A lot of us went. They liked me so much, they invited me. We went into their house, and their house was diesel dyke-y. They rode motorcycles and stuff, and they had that kind of masculinity in their house, I loved it. I said, "Does that mean you drove diesels?" and one of the Judys says, "No, but I could drive any damn thing."

They fed us, and we laughed, and we talked. They were much looser than when I'd see them in the bar. I got to see them laugh and smile. I hardly ever saw them laugh or smile in the bar because they were on duty, honey. They were protecting us. Shit went down in that bar. People came and harmed us. Once, people were shooting at us when we left the bar because it's open carry state, a Republican state. These two lesbian bar owners, they open-carried sometimes, and they shot back.

We had birthday parties at that bar, we had fundraisers at that bar, we cried at that bar—oh, it really helped me. It wasn't great to be in a bar because alcohol is not a great thing, but, like I said, it was lifesaving. I had my first lover from there. It was family, and we mixed and we mixed deep. We didn't just get together at the bar: we had parties in our homes, movie days, barbecues, all of those things because from there, it was a nucleus.

Those things were born that we so needed.

BAMBY SALCEDO: When I was twelve. I was living two different lives. I had my street friends—my gang friends—and then I had friends who were queer and gay and trans. We were part of a fan club for Menudo, and we'd gather and do queer stuff—very queer!—there in the park. The group ranged in age from twelve to about eighteen.

So they said that they were going to this gay club, which in

Guadalajara at the time was called GOHL: Grupo de Orgullo
Homosexual de Liberación. Homosexual Pride Liberation Group. It
was a house. During the day, they would do HIV prevention and stuff
like that, and then at night, they would convert it into a club. A big
house, with lights and a DJ. That's how they built community.

The others were going. They said, "We are dressing up."

We went to somebody's place. I put a dress on. My first time. It
was a long white dress, too. It was beautiful. At that moment, I felt as
if I was Cinderella, as if that feeling that I'd had many years before
came back again.

That very moment was my aha moment. It was just beautiful. I felt
beautiful, ready to face the world. Like: I'm here.

It was the best. That night was magical. It marked my life.

Such moments mark you for life.

FRESH "LEV" WHITE: By the time I'm fourteen, I come out. By the time I'm
fifteen, I'm in male clothing almost full-time. And that was through
the help of the butch-femme community I connected with.

So, I'm fourteen, and I make out with a woman who is an inappropriate age. I remember I broke down crying afterwards because I
was like, "Oh my God, I'm gay!" That freaked me out. And then, I just
went dancing—jumping—out of the closet.

Shortly after that, I was told by this butch-femme community I
needed to choose what my role was. "What's going on in bed?" We
talked about it, and they were like, "Look, you need to decide if you're
butch or femme. You need to choose."

They were inhabiting that butch-femme culture and sensibility.
They made me choose a role.

That role ended up being stone butch. Really extreme, hardcore.

JOAN BENOIT: At Eastern Michigan University, I got on the softball
teams. Everybody's queer and out on the softball league, so that was a
no-brainer.

It was all about androgyny back then. There was no butch-femme language, really. That was stone butch stuff. It wasn't us.

FRESH "LEV" WHITE: I started identifying as stone, but also, the outward identifying was baby butch. I love that. I was really loving being butch. I loved this idea of being a masculine female. I started identifying that way, and came out of the closet really big. Before you knew it, I was in the Village wearing buttons and pins, and I was like, "I'm gay all over."

In ninth grade, I left school. It was around 1977. I had already started bouncing at a club called Chap and Rusty's, down in the Lower East Side of Manhattan, in New York. So I'm fifteen, I'm going downtown in my dad's suits. My dad sort of disappeared into a bottle once my mom died. We didn't have a lot of communication. We had a lot of struggle. But he taught me how to tie a tie, he let me borrow his suits. We never ever, ever talked about me being queer.

I remember going downtown and getting off the subway, and being greeted by the ladies of the evening who were just validating my butchness. They were all trying to pick up on me, flirting, catcalling, and all of this. And one night at this bar, a queer bar, some of those ladies came in really late, and then, they realized that I was butch.

They had been reading me as a cis man.

I was read as cis man often. If I wore a suit, there was no question.

And that's when I also found out some of them were trans. There was no mystery for me. It was just, "Oh, okay, cool, this is who you are." Here are these people, they're living into themselves. It was more of a celebration.

So, after that, they would show up at the bar that closed sometime between five and seven in the morning, because we were mafia run, so we had some dealings going on with the police. I used to take the alcohol out to the police at four in the morning, when the bars are supposed to close. I'd take them the cases of alcohol. That was my job.

Then we'd be able to stay open until six, no problem. Crazy times, New York City.

And I survived it. I'm still here.

C. NJOUBE DUGAS: I started going into the clubs at seventeen. They let me in at Amelia's, a lesbian club—the club to go to.

It was segregated. White people stayed downstairs; Black people went upstairs.

TINA VALENTÍN AGUIRRE: Amelia's was a lesbian bar on Valencia near Seventeenth. "Colors" was what they called the Latina lesbian night once a month, maybe every two weeks.

C. NJOUBE DUGAS: White people didn't even go upstairs. You don't go upstairs if you're white, period. And you could be downstairs if you're Black but only during certain hours. I mean, it wasn't like there was a rule, that's just how it was.

I'll never forget when I first got in, it was crazy. It was me and my friend Cynthia. Cynthia says, "Let's try it, let's just try it." We're standing outside smoking cigarettes, trying to be cool. There's this big woman at the door, the security, so we walk up in there with fake IDs. Terrible IDs. She gives us a hard time and says, "Okay, you all go straight up, sit in the corner, and don't go near that bar, there won't be no problems." So we ran up there. We're just looking around trying to be cool, and we're watching all the OG studs. OG—they're probably twenty-five, thirty! But they look OG. And that's when you could smoke in the clubs, right? They sit there smoking their little cigars or their pipes or whatever. We just watched them, to see how they moved; we're trying to get some pointers in there.

They came over to us: "What you little youngsters doing up in here?" Look at me, I'm sixty now, so you can imagine at seventeen, I probably looked twelve. So they would give us a hard time.

Once we got in there, we could get in there all the time.

I was told I was a stud. It was like, "Look at you little studs."

We were like, "Oh, we studs, that's what we are? Okay." Okay, so we need to get our gear together, we need to get our clothes together, you know what I mean? In the white community, there was butch and femme, and butch was a white woman who was masculine presenting. In the Black community, it was that you're either femme or you're a stud, and the stud was masculine presenting, so I just took that term. I didn't question it. I looked more like them, I'm good to go with it. So that was my reality. There was nothing else. Every now and then, we had people come from the East Coast, and they took on the term bull-dagger, and I was like, "Oh, they are tough."

And, oh, man, it was crazy because these OG studs, they told us so many stupid stories.

They used to tell us, "Oh, you-all don't know nothing about being with no women, you-all don't know this, you-all don't know that."

We'd sit there and talk a little shit like we knew something. We really didn't know much of nothing.

And they said, "Oh, you know how to eat pussy and blah, blah, blah?" And one said, "Well how you know you're good, I'm going to tell you." And she's like, "You know you're good when you eating it, you could just take a tangerine and peel off that skin with your tongue without using your teeth and without biting into it, that's when you're good."

Do you know how many tangerines we went through? Me and Cynthia used to sit there for hours. "Damn, I bit it!" Oh my God, we would sit up for hours with that crap.

DONNA PERSONNA: When I was in high school, I'd go to gay bars and go home with guys. The object was to never see them again. It was anonymous sex, and just once.

I ran into guys that used to bully me in school. They wanted to take me home. I remember this one guy, he wanted a trick. I said, "I don't want to go with you. You hated me in school, you bullied me."

And he said, "Well, it made it easier for me, when I would bully you. I could play football. I'm sorry."

I said, "Well, I don't want to go home and have sex with you now, you traitor. I was shit to you then, but now I'm cool? I have a long memory."

You hate me because I'm effeminate. Now it turned him on for some reason. To me, those were not the people, they were not on my side, they were not for me. I mean, I guess it can be forgivable. The fault is not his. I don't want him not to play football in high school if he can do that. He was put into a world where he took a choice, he made a choice, to have a better experience in school. I can't fault him for that, but for him to give me a bad time because I was effeminate? That's not nice.

I said, "Get out of here, I'm not going home with you, I don't want to be a part of that club."

LANDA LAKES: One of the things about being half Native is that often I had long hair. The beauty of that is, if you wanted to dress like a girl, it was very easy to do. I'd often wear ponytails and go somewhere. Once I hit my teenage years, me and my friend Felicia were able to get into a lot of clubs and just sort of blend in with all the other girls.

Me and my good friend Phillip, we used to cross-dress. It was the eighties, so we would go out looking like all the other eighties girls, to these young people clubs down in this area called Bricktown, in Oklahoma City. We had been practicing for a long time on our voices, too, so they could sound as feminine as possible, and so when we went to those clubs, we'd also use these fake voices that we had accumulated over time. We'd freak out whenever somebody would ask us for our ID. We knew then we needed to take off.

TINA VALENTÍN AGUIRRE: We created our own languages, our own codes. There wasn't anything in the media that looked like us, that we knew of, and queers were on television in really horrible, in stereotypical ways, although sometimes they were interesting. Our codes, for us, revolved around Wonder Woman, and how in *Charlie's Angels* there were strong, feminine characters. Culture Club. Prince. Little Richard, Boy George, *The Hunger* with Catherine Deneuve, David Bowie, Annie Lennox. It wasn't really our language, but we learned to adapt some of those codes.

What we recognized was that we were goth, so it was easy to say, "Oh, I'm a goth girl." And what that means is yes, we use makeup. In ninth and tenth grade, we would go to the bus stop, and people from the neighborhood that we knew from elementary would all get onto busses, and they saw us wearing makeup. And for me, the euphoria, the joy, was: We're doing this, even though you don't like it. And even though you don't accept it, and it's not your business.

Sometimes people would ask us, "Why do you have makeup on?"

And usually we would just say, "Oh it's Tuesday." Or, "We look pretty." That's it. Why are you asking me this? This should not be a thing.

In high school there was an underage dance club where it was queer-, it was bi-, it was trans-friendly, and we would go and just were all playing out these things. We found ways to make it work, but it really was not like today. It was very different.

What we were doing was also genderqueer. I kept that part with me. I learned pretty early on, people saying, "Oh, they're not one hundred percent on one side of the gender spectrum," and I thought, "Yes, that's me."

ADELA VÁZQUEZ: At thirteen, I came out to my family.

My grandmother told me, "This is your family, this is your house." After that, who was going to stop me? You know what I mean?

I was in boarding school, in Cuba—fourteen, fifteen, sixteen; this is when your hormones are jumping. My free time, the summer and stuff, I would go on my own to places and make friends. And I had queeny friends. We'd go out to concerts, and we'd go to dance, and we'd go to quinceañeras, with makeup on. I remember going to school with a face full of makeup. They sent me back home, but— full-on. It was full-on makeup. I was very daring. The fashion was bell-bottoms, big buckles, very tight. I was in line waiting for the bus and people would refer to me with female language. They didn't know if I was a man or woman. I started super young.

With all this beautiful life, from age thirteen to twenty-one, I went out every night, just to hang out with my friends.

MS BILLIE COOPER: When I started hanging out at the clubs, it was a time when I was not only finding more out about myself, but I was getting to know my community. We were meshing together, because we were gay; we were queer; we were homosexuals. We would go to clubs that were off the beaten path. We would go to clubs that opened up after 10 p.m., or after midnight. It could have been dangerous, but it wasn't. This was in like 1971, or '72, when I was going into high school.

You know, people around me used to get jumped and beat. I was so lucky that I never got jumped, or I never was put in a compromising position. Back then we didn't use the word *phobic* too much, like *homophobia* and stuff like that. But it was there. Black people, white people, Spanish people, queer people, we pretty much got together and stayed as one.

It was a nice time; I found community. I found best friends.

CRYSTAL MASON: I was in this small bookshop in Richmond, and on the bottom shelf was *On Our Backs*. I read some of the stories in there, lesbian erotic stories. I started realizing that it was possible to have not just emotional relationships, but also sexual relationships with women.

STORMMIGUEL FLOREZ: In the early nineties, I worked at the feminist bookstore. There were a lot of books coming out at the time about

BDSM. Telling you how to do things safely. It was really important information. People do S/M and don't necessarily do it safely because they're not taught.

So I was telling the bookstore, "We need to carry these books," and they were like, "No, S/M is abuse." They didn't sell *On Our Backs*; they didn't sell the BDSM books. We would argue. It was complicated.

CRYSTAL MASON: With *On Our Backs*, it was amazing, just being able to put words and actions together with these feelings. It was really exciting.

The thing that really brought it home for me is that during all that time that I was, I would say, emerging, I met this guy named Frank. I was twenty-two, and he was beautiful and very kind. Somehow or another, we fell into dating. He wanted to marry me. In my head, I was almost going along with it because it felt like the train was going by and the last car was about to disappear, that's where my straightness was. It was like, if I was going to be straight, this was my last chance.

I realized how silly that was and how awful it would be for Frank. Then I was a full-on dyke.

CHINO SCOTT-CHUNG: I came out to myself in high school. In Denver, Colorado, in the seventies, there was no way to come out. There were no community centers, most of the queer life was in the bars, and I was too young. So I joined the Army, and that was one of the reasons why I joined: to come out. Also to leave home, to get a college education, and to learn a skill.

I joined the Army in 1979. I was in through '84. It was funny—there were indeed a lot of lesbians in the Army. I went to AIT, which is Advanced Individual Training, as a mechanic. The barracks where we lived was a four-story building, mostly men. There was a hallway that was covered by an olive-green tarp, and that's where they put all the lesbians. I wanted to stay in that hallway! But I never got a chance.

I imagine all the lesbians back there having a great time and partying and just enjoying life, and that's why I also wanted to go.

That's where I came out: in the Army.

MS BILLIE COOPER: I signed up to go into the Navy after high school. I was questioning whether I was man enough to go in, because so many people on my block were saying, "You'll be back, they don't want you, you aren't going to stay there long." But they signed me up, and I went into the US Navy in 1976.

It wasn't Don't Ask Don't Tell. It was "don't even bother us, we don't care." All they wanted was a body. It was right after Vietnam. So I just went in. You know why I went to the Navy? Because of all these commercials on TV: "Be all the man you can be in the United States Army, Navy, or Marines." And I said, I need me a couple husbands.

I just wanted to go, to get away from Philly, to do something different, to be a man, try to be a man; that was hilarious.

Back then, you know, they did tell me I was different. They never called me a homosexual, or faggot or nothing. But I was different; visually different. People could see that I came from a different realm.

The Naval Investigative Service, the NIS, came to my compartment, where I was sleeping in my space there, in the dormitories, and tore my cabinet apart, tore my bed apart, tore all my stuff apart, because one of my girlfriends in New York was writing me letters addressed to Miss Donna Summer. She would send me like a couple letters a month. They came asking me who was Donna Summer.

And I said, "I'm Donna Summer, honey."

I'll never forget the look on their faces. I had to go to another Captain's Mast and explain myself.

CHINO SCOTT-CHUNG: I came out to my mom and my sister when I was twenty-one.

It must've been 1981. I had gotten in this really bad accident in the Army: I was bleeding some brakes, and a truck backed up over me in the motor pool. The guy didn't have rearview mirrors. He caught the left side of my head, tore off my ear, split open my head. They had to piece my ear back together and sew my head. It was very intense.

They sent me to Chapel Hill, North Carolina, to the hospital there. In the hospital, I remember I was like, "Okay, I'm going to come out to my mom because I could've died." I thought, "I want my mom to accept me, if she can, and this could be my last chance."

When my mom came to visit, I was lying in bed with this big bandage wrapped over my head. I said, "Mom, I'm a lesbian." At the time it was either lesbian or gay; there was really no other word.

My mom said, "I know."

I was shocked. I didn't know she knew. I go, "You do? How long have you known?"

She's like, "I've known since you were fifteen."

So that was nice. She knew when I knew. I knew for sure I was a lesbian at fifteen. I guess moms just know those kinds of things.

STORMMIGUEL FLOREZ: We had a term in high school that we used when somebody kissed a girl for the first time, and that was that you were wrecked. It didn't feel like a derogatory term. So I was wrecked. I was fifteen. I learned that I was indeed queer. I don't think we were using the word *queer*. It was May 22, 1987, my wrecked anniversary, the day I kissed a girl and I knew. It was just like: absolutely, this is it. I suddenly had no shame, no question in my mind about whether or not I was gay. That switch happened immediately.

I was still kind of masculine. I was developing a more punk aesthetic, which is in some ways very gender-neutral or agender.

That summer after I came out, I just had fun. I wasn't out to my parents yet. It was hard for me not to tell my folks. I wanted to tell them, I wanted them to know this about me, but we weren't close like that. I wanted to know them, I wanted them to know me, I wanted them to be interested in my life, and they were just not, especially my mom. That just wasn't her style.

One day, I was having a particularly bad day. I was seeing this girl, and she broke up with me. At that point, I was already ditching class, so I left school. Something in my mind was just like, Okay, I'm going to go to my two friends, they live on the same street, I'm going to talk to them. They're always home. But if they're not, it's a sign; I'm going to go home and come out to my family. I'm going to write a note, tell them I'm gay, and run away.

So I go to the first person's house, she's not home. Well, that's weird, she's always home. I go to the second person's house, she's not home. I had made a commitment. I'm true to my word. I went home, I wrote to my parents: "I want to let you know I'm a lesbian and I'm running away because I figure you'd kick me out anyway,"—which was not true, I just didn't want to face them.

I left them that note, grabbed a couple essentials, a backpack.

I ended up hanging out with another friend that night who talked me into calling my parents. We went to a pay phone. I called my mom and dad's house. My dad answered. "Where are you, mija, are you okay?"

"I'm okay, I'm at a pay phone, I'm safe, I'm okay."

"Come home, come home."

"Not tonight, Dad, just give me the night."

And my mom picks up the phone. "You get home right now, you have no business being out there—" She just went off. I'm crying, and she's yelling.

"I'm not coming home tonight, Mom."

She says, "You get home right now."

This dramatic phone call. Finally, I just hung up on her and cried a lot. The next morning, I went to my dad's work. He said, "You should go home, your mom's really upset."

I went to the house, and went inside. My mom was in there. She was vacuuming, tears down her face, all swollen. She stopped the vacuum, she hugged me, and then she started yelling at me. My dad came home, we all sat down and went at it for a while. My mom telling me I'm too young to know this and that I have to change, she should've known. "I shouldn't have let you dress like a boy." This is where that comes in: suddenly, it wasn't okay for me to be masculine. "You're so easily influenced." She just really couldn't imagine that this was something that I was choosing for myself, and it was actually who I am. "You're going to have to go see a psychologist, you're going to change."

And I said, "No way, I'm not going to do it."

My mom was like, "No, no, no, you're going because you're going to change." She was just not having it.

My mom is Catholic, I grew up Catholic, we went to church every Sunday. We had a Bible in the house that I don't think we ever cracked open. Suddenly, my mom that day became very religious. She was just like, "That is evil. It's against God."

I'm just like, "Okay, I've never heard you be so Catholic. You're saying evil? I've never heard you utter that word."

She took me to the doctor.

The doctor said, "What's going on?"

And my mom said, "Well, you know, my daughter thinks she's gay."

And I'm like, "Mom, I know I'm gay."

And the doctor, Dr. Prado, said, "Well, okay, I can give you the name of a good psychologist, but I can also tell you that her being gay is a lot safer than her sleeping with every boy on the block."

It's funny that those are the two alternatives. But I was so pleased that she said that.

My mom, of course, was not.

TUPILI LEA ARELLANO: When I told my father, I used the word *lesbian* because that's what we used then.

And he said, "I don't ever want you to use that word again in this house."

I said, "Lesbian, lesbian, lesbian, lesbian."

I kept saying it over and over. He knew it wasn't going to fly, like he was trying to get mad.

I said, "Look at me, here I am telling you a very important part of my life, and you're focused on that word." I said, "You know the friends who come over here with me, that you love? They're all gay."

"No way, no!"

And then he started going down the list, every one of them. He already was attached to them, they were so kind to him, they'd come over and help us cook all the time. That really helped.

Then my dad became one of my best allies. He let me bring my girlfriends over and sleep with them in his house.

My brother once said in front of me, "How come Lea gets to bring her girlfriends and everything?"

And my father said, "Pendejo, she can't get married, you can. So when you get married, you bring your wife over here."

JOAN BENOIT: I was disowned when I was in college for being queer because my family is Republican, and in Michigan, and Catholic, and that was what the priest told them to do. It was my chosen family that gave me life, saved my life, created a safety net. I was nineteen. I was a child. I was sleeping in my car for a good six months. Showering at friends' houses, parked in front of a convenience store where my cousin worked the midnight shift, so I would have a safe place to sleep. It was the chosen family that not only saved me, but raised me. They taught me values, how to be there for each other. And I think the chosen family really solidified in a way that probably would never have happened if I weren't disowned.

The first holiday after I was disowned, my parents granted permission for me to come home for that holiday. And my mom said, "The only way we'll let you into the house is if you get tested for HIV."

I said, "I won't do that, it's an impossibility that I have it. There's no way that I could have contracted it. I'm in the safest population there is. The only ones not getting it are lesbians. I won't get tested."

So, I didn't go home.

I don't think I stepped foot in that house after that for at least—seven years? Eight, ten years? I don't know.

I'm grateful for those years in so many ways. You hear "disowned" and think, oh, how awful. Heartbreaking. But I grew in ways that I never would have if that hadn't happened.

There was no fallback anymore. My mistakes were mine to own. And I had to learn that there were consequences to my actions in a way that I probably wouldn't have earlier. Up until that point, I was a little wild and carefree. So I learned confidence. I learned that I could accomplish a lot more than I thought I could, that I could stand on my own and thrive.

When I got disowned, I got involved with Native stuff in college, and when my aunt mom adopted me I really got involved. She was really involved in the Native community in Michigan. She knew everyone, she was at the reserve all the time, she married a Native guy, her children were Native. If I hadn't been disowned, I would have never learned all of that.

ANDRÉS OZZUNA: I had some gay friends. Sometimes we'd go out at night, in Buenos Aires, and the first time a girl kissed me was at a bar, I don't remember her name, nothing at all, I swear I don't remember almost anything about her. But I was at this bar, and a girl kissed me. I think in that moment, I was so overwhelmed I couldn't even see. I didn't understand a thing. But what an incredible sensation in the body, oh, I remember the feeling. I remember the feeling more than the person. It was very intense, through my body, and from then on, I thought, yes, obviously.

At nineteen, I had a girlfriend, then another girlfriend, and I'd try to spend as much time as possible at my girlfriends' homes—not the first one, she wasn't accepted in her family either so we'd spend all afternoon or all night until morning in the plazas of Buenos Aires. I was out on the street a lot because I didn't have anywhere to go. I'd come home late. In Buenos Aires you can stay out all night and go home at six in the morning, so I did that a lot. The years passed that way. I had no plan except to survive, you know?

When I was twenty, my first girlfriend and I went to an underground gay place, and we were arrested there. This was in 1990. It was horrible. It was one of the hardest things that's happened in my life, for not having anywhere safe to go.

The place had no name. It was in downtown Buenos Aires. There was no sign on the door. You knocked and went down some stairs, it was underground.

In those days—and before then, too—if you were on the street, they could—well. In the military era, forget about surviving. Later, after democracy started in '83, there were still a lot of coups during the transition. They were trying to overthrow the democracy. So even though we had a democracy, it was very fragile. And the military still had a certain power. The society was still conservative, structured. Democracy didn't happen just like that. So the repression from before was still around. And, obviously, in the dictatorship era, they killed gay people. They were disappeared. Anyone who expressed themselves, everyone who went beyond the parameters they had that were extremely conservative. Anything different from what the military thought—anything—made you a subversive person. So if you weren't conservative, orderly, all of that, you were subversive, you were a problem, and as a result they'd take you and torture you. And kill you. If you were lucky, they'd kill you directly without torture. And then they'd basically throw you in the river. They could do anything to you. To gay people, of course, but also to artists, people who expressed themselves or wanted something else.

In 1990, the Falcons were still on the streets. Ford Falcons used by the police. And thousands of times, I'd be waiting for the bus, since I was on the street so much because I couldn't go home, and they'd ask you for your documents.

That's why it was always good to have long hair, to be a woman who looked like a woman. If they saw something strange, they'd take you. Living in Buenos Aires, I always presented as feminine. I'm not going to say super feminine, but feminine. Long hair. Because it was a way to survive.

So we were in that place, down the stairs, sitting together, my girlfriend and me. And down they came, fast, so fast, that in one second they were standing right in front of us. We were just talking, and then boom, there they were. "Documents." We couldn't do anything. And they took us.

They just took us. It was nighttime, or maybe early morning, three in the morning or so. They put us in a car, along with others. I never found out where we went, we were loaded into the car, I don't know where they drove, I don't know where they stopped. They basically treated us like cattle. They made us all go into a room. It was like a school, you know? A big room, like a classroom. They took everything from us, documents, money, everything we had. Our shoelaces. It was winter. They sat us all there, wrote things down, I don't know what they were doing but they did it to each of us.

At one point, these men come in, with faces just like Nazis, perfect uniforms, their trousers ironed, the whole thing. And there's a gay kid with us who stands up and says he wants to call his mom. And one of those men says, "Who is it you want to call?" He grabs him, hits him in the head, starts beating him, *pah, pah, pah, pah, pah.* He grabs him by the hair and drags him by it, takes him away. That's how the night started.

So then it was, like, "Fuck." You know? My thought was, "What do I have to do to get out of here?"

I thought it was my last day, that they were going to kill us. It was a horrible situation, of not being able to do absolutely anything other than keep your head down and try to survive.

After that, they took us to a kind of patio with cells. It was all dark. In the patio, they opened doors made of solid metal with just the tiniest windows, and they put us in the cells. Dark. You couldn't see anything. You just heard voices.

We were with a lot of people.

We were cramped in there, standing, or sitting on the floor as if standing. They didn't let us out for twenty-four hours. They didn't let you talk to anyone, or leave the cell, they'd hit the doors all the time, *bah, bah*, you'd hear all sorts of blows . . .

You'd hear them beating on the doors, then you'd hear screams. But you couldn't see anything because it was so dark. All you had was that tiny little window at the base of the door. All day in the dark. Just, there. We didn't know where we were. Cold, cold. Winter in Buenos Aires is cold. It doesn't snow, but it gets very cold. And there was nowhere to sit: the cell was tiny, and we were the last to come in. There were others who'd already been in there, many trans women or sex workers who were also being treated this way. A whole lot of other people, although I didn't really know who they were, it was so dark, you couldn't see anyone, see anything. They didn't let us out, didn't let us use the bathroom, didn't let us eat, nothing. No water, nothing, nothing. And what's more, the guys, the gay men who were there, were tortured and killed there. As soon as we arrived they started getting beaten. Right there in front of everyone: we were all there and it would start, *pah, pah*, bleeding. Dragged by the hair. Taken away. The message was: this is what's going to happen to you.

It went on until Monday morning. It had started on a Saturday night. On Monday, the police commissioner came.

The crime was, to have been there. In that place. We hadn't been kissing, or even holding hands, we were just talking. But still: I denied it. Constantly. My girlfriend and I were from the provinces, not the capital, where all of this was happening. So when that guy passed, beating on the doors, I'd say to him, "Pardon me, sir, I'd like to speak to someone because it seems I've been brought here by mistake." I spoke very politely, with respect, because what would happen if I spoke any other way? I knew he could just say, "Hey, you bitch!" and I wouldn't have lasted two minutes. So that was my strategy: to deny it, and to speak to him well, really well. I also felt responsible for my girlfriend at that point. Plus, we were incredibly cold. I remember that cold. It was horrible. So every time the guy passed, I said the same thing.

And finally, on Monday, they let me talk to the police chief, or commissioner, I don't know who he was. I acted very feminine with him, it was the only way to get out of that place. I told the man that we weren't from here, that we didn't know where we were, some young guys told us we could go to that place downtown and so we stopped by, we'd just arrived when this happened, and we'd had no idea, we were basically two stupid girls from the province. Innocent, I said.

And the guy says, "Well, next time you come to the capital, come talk to me and I'll tell you where you should go."

And I said, "Of course, sir. Of course."

And so they let us go.

But to not have any control over your life! Because it looked like they were going to torture us, and kill us. Because that was part of our past. I think it saved us that we were women.

I have so much fear. I was afraid because I'd think, well, I was lucky that one time. I was so afraid of the police, even when I came here to California. After I got here, years after this happened, it was still with me. Once, I was in the Castro District with my girlfriend at the time, and sometimes the police would walk around the Castro. Now in the Castro, the police are gay! But at the time, I didn't know that. So we see the police and we flee into a store and stay there, hiding. I was terrified. I didn't speak any English. It was a store that sold magazines, and my girlfriend and I grab a magazine and pretend to read it. Gripping that magazine. How ridiculous! But at that moment—I don't know. It was survival instinct.

It's taken me a lot to be myself. It took a lot to get to where I am. Maybe it's the repression, or something else, but I have such a strong survival instinct in me that sometimes I don't allow myself things. And that's marked me, made me say, "I can't let anything show, because I might get killed." Which is a shame, because here, I could have expressed myself more fully earlier. It took so much for me to be able to walk down the street holding someone's hand and feel okay, even in the Castro. This isn't Buenos Aires, but it's as if Buenos Aires is here with me. I escaped but didn't escape, you repeat your story in the new safer place. It took me time. And there are older people in Argentina, friends of mine who were gay in that time, who still don't like to express themselves on the street. You absorb that, and it's hard to get it out of you.

So what did I do to heal? Over time, I tried to find ways to feel safer with my own self. But it still took a lot. Especially around masculinity. Being butch, then trans. When it comes to femininity as survival, you could say, well, women aren't safe. No, they're not. But at the same time, I had this feeling like, if you let your masculine side show, it's worse. You're in deeper shit. You're less safe.

SHARYN GRAYSON: As I grew into young adulthood and began to understand a little bit about gender, I felt that I was always the same person. As an older young adult, we had developed terms, terminology, and definitions, and I kind of began to understand. But then, I'm like, "I don't really fit into that. No, that's not really who I am."

Effeminate.

Sissy boy.

Oh, gosh. There were some much more negative terms.

I'm like, "No. That is not a complete picture of who I am."

Even though people were telling me, "This is who you are."

And I'd say, "No. No. No. Not really."

No, that wasn't me.

KB BOYCE: When I moved out at seventeen years old, I wound up living kind of on the border of the West Village, around some gay bars. I took the opportunity to be like, "I am free. I can go to gay bars if I want to."

I quickly realized that I did not identify as a lesbian. I didn't quite know what to identify as. I didn't have the words. So I started calling myself queer. Back then, that really wasn't in vogue yet.

CHINO SCOTT-CHUNG: *Queer* was actually a very derogatory word, and we didn't use that, it was something that was very hurtful at the time. Now, it's a great word, because it encompasses all sexualities, all identities within the queer community—trans, lesbian, gay, bi, gender fluid, nonbinary. It's a beautiful word. An excellent word and an excellent identity. I call myself queer and trans now, but back then, we didn't use the word *queer*.

YOSEÑIO LEWIS: It's still hard for me to say the word *queer*, because that was the slur that was used against me when I was a kid. That was the slur I heard when somebody was running me off the road. That was the slur I heard when somebody had thrown things at me. That was the slur I heard when I was walking to school in my town, and one day, I think I was maybe fifteen or sixteen, somebody decided to pull up real close to me, and had a shotgun, and I felt it in my ribs. And they said, "You fucking queer, I'm going to shoot you!" My logic brain was, "Okay, how do I get through this alive?"

It was: "You're queer and you're bad, you're worthless, it's not a problem for me to eliminate you." I've had that my whole life. I also have that because I happen to be Black. And because I happen to have names that people couldn't pronounce, so therefore it was foreign, and it was wrong. I was too dark for the Latin people in my world, and I was too Latin for the Black people in my world. "Oh, you're different. I don't understand it." All my life I've had that.

I do use the word *queer* now. But I understand some of the older people who say, "I will never use that word! That word was used against me."

KB BOYCE: I was so ecstatically happy when *queer* as a term did come into vogue. I remember when I found it: it meant the world to me because I was like, "Exactly! That is exactly what I've been feeling. This makes sense, you know?" It made me feel like part of something, which is what had been missing for my youth, my growing-into-myself years.

Still, older lesbians or gay men would say to me, "Don't say that! That's not a good word, that's bad. Don't say that."

And I would say, "But I feel queer because I'm not a lesbian and I'm not a gay man. I don't know what is going on."

So yeah. I was aware that I was different, and I just spent a long time trying to figure out what that meant.

It wasn't until later that I began to find out about the possibility of transmasculine existence, and found some of the words.

PART TWO

* * * * * * * *

FORGING LIVES

* *

FOUR

Migrations

ADELA VÁZQUEZ: This is how I value my life: I'm an immigrant, I've been here forty years now, without any kind of guidance.

It's like being born again. You have to leave your life behind to find another one, and learn the ways of this other culture: the new life. From zero. From zero. You are new. It's like you just came out of the womb, but you don't have a mother. You're on your own. That is not easy. You have to be very strong, you have to be very smart, and you have to navigate waters that are very turbid.

ANDRÉS OZZUNA: I think that, when you're an immigrant, you contribute something to the community where you live. Your perspective, your way of being. A different way of looking at things. And it can be—how to put it? Not welcome, maybe. But it can have value.

BAMBY SALCEDO: I'm a woman, a trans woman, a Latina, immigrant, undocumented woman.

When I came to the United States I had just turned sixteen.

From the age of twelve, I started getting incarcerated in juvenile detention centers in Mexico. That's how it went from age twelve to sixteen. I was in and out of those correctional facilities. The last time, my father came to visit from the United States. He sought me out, and that's when I met him, there in that facility in Guadalajara. He asked me if I wanted to go to the United States and join him. When I got out that last time, my mother didn't know what to do with me. I saw no future in Mexico, none. So I decided to go.

The truth is, I didn't know what awaited me in the US. But my life in Mexico at that point was one of the streets, drugs, crime. All I could see for myself was more time in prisons, or I might end up dead, murdered. So it seemed like the only option.

I came with an uncle of mine, Tío Eloy. We went to Tijuana and crossed the border. It was easier in those days. We crossed over on the beach. We arrived in Los Angeles, my father picked us up, and then we went to a small town where my father lived at the time, in Central California, called Visalia. My dad had his own family, with other children, so I wasn't very welcome in that house. My dad sent me there to work instead of enrolling me in school and helping me that way.

I mean, I did want to work, because you hear about the United States and how dollars can be made there, and I came with that goal: "I'm going to earn dollars and help my family."

So there I was, working. I worked in a tortilla factory, putting tortillas in bags. It's heavy work. I had no papers at that time. So I was exploited, as a minor. I worked long hours, and they didn't pay me the overtime they should have. No breaks. That tortilla machine spitting out tortillas, and me there catching them, putting them in bags. It was too much. Around that time, I was also introduced to more intense drugs. Cocaine. Heroin. I had started injecting heroin when I was seventeen, a year before I came here, to Los Angeles.

And this is where I've always been since, where I started getting arrested here in the United States. Because of my drug addiction, it took me four periods in state prison, and many in Los Angeles County jail, as well as deportations and time spent in immigration detention centers, before I could finally reform my life.

ADELA VÁZQUEZ: After I finished school, I could not stay. I couldn't stay in Cuba. Cuba was too small.

I knew that I needed to leave because everybody was going to jail. In Cuba, they take you to jail for the smallest things.

And it was pretty much against the law, being gay.

NELSON D'ALERTA PÉREZ: In Cuba, we were very oppressed for being gay.

ADELA VÁZQUEZ: I knew that I wanted to leave. I knew since I was ten. This is my dream come true: coming to America. I knew that I had to leave to be free, to be myself.

Okay, so I came to America in 1980, in the Mariel boatlifts. And I loved the fact that I left that way. It was an excitement: oh, my God, I'm leaving Cuba, I'm leaving this motherfucker behind, you know what I mean?

I had to leave to save myself. And I had to let in a new culture— which is fucked up because I was twenty years old. I didn't know how to talk, I didn't know how to get anywhere, I didn't know anybody.

NELSON D'ALERTA PÉREZ: I left Cuba in 1980. I received political asylum through the Peruvian Embassy. That was a moment that really marked me, because it was the bridge for me to come to the United States.

I was working in a tourism office. I read in the newspaper that the guards had been removed from the Peruvian Embassy, because there had been a shootout over some people who wanted asylum. And Fidel Castro decided to remove the guards. I joked with my friends: "Well, now we can all go have tea at the embassy."

After that, I went home, without thinking more about it. But my lover at the time came to me and said, "Did you know there are a hundred people taking asylum right now at the Peruvian Embassy?"

I said, "What?"

He said, "Do you want to go?"

"No," I said. "Not me."

But I was mad with desire to go; I couldn't take it anymore.

It was the persecution. It was so tough. Terrible, terrible. At one point I was detained by state security, for holding a drag party in my home. They took it to the higher levels. They interviewed me. Tortured me. I was tortured horribly. I still have aftereffects to this day. It was really hard, something I don't understand. I said this to them: "I'm gay, yes. And I'm transsexual, yes. I'm a woman, I dye my hair, I wear makeup. What's behind all that? Nothing. That's all it is. What are you looking for? Something political, that isn't even there?"

I was one of the few, the 10,800 people who received asylum at the Peruvian Embassy. We spent 1,001 nights there. My asylum was hard. I spent fifteen days without food or drink. I lost my strength; I fainted. Then I rallied. I won that asylum. I won it.

ADELA VÁSQUEZ: When I arrived, I had my ups and downs. I came from Cuba to Key West, in Florida, and from Key West I went to Arkansas. I was there in a fort being processed by immigration and so on for a month and a half. And then from there, I went to Los Angeles, California. I stayed there until March of 1982. Then I went to Dallas, Texas, where I met Nelson D'Alerta Pérez, who would become a life-long friend and who I live with now.

I arrived in San Francisco in 1983. I came here with my girlfriend, who at first was roommates with Nelson, and that's how we all came to live in Nelson's apartment.

I immediately liked San Francisco. I remember taking acid the third day I was here. I walked around and I was like, "Oh, yes. This is home." I got lost and everything. I loved it.

I have beautiful friends here. I have lived here many years.

NELSON D'ALERTA PÉREZ: Oh, my life when I arrived in the United States was just wonderful. I'd dreamed of it so much that I didn't even miss my family or my country. Even now, I'm celebrating my arrival in the United States, after forty years. To me, this country opened its doors, and I'm very grateful that it did.

Although, when I first arrived, I had major problems for being homosexual.

I was interviewed by a man from the CIA. They were worried about people coming from Cuba as infiltrators, so they were interviewing those who arrived, with many very specific questions. It was all very serious. There they were, asking, "Have you ever been a communist?"

"No."

"Tell him I'm going to ask the questions again. If he lies, he won't get papers. One more time. Have you served in the Army."

I said, "No."

"Why not?"

"Because I'm homosexual."

Oh, my god.

He shouted, "There's a homosexual here! A homosexual!" And on my file, which was yellow, he stamped the red letters HOMOSEXUAL. Look, I still get goosebumps when I tell this.

How did I feel? Like I come to this country seeking freedom, and this is the face they offer me. Where do I go now? Where can I live? But at the same time, I was fighting for my rights. "No, no, no, you are mistaken, sir."

So they sent me to another man, and he was very vulgar. He said to me, "Do you do oral sex?"

I said, "I do oral sex, yes, but I don't think I could perform it with you because you seem too small."

The man froze. He said, "I could slap you."

I said, "No, if you slap me, I'll slap you back."

That was very traumatizing for me.

All of that was very violent. Everybody around us, laughing.

Fear, fear. Disgust at having this thrown in my face. Repulsion that I'd had my rights violated yet again. After the long asylum, when this happened, it was a shock.

It took me ten years to get a green card. They wouldn't accept me. There was a law that if you were homosexual, you couldn't enter the United States. That law was still in effect, then. For being who I am. That made me feel awful.

I felt exhausted, but I said, well, I'm going to keep on. With my truth. I'm going to get through this.

And still, I'm very grateful to the United States for opening doors for me to be here.

Here, in the US, I've achieved many of my dreams.

NICKY CALMA: I'm originally from the Philippines. I moved here in 1989 to explore the true me, the real me. I was around twenty. It was very challenging. I didn't have it that rough back home in the Philippines, but I had to leave because I was really searching. I mean: who am I?

We'd go to church every Sunday. My dad would make us read the Bible. And I thought, Okay, I need to get out of here.

An opportunity came. I had the chance to come here to the United States, and then I just worked my way to make the United States my permanent residence. It was here in the United States that I started to think, who am I? Who really was I dealing with in front of the mirror?

The chance came in 1989, with a group of friends. One of them is a leading actress in the Philippines, and she was contracted to do a show here in the United States for her fans to see her. I was her only friend who had a visa, who could come to the United States. And none of her assistants were granted visas. So she said, "I'd like to hire you to be my production assistant for the show."

I took advantage of it.

And then, I told my mom, actually: "I might not come back. I'm just going to live it out there." She knows that I can be very independent.

When I got to the US, I told my friend, "Hey, I'm going to stay behind."

I had to survive. It wasn't easy for me. It wasn't like I had a place to stay. I only had, I think, $500 with me, and my two suitcases. I didn't know the system, I didn't know how it worked. And then, you know, you get to meet people. And that's when they got me into doing sex work. They said, "Well, you're going to get paid to do this. You like to do these things."

That was in '89. And since then, my eyes were opened to all of these concepts. I read articles about Christine Jorgensen. Transgenderism. All this stuff. That's what made me stay.

ANDRÉS OZZUNA: I had this girlfriend whom I'd met when I was about twenty-five. I lived with her in Buenos Aires. I worked, and so did she. Her class background was a little different from mine. She had a brother who lived in San Francisco, California, and at one point, we went on vacation to visit her brother in San Francisco.

I didn't even know that San Francisco was a gay place. I found that out by coincidence while we were there. All because we were visiting her brother. We just happened to be there in June, for Pride—by coincidence.

When we found out, I said, "This is fantastic."

We went to the Castro District, where all the gay people were, all of this and that, all the Gay Pride. It was—oh, my God! It was incredible. When I went to that first Gay Pride, I had the most amazing time. I saw all those people walking and spent the whole time crying on the street.

It was so moving to see all the different kinds of self-expression. But I remember one thing specifically: a woman or man with a sign that said, "I am a proud parent." Okay, when I saw that, I almost died. There I was, crying. Yes. It was really so moving.

We saw all those gay things, and then when we returned to Argentina, she said to me, "I want to leave here."

So I say to her, "Let's go."

And we went.

Just like that. I had nothing to lose. An office job, that's it. But I basically had nothing.

I was twenty-eight years old.

In 1998, we came with a single suitcase. With no English, nothing. I didn't speak a single word.

When we arrived, we went to live at the brother's house, and said, "What now?" That's how it was.

I remember that we sat on the porch—you know how, in San Francisco, there are stairs up to the houses? We're sitting on those front steps, and I say, "Well, what's next?" We had no plans. No idea, no papers. We had nothing. So we started putting up signs offering to clean houses. We started cleaning homes without speaking English or anything. It was hard, because we had no car, no money. We'd go by bicycle, clean the houses, it was all very physical, you know?

It was like that for many years.

Eventually, things changed, but for years, it was a kind of survival instinct. The good thing is that I kept going to school, then university, and eventually built a career. I graduated from San Francisco State University when I was almost forty years old.

CHINO SCOTT-CHUNG: As I was growing up, we used to drive to San Francisco, because my dad loved the food. We all loved the food. We came to San Francisco to eat dim sum at the Jackson Street café. My dad could always find Chinatown by seeing the Transamerica Pyramid building. We'd drive there, every five years or so, and we'd have dim sum and clams in black bean sauce, my mom's favorite.

When I was fifteen, my brother and his best friend Wayne decided to drive to San Francisco, as a vacation. I was fifteen, and my brother and his friend were seventeen. They organized the trip, and I was like, "Oh, can I go?"

They said yes. My sister came, too. We took off in Wayne's van to San Francisco, and of course we went to Fisherman's Wharf because that's where all the tourists went.

I had long hair at the time. I remember I had these jeans that were kind of sewn squares. I remember for some reason that I was wearing them. We were walking up a hill in Fisherman's Wharf. It was a very steep hill. I remember the image of myself walking up this hill in these jeans, panting and having a hard time getting up the hill, and the image of the sidewalk right in front of my face. When you're walking up those steep hills, that's what you see. It's really close. Wayne and my sister and my brother were way up ahead of me, and I was panting up the hill.

I looked over, and there were two women holding hands walking up the hill, walking past me.

I just remember going, Oh my god. I had never seen that before in real life, two women holding hands, being together so out and so visible. I remember looking over. Probably my mouth was wide open. I was like, "Whoa!" I don't think I said that, but I remember feeling that inside.

These two women looked over at me. One of them had long hair, wavy brown hair. They were both white. The one with long hair said, "Hi!"

And I'm like, they actually said hi to me! These two lesbians, so visible and out. I was just so impressed as a young person, I couldn't even believe it. I was like: I'm moving to San Francisco. That's the moment I told myself I would move here.

I was fifteen. It was 1975.

I moved here in 1986, to San Francisco in the Bay Area, and was able to really come into my own, into myself and my identities as an Asian Pacific lesbian.

DONNA PERSONNA: In San Jose, I didn't want to be flamboyant. That's a word they use: flamboyant, or screaming queens. I was protective of my family and all that that entailed. I didn't want anyone to ever come and tell my siblings this or that, or my parents.

And this is a humorous story: my father, a Baptist minister, sometimes would go to San Francisco to do a substitute sermon, and so I would go along. I'm in the car, and I remember seeing guys, like they're nineteen, twenty, or something, and they had arched eyebrows. They looked like guys, dressed like guys, but I thought, wow, those eyebrows, they've been plucked! So something in me said, I want more of that, I want to see more of that, I want to learn about what that plucking is. I knew I wanted to come back to San Francisco.

TUPILI LEA ARELLANO: I arrived in the Bay Area at twenty-eight years old.

One of the reasons I left Tucson was because of the Republican state, but also the racism and more and more white people moving there. Politically, I needed a progressive place, and I needed to feel safer because I had been targeted because of my gender and the way I looked. I needed to get out of there. I was in my twenties. I wanted to get sober, and I did. I also wanted to have spiritual teachers, and I wanted to have more queerness, I wanted to have art, I wanted to have the ocean, I wanted to have the Bay Area. I was suffering in Arizona.

The Bay Area is one of the epicenters of queerness, of art, of Yemanjá, of dance, of teachers.

It's an epicenter. The menu is so abundant. First of all, very progressive commitments to social justice. And the art! The art is phenomenal. Oh my God, the teachers there, some of the most incredible teachers internationally—spiritual, sacred teachers are there. I was walking my way home to be rooted in my Mexican Indigenous sacred roots.

There were many places where I could go where I didn't have to deal with heterosexuals. Those places were already established before I got there, and the people were committed to keeping each other safe in ways that I'd never experienced.

I studied with folks in the Bay Area, and they taught me how to find the grace in everything, every chingazo, every cerote, everything.

You know what a cerote is? It's a turd.

We find the grace because that turd is fertilizer, it really is.

In the dung of deer, like up on Mount Lemmon in Arizona, that's where you find more mushrooms, you know?

So I'm just saying: I learned to do that.

VIVIAN VARELA: One of my first experiences with the Bay Area Lesbian of Color community was when I traveled there for the Califia Women of Color Conference. It was fantastic. It was mesmerizing. Community, home, this is real, this is who I am. Women with different body shapes and dressed so differently and free. Some would do rituals. It was amazing.

I was living in LA and I had a job, and I said, "You know, either I do this or not."

I got a friend to sublet my little house in Glendale and I moved up there. With no job. I packed up my car knowing just a few people. I couch surfed a little, spent some time living in my car, got a job at Pacific Bell.

STORMMIGUEL FLOREZ: I live in San Francisco, California, and I've lived here about half my life now. I moved out here when I was twenty-five, and I'm about to be fifty-one.

Around that time, before I came, I'm still playing in my band, we're doing pretty well, and we started to tour a little bit, but there was a point where it was just not the best group of people to be working together. It was kind of like a relationship where, "Wow, the sex is great, but we fight all the time." The sex was us playing music together live. That was the most exciting experience for me, the most wonderful, deep connection I could have with other humans. The bass player in that band was my primary partner, who I was going to move through my life with. We weren't sexual. Music was our marriage.

A lot of hard things happened in that band. I was starting to get migraines and get sick because I was so stressed by the interpersonal dynamics. After we did a tour, a couple people in the band were threatening to quit, and then I would be the one trying to make the peace. I hit my wall. Something in me clicked: "Oh my God, when we get back home from this tour, I'm quitting the band, and I'm going to move to San Francisco." It just was this voice, this thing that came out of me. We were in a car together, it was nighttime, and I was quietly weeping, turning my head. They didn't know. I was just like, "Holy shit, my life is about to change again in a really big way."

We got back home. I quit the band. Almost exactly a year later, I was in San Francisco. I didn't know anybody in San Francisco when I made the decision. I had never been there.

When I first moved, I went to Folsom Street Fair. It was amazing. It was just like, whoa, going from the Albuquerque leather community to Folsom Street Fair, which is the biggest leather or BDSM event I think in the world. It happens annually in San Francisco. Leather people everywhere, demonstrations everywhere, stages. It was just mind-blowing.

CRYSTAL MASON: I was still in Richmond, but I realized that this wasn't just a fad or some passing thing and that marrying Frank wasn't going to change anything, So I moved to Washington, DC, with my sort of gay daddies. That was where my more sexual dyke life started.

More and more, my own consciousness was growing, and my political analysis. I had read a lot of feminist literature: *This Bridge Called My Back*. Stuff from the Combahee River Collective. Also, Audre Lorde, right? In *Zami*? To name myself, understanding that if I didn't, other people would name me anyway.

My own book started to open. It was exciting.

By the time I moved to DC, I was starting to dress more masculine, but still not quite in that identity as of yet. That happened more when I moved here to San Francisco in 1989.

It wasn't until I moved out to San Francisco that I really started to see a lot of possibilities.

KB BOYCE: I had little to no experience with any trans guys until I moved to the San Francisco Bay Area. I was about thirty-three. It wasn't until then that I really began to know more about the transmasculine side of things.

I became part of a community that was all types of queers. I mean, there were some trans folks, there were queers; you know. A queerdo

community. A bunch of young punks and queerdos. Even though
at that point, I was beyond my punk life, I wound up in all types of
bands playing all types of music. In the nineties, I was about that hip-
hop and trip-hop thing, but the queer community was very punk. So
I wound up being friends with some punk icons who happened to be
part of the trans and queer community.

That's where I started finding more of the language around how
I felt.

TINA VALENTÍN AGUIRRE: At Stanford, I was having a culture shock,
because it was so clean and antiseptic. I came to San Francisco and
decided I need to find myself here. I already knew some people, and
I could tell: "This is where I fit in, this is where there are people like
me." I had started traveling into San Francisco and going to Esta
Noche, a bar that was on Sixteenth Street, a queer Latino bar, where
there were lots of drag performers.

TUPILI LEA ARELLANO: We partied with men, Latinx men, at Esta Noche.
It's closed now. That was where I first saw more trans folks than I had
before. That's who was really in spiritual charge of that bar: Latinx
trans women.

TINA VALENTÍN AGUIRRE: That block connects with Valencia, which had
at the time a very strong lesbian presence, and that particular intersection of Sixteenth and Valencia was a mix of all that. And it was
amazing.

So, I moved to San Francisco and dropped out of Stanford. I
started doing community outreach on Sixteenth Street. At the time, I
was a volunteer passing out condoms for the Latino AIDS Project.

LANDA LAKES: I went into the US Navy, because Desert Storm was going
on, and it felt like the only way for me to be a warrior within the
Chickasaw system was to serve in the military. So I was like, "Well, if
I do this, it will make my dad really proud."

That's how I ended up out here, in San Francisco. My ship was anchored here, in the San Francisco Bay. And after the military, I settled here in San Francisco. That's how it happened, in 1992. It was the first city I lived in.

Do you want to know the truth, the truth of the matter?

I'll tell you something that's really, really honest: my grandpa died, and I didn't want to go back. I decided I wanted to be away.

I came out here and I was like, where's the Native community? I need to find the Native community. So that's what I did early on.

Finding the Native community was somewhat difficult. I really didn't find the Native community out here until BAAITS [Bay Area American Indian Two-Spirits] started. One of the things that the founders did was make sure that it was a clean and sober space. That was extremely helpful, at least for me.

MS BILLIE COOPER: The Navy sent me to Pearl Harbor, in Oahu, Hawaii, and I did my last four years there, 1978 to 1982.

I was queen on the base, honey.

My first day on Pearl Harbor, it was Halloween, and it was a big bash at the enlisted men's club. I entered the contest, me and this female. We didn't know each other, and we got together. We had like twelve hours to put together a routine and get costumes. And we did, and we won $150. All the while, while we were dancing, people were clapping and screaming, and telling us how fabulous we were. I was called a faggot by some people. And there was a whole lot of racism there at that time, in Hawaii. But most of the people in the enlisted men's club that night at least were acting like they liked me.

I got out in 1982 and moved to San Francisco. I've been here ever since.

I've been here forty years.

When I came to San Francisco, I fell into drugs, and addiction. I used for over twenty years, Crystal meth, cocaine. Crack hadn't come out yet. When that came out, that was all she wrote.

C. NJOUBE DUGAS: I turned twenty-one, so I'm me, can't nobody stop me. I moved out. I'm grown, right?

I ended up getting in a relationship with this woman, and we decided to move to Sacramento, California. Getting work in San Francisco was really difficult at that time. There was just no work out here. It was 1984. Unemployment lines were crazy. So we moved to what was then the queer area of Sacramento, downtown in that J Street Corridor. We were in the safe zone, or at least what we thought was the safe zone.

You had to be careful at night. I had an experience where someone threatened to kill us with a gun, because of homophobia. They didn't actually touch us, but just the threat alone was enough. I'm walking down the street just trying to get to where I'm going, not bothering anyone, and they threatened to shoot me with a gun.

At that time, a lot of people carried guns in Sacramento. I didn't even know I was visibly gay or visibly anything, I was just who I was. But the world let me know: I see you. Like we got all these social control agents, particularly in the Black community, telling you what you need, ought to, and should be doing, and it's like, "Whoa, I don't know you."

Sacramento allowed me to build up some community. We were tight-knit, since it wasn't necessarily safe all the time. We literally stayed right in that corridor the whole time we lived there. We didn't go past Twenty-Ninth Street. We went as far as Old Sacramento downtown. We didn't move outside those zones.

The queer community was segregated. There was this one club in West Sac, and it was for Black people and people of color. Very few white folks went there.

There was also a bar in downtown Sac, and I went there. I'm like, "This is my neighborhood, I'm going there." But it wasn't welcoming. It was mostly white. Latinos and Blacks went there, but usually after work. That was it. We didn't go there at night because it was essentially an all-white club, and we knew that, right? It was just like,

"Okay, it's seven o'clock, let's get out of here because now they're getting ready to do their thing." We didn't mingle like that.

Sacramento, at the time, was a little bit more sleepy. We had our little barbecues in someone's backyard. We stayed close like that.

CHINO SCOTT-CHUNG: I actually got gay bashed in San Francisco, in Duboce Park, with my lover at the time. She was a Latina lesbian. We were in the park, swinging on the swings, holding hands, and we got beat up by a gang of teenagers, young men. We both suffered concussions. That was how it was back then. That was the environment, the environment we lived in. That kind of thing just was possible. There was a lot of hatred against gays and lesbians.

The day after that, I went to San Francisco Gun Exchange, and I bought a gun. I had been in the military and I knew how to shoot. I got a holster, and I wore it when I went out. Because I was really terrified of something like that happening again.

YOSEÑIO LEWIS: I lived in San Diego for eleven years. I went to college there, and then I just lived there because I didn't know what the hell I was going to do. To be honest, I had not expected that I was going to live that long. I thought I was going to die by the time I was twenty. I thought, "I'll be cut short, I can't live past twenty, because I have no value."

Then when I hit twenty-one—it's, like, what the hell am I supposed to do now?

When I came to California, I was a stuck-up, prejudiced asshole. I treated people poorly. I told people to their face that they were going to hell because they were gay. I spent hours at the chapel on campus, on my knees. I would write letters: if you'd only let go of this bad part of you, so much good could be in your world.

VIVIAN VARELA: Here I go, plodding along and doing my missionary work. I think part of me was really ruled by fear. Afraid of—I don't know. I kind of want to say, afraid of myself? I felt like I was hiding something. Being in church, I was hiding my sexuality. For sure, I felt afraid of that.

YOSEÑIO LEWIS: So I'm in California, finishing school, trying to figure out what I'm going to do with the rest of my life. And here's somebody else from Rhode Island, a lesbian involved with another lesbian who wants to live with me off-campus.

I said, "How can you be from Rhode Island? We didn't have homosexuals in Rhode Island."

And Jane sat me down and said, "Look, first of all, there are plenty of homosexuals in Rhode Island. I was one of them. And number two, we are not what you were told we are. We're not unhappy, we're not suicidal twenty-four hours a day, we're not evil people who are trying to destroy childhoods. We're just like you: human beings trying to make it in the world, trying to have a good life. And we happen to love each other."

And it clicked for me that all the prejudice and bias that I had grown up around was now being challenged.

I am forever grateful to her, because she opened that door. She unlocked that space in me, where I could say, "Everybody has their own unique way of being. And we don't have to listen to the crap that we were told as kids."

ANDRÉS OZZUNA: I haven't lived here all my life. It's an interesting contribution: to see where we all come from, what we each bring.

JOAN BENOIT: I moved to Seattle, because I had to get the hell out of Michigan. I was going to die if I didn't leave, so I left.

Seattle is where my friends started identifying me as butch.

"Butch, like Joan."

And I'm like, "What are you talking about? That's not how I identify. I don't identify as butch."

"Well, if you're not butch, what are you?"

I'm like, "I'm Joan. I defy any categories. I'm not going to fit myself into that category. I'm just who I am."

Butch-femme was making a comeback.

When I came to San Francisco, that's when I started identifying more with butch.

After Seattle, I thought I was going to move to a bunch of different places, to see what I liked. But I got here, to Oakland, and it was home.

TUPILI LEA ARELLANO: When I moved there in '81, Oakland was the city that held the most lesbians per capita, internationally.

I said, "Oh hell, yes."

I said, "Woo-hoo, bring them on."

I wanted to be there for that, and, oh!—did that pay off.

JOAN BENOIT: I've been in Oakland now for almost thirty years.

It was an interesting time to land in the Bay Area: 1989.

I felt like my queerness was irrelevant. It wasn't the first thing that presented to anyone here. It was secondary. I was "that lesbian" second. I was Joan first.

FIVE

* *

Intimacies

NICKY CALMA: You know, we always look for love.

CRYSTAL MASON: I ran into the problem often where, as dykes, it was hard sometimes to tell if anybody liked anybody. It was hard to tell if you were on an actual date. There was that thing of everybody waiting to be asked.

I used to say to myself often that I didn't know the rules. But what I came to learn is, we were all making up the rules as we went.

TUPILI LEA ARELLANO: Teresa was my first lover, my dear friend.

I think she was twelve years older than me. A beautiful soul and spirit. She was very butch. She was relentless, and I'm codependent, and when I told her, "Look, we're not going to be together that way," she hit the windshield with her fist and cracked it. That put me in a codependent stupor of safety. I said, "Okay, we can try being together." That was my life-saving reaction growing up.

I gave it my best shot. She didn't do that ever again. We did have one physical altercation. That was it. I just said, "I promised myself I would never engage in domestic violence. Goodbye." And I left.

We were together for three years, and friends for many years after that.

When we were together, one night she called me Otto Preminger.
I said, "Why are you calling me Otto Preminger?"
She says, "Because you want to direct our sex."
I go, "Well, you want to direct our sex too."

She says, "Yes, but I'm who I am."

I said, "Yes, I'm who I am."

I had long hair, so there was some wishful thinking on her part.

I had braids, and things like that. That was very early. I was just coming out more and more, and really taking charge of my gender.

That long hair gave me permission to shape-shift a lot depending on what I would put on, and I still needed that shape-shifting safety then.

MS BILLIE COOPER: I successfully went in the service in May of 1976, and stayed until 1982. I got an honorable discharge. But in the Navy, I found out about international men, and I fell in love. I remember my first time falling in love, with this guy from Guam. He was just so pretty; his skin color was so pretty, I just fell in love with him.

C. NJOUBE DUGAS: In the early days, I really didn't associate with white women at all, not because I tried to avoid them, but because we were separate. I guess we just naturally separated or there was an unwritten rule. I never really saw Black women with white women in the community, as a regular thing. That started later.

Initially, it was frowned upon, I would say by mostly the femme women. Typically, when I saw Black women with white women, it was usually a Black stud with a white woman, not necessarily a Black femme with a white woman, and Black femme women didn't like it at all. They were like, "What the hell? Why are you over there, why would you separate yourself from the Black community?"

I just internalized that as no, that's a definite no, you do not date white women, you do not date outside your race. Not that I didn't! But early on, I internalized it like that.

I navigated the lesbian and LGBTQ community really by listening to Black women, and the expectations that were put on us, right? If you're going to be a stud, be a stud. This is what studs do. This is how studs act. This is how studs treat their women. And you never date outside your race.

I felt like the conditions of stud were a requirement. I had to do this, I had to do that, I had to do the other. I'm like, I just want to be free, I just want to just do me. I don't want these rules and regulations.

It's very aligned with what it means to be butch. First of all, the women that you chose had to look a certain way, had to be feminine all the way. They could not carry any masculine energy whatsoever. You had to dress a certain way. It almost played the male in a straight role, bring home the money, you know what I mean? The femme was expected to do all the cooking, all the cleaning. It was just like, Wait, wait, that doesn't work for me, I need some collective cooperation, we both work together. But femmes also played into what it meant to be a femme, you know?

In the early eighties and through the mid eighties, I just felt like: I'm going into this community because I love women, but I feel again I'm in this box. This is not what I expected.

There's more acceptance now. I think that started in the nineties. By the nineties, people were just kind of like, I just want to be free, this is ridiculousness, love who you love.

TINA VALENTÍN AGUIRRE: Robert, my first partner, was an Italian man who liked to go to Esta Noche. I found out he was HIV positive after I moved in. I didn't know beforehand. We were safe. However, I understood that construct, which is kind of a stereotype, where I was a young person of color dating a white man, Italian, who really looked Latino in many ways and was comfortable with Latinos but was not Latino, and was eleven years older than me, and was HIV positive.

Sometimes those stereotypes are out there because they're based in some kind of reality.

CHINO SCOTT-CHUNG: The first Asian Pacific lesbian retreat I was ever at was in 1988.

That's where I met Kitty Tsui, one of the organizers. She became my first Asian Pacific lesbian lover.

Kitty was a bodybuilder and a poet. In fact, she had published a book, *The Words of a Woman Who Breathes Fire: Poetry & Prose*. She wrote a poem about me, and put it in her second book. I have an original, signed copy from her of the actual typewritten poem, because back then we typed.

We got together there at the retreat. It was a tumultuous relationship. I had only met one other Asian Pacific lesbian in my life, a Japanese woman who I went to the retreat with. When I walked into that retreat, there were seventy-two Asian lesbians and probably bisexual women. It was at Valley of the Moon Retreat center in Northern California, kind of up there towards Napa. It was night. There was a campfire, guitar, singing.

I couldn't believe it. All these women. I was like, "Oh my god."

I had never, ever, ever, ever seen or experienced anything like that.

Powerful, beautiful, strong, butch, femme, mostly androgynous, because back then a lot of Asian women were androgynous. But Kitty was very butch, so she really stood out.

There was a talent show, and Kitty—I'm trying to think of what her actual talent was. It didn't matter, because she was so cut and built. She was dressed in a leather bikini. I guess her talent was showing her muscles.

So she was on stage, showing her muscles, and her bikini strap popped off. It was the most amazing moment. Everyone was like, "Oh my god!" People were screaming and laughing.

I'm trying to think of what Kitty did, if she tried to cover herself. I don't think she did. I think she just kept posing. Yes. An amazing moment.

I don't even know how to explain it: just so validating and so beautiful and open and strong and powerful and diverse. In my own

internalized homophobia and racism, I imagined Asian lesbians as—
well—that everyone would kind of look the same, or act the same. But
everyone there was so different, you know? Filipino women, Chinese,
Japanese, Korean, Vietnamese, women who were adopted into white
families—and the workshops reflected that.

Looking back, it was a fucking historical moment. Oh my god,
loud and proud. And you think about Asian women stereotypes of
subservience, all that bullshit, not being able to speak, being silent,
being unheard, that was not the case. It was the opposite of all that.

I thought, "Oh, my god, how do I even understand this, or
incorporate it into my own life?" I had no idea, but I joined the organization right away.

FRESH "LEV" WHITE: When I was a bouncer in New York, I had no idea
how bad the neighborhood was that I was in. It was pretty bad. The
ladies of the evening, as I called them, would come and pick me up,
take me to breakfast, and walk me back to the subway.

I remember, during that time—a flash just came—being on the
subway, and this guy comes up to me, and he's talking to me and
starts flirting with me, and he tries to kiss me. He's a cute young guy,
you could tell he'd probably been drinking.

And I'm like, "I can't, I'm gay."

And he's like, "Yeah, me, too."

I'm like, "No, I'm gay."

And he's like, "No, me, too."

I didn't understand that he couldn't tell I was not a guy.

So, yeah, those middle years were me really embracing myself as a
masculine female.

I didn't know any trans men. I knew butches, trans women, and
female, that's it.

ANDRÉS OZZUNA: When I was in my twenties, the women in Buenos Aires
didn't like it when I let my masculine side show. That's very common

in Buenos Aires, for butch women to be seen in a negative light. These days, there's a queer vibe, that says, yes, okay, you're genderqueer, but still I don't know whether that's acceptance of masculinity or of queerness. Masculinity is another matter.

And back when I lived there? Forget about it.

There was this idea of, I don't want to walk down the street with someone gay, with a dyke who looks like a dyke. Of course. Because that was dangerous. They're going to get us, they're going to round us up and throw us in the river.

So if you were walking down the street with someone who appeared gay, it was a matter of survival.

YOSEÑIO LEWIS: Everybody thought I was going to come out as a lesbian. I never did. I never identified as a lesbian, I don't know much about lesbian culture. I never tried to be with a woman as a woman. That was a foreign concept to me.

I did not have consensual sex until I was twenty-four. I knew what it was like to have attraction. But I also knew, you don't acknowledge that, you don't try to be with women because that's wrong, dirty, you're going to hell. I didn't express my desire until I was twenty-four. I ran from it for a very long time.

I did not think I deserved to have sex, did not think I deserved to have a sexuality.

At twenty-four, I had sex the way I wanted to have sex for the first time in my life.

And I told the person at that time, "If you are going to be sexual with me, this is what you need to know: you're not being sexual with another woman. This is how I see myself. This is how I walk in the world, even if I never say the words. I see myself as male, as a man."

We had a lot of conversation before we actually had sex. "I need for you not to be thinking, whatever you have in your head about what you do with women, you might be able to do some of that with me. That will turn me off completely. We have to find words that we can use, and we have to find actions that we can engage in that don't minimize my masculinity, but also don't threaten your femininity or, possibly, your desire to be with someone who identifies the way that you do."

It was fraught. It wasn't just, roll in the bed, have a wonderful time. It was a lot of work to get to that point. I appreciate her for taking that chance with me, for going down that path. She didn't have to.

We had to have a lot of conversation before we could get to the place of, "Okay, now we can fuck like bunnies, we can just do what we want to do."

And that was my introduction to kink: realizing that if you talk about what you want, how you see yourself, what you're willing to do, what you're not, then you can go and have fun. But you have to do that work ahead of time.

STORMMIGUEL FLOREZ: I had invited this girl to this party, and we ended up making out in her car. I was twenty. She was from the Midwest and had just moved to Albuquerque. She started dropping little hints about BDSM.

"So, you like my earring?"

It was like a little cuff. I was like, "Yes, that's cool."

"Do you know what it means?"

"I don't know."

"Do you like handcuffs, you're into handcuffing people?"

It was very interesting. She eased me into things.

Before that, I had a girlfriend that wanted to tie me up, and I was like, "You're never getting close to me with that. Hell, no."

I started becoming intrigued with this new person. We developed a relationship and started playing together. I started learning about this whole new world of BDSM, and the leather community. There's actual community, and protocol, and ways that people interact in the world, so many freeing and liberating ways of getting to be sexually, within these parameters. If you're doing it in a way that's ethical, it's very contained, it's very safe. It's some of the safer sexual interactions I've had, because there are agreements, there are safewords, there's ways that you talk about things, negotiate things.

This is where I learned how to talk about sex: what I like, what I don't like, how to ask other people what they like, what they don't. All these amazing things. About safe sex, about consent in a way that I never talked about it before. Getting to be involved in this community was hugely liberating.

BDSM was the space where we were getting to play with gender dynamics, and play with gender roles. It felt very intertwined.

That was, for myself, where I got to start expressing and playing with gender in a more outward way. For the first time since I was a kid, really. Because I had a partner who would call me "boy," and I just thought it was so fun and titillating that she was calling me her boy.

Those early years in BDSM exploration gave me the room to play and explore. To play with using masculinity as an identifier. To be somebody's boy, to be Daddy—just to play with those roles. BDSM really allowed for that. It was: "We're going to have a playground, and get to do all of our fantasies here, and also get to find out who we are, what our limits are, what's deep in there, what have we not gotten to explore about ourselves?"

BDSM is such an amazing playground, and arena, for us to explore.

That was the place where all these things got to happen.

YOSEÑIO LEWIS: I want to learn. And now I'm learning, yes: I want to know about kink.

How do you get to a place where one or more people enjoys the sensation of pain?

I enjoy the sensation of inflicting that pain. How did I get here? My whole life, hurting someone is bad. You don't hurt people.

Except there are these people who say, "Yes, please hurt me, because I get off on it."

"How can you—that's wrong! That's disgusting, that's—Oh, but I like giving it to you. Wait, what does that make me? And how do I figure this out?"

DONNA PERSONNA: I went home with gay guys for a lot of years because that's all I knew, but I never felt gay.

I didn't put on a dress until I was fifty-nine years old. But I've been married twice and those were not gay people. Like one: before he took up with me, he was with a woman, a Mexican woman. We were together for fifteen years, and then I left him, and now he's with a woman again, a biological woman. So these are the things that made me think, "Maybe I'm a woman."

Gay guys? I was with them, but I was always the woman in those gay relationships, you know what I'm saying? I don't have to get too graphic, but . . . tops, bottom, this and that. Intimacy. I've played—I wasn't playing—the role of the woman. That's what they wanted. Once in a while, they wanted something else, they switched roles, and that was the last time. I wouldn't do it. I couldn't. It wouldn't happen.

Another thing: I only do what I want.

Sometimes it gets me beat up or whatever, but I'm not going to do what I don't want.

I acknowledged who I was with bravery.

CRYSTAL MASON: I wasn't much for packing. I liked it from time to time. But it wasn't a big part of my identification, because for me, what mattered was a combination of my own imagination and being in relationship with people who saw me the way I wanted to be seen. I didn't ever really need to pack, if that makes sense, to feel a dick—to feel that energy—because I feel like, with my own imagination in combination with the way I wanted to be seen, I didn't need that. It was already present in me.

I don't see anything wrong with being a woman. I'm not a person who needs to be identified as a male. It's not like I feel joy or disap-pointment either way. I guess now, at this point in my life, I'm more interested in just trying to be happy in this body, in this world, experiencing everything that I want with who I want—with consent, of course—and not really thinking about, "Is this something a man does or something a woman does?" But thinking more about, "Does this feel good and right to me?"

TINA VALENTÍN AGUIRRE: Some people thought "Oh, you're not femme enough," or "You're not a woman." And they would think that they could treat us different.

I never cared about that stuff.

Sometimes people would say "Oh, you're not this or that"—let's say at a trans bar, where men are looking for trans femmes. It's this own kind of thing. There were times when trans women who'd had medical work done would think "Oh, you shouldn't be here," or "You're not a woman," or "You're not trans enough." At the time, trans really meant that.

I would say, "Well, let's see how this plays out."

Because they would often think, "Oh, nobody's going to pay attention to you. You don't fit in here."

And I'd be like, "Okay, let's see who actually gets what's going on."

And it always happened for me.

I think people pick up on what you are, even if it's not one hundred percent a binary, and people are attracted to you, it doesn't really matter. It's up to me to say yes or no. I know that, I've always known that.

It doesn't always make sense. Attraction, who we love, is not always rational. I learned really early on, "Oh, I don't need to analyze this. I don't need to understand it completely. If somebody is into me, and I'm into them, then that's the deal."

What I learned later was, I need for this other person to be okay enough with themselves that we can be out in the open. Because it's really easy for people to be on the down-low, dating trans people, and what I learned was, well, no.

I am public.

The work that I have done in the community has been very public-facing,

LANDA LAKES: When I settled here in San Francisco, I was already in a relationship. My boyfriend at the time didn't really broaden my horizons at all. He didn't want to go out, he didn't want to enjoy the nightlife, he wasn't into anything much, other than being a homebody.

So during those early years in San Francisco, it was very difficult. I wasn't finding new people in the community. I couldn't even find a supportive Native group that I wanted to be a part of, so there was a good span of years where there wasn't a lot for me.

It was a very depressing time. Sure, I was in a relationship, but what a sad one.

Throughout the whole nineties, I was with my ex, and nothing really happened. For like ten years, I stopped. You know, when I first met him, I was in drag. But he hated drag, and drag queens, so when I was with him, there was no drag.

But throughout this whole time, I always held onto women's clothes.

In 2001, I broke up with my ex. I was tired of pretending to be his cousin. It was so weird that we were in San Francisco where everybody's out, but he was not. He was still closeted. I just wanted that freedom, I wanted to be out, I didn't want to be in a closet anymore, and I definitely didn't want to be with him anymore. Once I was out of there, as soon as I was out of that relationship, I was back to myself again.

ADELA VÁZQUEZ: After I came here, to the United States, I discovered that sex was a way to obtain things. I discovered it was a power tool.

In 1989, I had to go back to Los Angeles for a minute because I was too into drugs. So I moved to LA with a friend, and there, I met up with other friends. These people were girls, and they were turning tricks and making money. I'm like, "Why not me?"

And I started to do that. I dressed up to prostitute.

I wasn't a good prostitute. Never have been. Because I'm too intense. I think too much. And I'm not really comfortable with being an object, you know what I mean?

I was a prostitute for a very short time. I had to move from my place because this guy wanted to pimp me. I was like, "I don't want this." It was very confusing.

NICKY CALMA: In my early years in San Francisco, these folks were influencing me to do sex work. I met them on the streets. Most of them are trans women of color. African-American, particularly. At that time, they looked at the Asian girls as their little babies, someone who they can ally with when they're working. Because these are big-sized trans women, you know. I knew they were transgender. That's when I started confirming: "Okay, this community exists. This identity exists. I want to be this."

But I just got here. I'm starting a life. I was trying to survive.

Some of them really were very nice, and kind enough to let me sleep on their couch, in their living room, in their place. They tried to make things work.

At the time, my view of sex work was really more like what I saw on television back home in the Philippines, with the American shows. It felt a little bit glamorous, because when they leave the house, they're all made up, beautiful. It's the kind of dresses that I like, miniskirts and everything.

They would ask me, sometimes, just to hang out with them, because they're feeling a little bit nervous or anxious or scared that the police might come around and do a sweep. And they would ask, "Are you hungry? Here. Here's a ten, go get something to eat, and come back later."

I was very lucky. Because these people were nice to me. They kind of took me in. I learned to become street-smart. What to avoid, what not to get into. They never influenced me to do drugs. They did it on their own, but they were just really looking after us. I have so much respect for women—anybody—who does sex work. Because they were not only taking care of themselves, but they took care of this group of people, they took care of others.

I mean, sex work is not, come in at nine and leave at five. If you're really serious with it, you can't choose who you're going to be with. There's danger.

I asked them, "Do you tell them you have a dick?"

"Some don't know."

The first thing in me was, "So what happens if they find out?"

"Girl, that's when you get out of the car and you run."

"No, but that's dangerous," I said. "What if these people have weapons or something to hurt you?"

I had a good intro to sex work, because these were real things that people were telling me.

And then I tried to do sex work. I had to survive. I wore a wig. It changed my look and everything. I was the fresh meat out there. These women protected me. I mean, there were some growing pains, because some of them may have felt jealous. We were the new ones, the young ones that were being picked. Plus, there's this Asian factor: "Oh, wow, Asian." People use us as fetishes. At first I liked it, because there's validation. But that didn't last long. Especially when I heard someone say, "Well, when I saw you oriental girls . . ."

And I'm like, "You make us sound like we're oriental sauces or something."

The johns that would pick me up, or would choose me to be their flavor of the night, they were mostly good-looking men. I was young, and I was new on the strip.

It was cold, it was really cold. I told them, "How do you all keep yourselves warm?" That didn't click for me. They were using drugs so that they could stay up late and be on the streets until four or five in the morning.

I had so many questions. "What if they find out you have a dick, you're not a woman?"

And this one girl, I remember her name is Sylvia: "You're a woman! Just think about it, you're a woman! It doesn't matter what's between your legs. Look at you, you're a woman."

Coming from a Catholic family, sex is sacred, sex is something that produces life. So I had a little bit of dread. I was really confused.

Another piece that I was asking myself: I had a beard. I had hair on my face. I watched them shave, and I was like, "Hmm, if I shave, it'll grow."

They said, "Oh, you need to do electrolysis."

I mean, this was Transgender 101, 102, 103, everything. I was absorbing it. There's no amount that I can put of money for all this education that I was getting from these women. They were the ones who taught me everything. To be street-smart, to learn about trans-genderism, and all of these things that I needed to know to survive.

But after two months, it came to a point where I felt, "Hey, you know, I have options here. I have other things that I can do." Sex work wasn't profitable for me, because I only had one dress I wore all the time, and one wig that was synthetic. It was getting so bad. Even the girls that I was staying with were like, "Come here, we need to shop for a new wig for you." I was not concentrating on it. It was not something that I wanted to do.

I immediately tried to connect with some Filipinos. I was at Fisherman's Wharf, just walking there, and there was this group of folks in the back of Pier 41, all speaking Tagalog. So I spoke to them in Tagalog. "Do you guys know anything like, maybe, any jobs here or something?" I was willing to take anything.

BAMBY SALCEDO: Bob was, in many different ways, the love of my life.

I met him in prison. We lived together in prison, and on the streets. We did crime together. We got high together. We did many beautiful things. Obviously, when there's drugs involved, people are not the same, right? But when I met him, he was clean and I was clean, and it was a pure, beautiful love that we had for one another. He loved me as who I was, as the person that I am, and I loved him just as who he was. Yes, it is true that when drugs are involved, things become different, but our love was always there.

I mean—just meeting him.

If I was to die tomorrow, I know what love is, right?

I have known what it is to be loved, and accepted, and cherished, and cared for, and trusted, and all of those beautiful things, with Bob. I also have felt love from many other people, in different ways. But being in love, and loving someone equally, it's beautiful, and I can say that I have lived and experienced that.

NICKY CALMA: Years later, I found love, but the love I found was not what I thought it would be. I took a risk and moved to Dallas, Texas, for a short time, because he lived there. I gave up my job at Asian AIDS Project, gave up my cute one-bedroom, which was only, what, $550 at that time? I had a garden, I had a barbecue pit, and everything. Gave that up, and then it didn't work out. I came back here, and then I found myself homeless again, because I didn't have a place.

I gave my paycheck to that guy. I was in love.

When you're in love, it's "Take everything," you know?

It was a good lesson.

I came back, and I had supportive friends. I did a little bit of drugs at that time. I had to get my mind off what I was experiencing: "Damn, I've got to start all over again."

I didn't have a place to stay. I had this wonky, dinky Toyota Tercel that had all my clothes in it. But people were nice, very nice. They helped out.

And then I told myself, "I will never be in this situation again."

C. NJOUBE DUGAS: One-night stands were great. Get out of here—they were great!

Threesomes were great, everything was great. I mean like, whooo, you know?

I remember they had a bathhouse over on Valencia Street, when I lived in the Mission. I used to walk down all the time. That place was a hoot! Like, "Hey, let's go have fun tonight because I feel like just being sexual." And you could.

TINA VALENTÍN AGUIRRE: There were bars, and bathhouses, and sex clubs for everybody. There were lots of bars south of Market where you could have sex in the bars and sex clubs. There was a lesbian bathhouse that was super private that was on Valencia, but it wasn't really well known, and people were not supposed to talk about it.

C. NJOUBE DUGAS: It shut down during AIDS.

They don't have that anymore.

In the queer community, they don't have anything like that anymore for women.

TUPILI LEA ARELLANO: I consider myself a relationship anarchist. I have a commitment to love my friends as passionately, as deeply, and with as much commitment as I have only shared with lovers in the past.

To harvest and to give love in many, many places, to many four-leggeds, many butterflies, many humans, but not to get caught up in the closed system I believe marriage is, in many ways. Creating a nuclear family, buying your house, blah, blah, blah.

NELSON D'ALERTA PÉREZ: After I told off my mother for telling me to commit suicide, she learned, and the last time she came to visit me in San Francisco, she was different. I had a lover then, and she said, "But you two are just like your dad and me!"

And I said, "Girl, what did you think? This is the same. Marriage with all its curses and everything, or its joys. You know: a marriage. It's two people who join together, and their sex doesn't matter."

Then she said, "Yes, I understand now, I do."

These days, I have intimate encounters, but I don't want a steady relationship.

No. I went through a lot with my marriage. I'm taking a long break.

ADELA VÁZQUEZ: About five years ago, I stopped having sex.

I had a lot of sex in my life, I had a lot of dicks in my life. Plenty of dick.

DONNA PERSONNA: People are attracted to me. Men, women. It happens every day.

I'm seventy-six years old. I'm a good person. I have the "It" factor—I don't know—there's something there.

LANDA LAKES: My sexuality, I think, is a little bit fluid, but not completely. I find that in relationships, I have a tendency to be more with men than with women. Being with a man just seems to fit me a little bit better. I can be freer, I can be more aggressive. I think the aggressive part is the biggest piece. There's an aggression there, with a man, that doesn't happen for me with a woman. I think a lot of that has to do with just the fact that—I don't know—I guess there's this respect that I feel for a woman. Maybe there's this whole mother syndrome thing that goes through my head.

NICKY CALMA: My sexual orientation—it's kind of like a cross between straight and queer. A lot of revelations, for me, started when I was in my forties: about my sexuality, about who I'm attracted to or who I would prefer to be with. I dug deeper about sexual orientation then, about what it really is, for me.

VIVIAN VARELA: I can say even today that I am bisexual. Because, transactionally, I can have sex with a man and I'm okay with it. I have fallen in love with men. I have wonderful men in my life. Some are gay, some are not. But when I experience intimacy, there is no way that I can walk that path because I won't be happy. I will always look for a woman, or want to be intimate with a woman.

I identify the male part of me as attracted to women.

But I don't just fall in love with a woman because she's a woman. There are components to it; spiritual, intellectual, the creative, the humor. There's so much. A spiritual quality. There's something about being with a woman that is spiritually, intellectually, emotionally fulfilling.

There's something about the feminine.

There is no substitute.

YOSEÑIO LEWIS: With sexual expression, as with everything else, each time I hit a wall, it becomes, "Are you going to knock down that border to incorporate more of who you are? How am I going to work this out so I can be here, but be myself, all of myself? Be whole, and feel alive?"

* *

SIX

Transitions

DONNA PERSONNA: I know this: I've been transitioning since the day I was
born.

And everybody else I've ever met has been transitioning.

Everybody transitions. You go from an infant to a toddler. We
change. We have to fit in with the moment that we're living in. That's
not a bad thing.

MS BILLIE COOPER: My transition has been lifelong. Even before we were
using the word *transition*.

ADELA VÁZQUEZ: Many people think I had a sex change. I don't talk about
it with people that I don't want to fuck. Why should I talk to anybody
about my genitals if we're not going to have sex? I don't talk about it.
I'm discreet.

I've been asked when I was doing my nails. I always did my nails
for when I was working in an office, I'm old-school that way. And
I was doing my nails, and this Salvadoran or Nicaraguan lady was
there. She started saying things like, "You guys are so cute."

I knew where she was coming from, of course. So I was like, I'm
going to have fun with this.

After a while, she said only stupid things. "Are you complete?"

I'm like, "Oh, sure, yes, I have everything that I need—I have a
pair of hands and I have a pair of arms . . . I'm pretty complete."

She was like, "No, no, no. Down there."

And I'm like, "Oh, yes."

"Can I see it?"

And I'm like, "Would you show me yours? I'll show you mine."

I don't see people that are showing their genitals to each other just because. People are really insensitive when it comes to saying things to you. People feel that they have the right to tell you whatever. But you know, I always have an answer. If you have the balls to tell me things like that, I'm going to have the same back.

SHARYN GRAYSON: I started my transition in my second year of college. It was the late sixties.

It was strange, because I didn't completely transition. I did it in periods, in stages. My family was okay; it was me. I did not want to bring what I thought would be negative attention to my family.

It was this innate feeling that I knew who I was, but I just didn't have the proper tools and space yet. It was dear friends of mine who gave me the courage and the knowledge that this is who I was. And that it was okay to embrace and accept me. They would often tell me, "No, you're not gay. You're a woman. You're a lady." I've had so many of my friends during the years say to me, "We always thought of you as a lady. You've always been that. We just couldn't put you in a box outside of that."

Talking to these friends, and feeling really supported by them, helped me understand my real feelings, my true inner self. I was able to relax and say, "Oh, yes, now, that's who I am."

That's how I began to make the transition. I did not feel comfortable in any other realm, any other circle, any other group, until I made my transition.

And then, it was like, "Okay. This is me. This is who I am."

Everything was wonderful about it. Oh, my God. I had so much fun. I was free. I was myself. I didn't feel any fear. It was a different time. The early seventies. I was like a person experiencing Rome or Italy for the first time, and you've always wanted to go. The clothes, the music, the environments, just walking down the street with friends, and guys flirting. All of that. Just wonderful.

During my twenties to my early thirties, for the most part, life was exciting. It was thrilling. It was full. I was working. I had jobs. I was independent. Yes, it was really something.

BAMBY SALCEDO: You have to realize that when I arrived here, with my father, I didn't know him. I didn't have a relationship with him. I wanted him to love me, to accept me. So I couldn't be me. I tried to act like that person I wasn't—until I couldn't do it anymore. When I turned eighteen, I came to Los Angeles and started my transition.

In those days, there were no resources for us. Nothing. Anything you need, you would find it with other trans women on the streets. So that's how I started.

I started letting my hair grow, dressing up every day. And obviously, as a way to survive, I would sell my body. As a consequence, I got arrested and all of those things.

It was really hard for me, but at the same time it was beautiful, because I had people who were older than me, who are still my friends to this day. In those days, if you needed a hormone, they helped you get it. If you didn't have a place to sleep, they gave you one. They gave me food if I needed it, lent me makeup or clothes if I needed them. Despite all the survival challenges, there was also this beautiful component: the community, the people.

NICKY CALMA: I had an incident at Macy's. I was working at Macy's at the time, and I was becoming aware: "I think I'm transgender. I'm doing this."

So I spoke with my manager. "Is it okay for me not to wear a tie?" That was the requirement for a male sales associate. I explained to her, "This is what's going on. I'm taking hormones." I was doing electrolysis already, too. I was thinking, if I'm going to come to work as a woman, it has to be fully baked. Because, at that time, I would be perceived as a drag queen, or I would be ridiculed all the time.

When I got to HR, they were nasty. "Well, we want you to present yourself as the sex that you filled out in your application, which is male."

I could have stayed and prolonged that back-and-forth. But I said, "I want to start looking for a new job."

TINA VALENTÍN AGUIRRE: The concept of transgender, the umbrella of transgender, was really closed before. You had to have body surgeries. You had to, literally, for the US government. To be accepted as trans or the opposite sex you had to be in medical care, which is a very clinical way to look at this.

How that translated in community was, there were people who had medical transitions who looked down on some of us who did not have medical transitions, or were not on hormones, as not being trans. In the community, in the eighties, there was a separation between the people who had medical procedures and those of us who didn't. My trans mother Teresita did have breast augmentation. One of her sisters was Elena—they were sex workers together in the Polk and South of Market area—and Elena had full surgery and was designated as a woman by the federal government. She would lord that over us in a way. "Oh, you're not a real woman," she'd say to Teresita. "You're not a real trans person, you're a transvestite."

Teresita could care less. "Well, that's because I don't need all of that, I'm happy with what I am." She would say, "I'm a man and a woman, I am both. I'm not trying to fool anybody, that's what I am, and you like it or you don't, it doesn't matter. If you like it, you're going to pay for it"—because she was a sex worker. She didn't have any shame around that.

We were on a continuum of gender where some of us did get stuff done, not all of us did. And it was okay. My trans mother Teresita let us know it's okay, whatever it is, "I'm here for you and we're here for each other."

CHINO SCOTT-CHUNG: There was this gang of butch Asian women that I hung out with. We called ourselves the Sticky Rice Gang. We would play mah-jongg all the time. It sounds like a bad stereotype, but we really did do that.

I had a good friend in the group, her name was CJ. She's in the fire department. We were really tight, really close. She was very butch, and she passed as a man pretty much all the time. She also had a deep voice. A Black lesbian organization used to put on a butch drag contest, and CJ won because she was so butch. She was my role model. She helped me get a better haircut and wear better clothes, more masculine clothes. I really credit her for that.

Then there was an informal little group that started up called the Dragon Club. It was Asian transmasculine guys in the club. It was the early nineties. We would meet in Vietnamese restaurants in the Tenderloin. There was an Asian trans guy who came into our community, and we got to know him. A really, really nice guy. He was taking testosterone. He'd had top surgery, he was like a year out. I had never seen anyone who had had top surgery.

We were there having dinner. He was talking about his transition and his top surgery, and we were like, "Can we see it?"

He's like, "Yes, sure." He was really open.

So we went in the bathroom. Willy Wilkinson was there. I had been using the men's bathroom for a long time, but Willy said, "Should we go in the men's bathroom?"

We were all like, "Yes, yes, yes, of course."

And so we went in there. We locked the door. There were five of us there. Some guy knocked on the door.

Willy was so sweet: "What shall we do? We're not supposed to be here."

And I said in my deepest voice, "Occupied, go away!"

So the guy went away.

Our friend lifted up his shirt and showed us his top surgery. He had a really nice chest, his nipples looked really good, really natural. He still had the scar, but it was light and fading.

His chest just looked amazing. He was also lifting weights, and he looked really buff. To me, it was just amazing to see that. It was like, "Oh, my God. This is the future. This is what we can do, this is what's possible, right here in front of me." It just blew my mind. It was one of those moments where you know you're in it, you feel it, but you don't even know what it means. You don't know what the implications are, or how this is changing the world. It's like you're in a moment of world change. That was that moment for me, in that Vietnamese restaurant, in the men's bathroom.

ANDRÉS OZZUNA: It took me a long time. I was with women who didn't like me to appear masculine. I struggled, because I wanted to be accepted. And I had the strong sense that I wasn't going to be safe, you know? Plus, I didn't want to be a disgusting man, because that's insufferable. I had my own negative feelings about men. Not masculinity, but men. So do I want to be that man? No, a different one. But I had to understand that I can be a different kind of man. You can create your own manhood. You can create who you are as a man. I was socialized as a woman, so I have that thing about not taking up space. But then, I also don't want to take up space—I don't want to be that.

I had a lot of repression within myself. So it took a lot for me to take the step.

There was an element in the community around me, where it was okay to be butch, but not trans. This was mostly among lesbians. There were comments like, "Oh, that guy is gross." Someone with hair. "How gross." I was noticing all of that. I didn't want to be gross.

I still remember how, in 2005, there was a trans guy on the TV show *The L Word*. I heard it back then not knowing I was trans, but it must have been inside me because I remember the dialogue perfectly. One of the women says to him, "But why do you have to be trans? Why can't you be a butch?"

And that's the thing that really gets me. "Why can't you do things this other way?"

Because he can't. Leave him be!

FRESH "LEV" WHITE: In my early days in San Francisco, there was another butch who talked to me about wanting to transition, and I remember saying to them, "Why?" Like, "Why do you need to?"

Because I just didn't know. I was way into: you're this beautiful butch. Why would you?

This was the nineties. The crowd that I was involved with was still pretty butch-femme. I didn't know any trans men. I still only knew a few trans women. I didn't really understand it. Certainly, for trans women, I never even questioned it. I'm not exactly sure how much that is something to do with my position on patriarchy. But I, myself, had some learning to do.

STORMMIGUEL FLOREZ: A lot of people who once identified as dykes have transitioned. It was interesting. Some of the hardest conversations I had early on were with other butches who felt like they were being left behind, or like they were feeling pressure to transition. I just tried to be present for those conversations, even though it was hard. It hurt my heart, that my transition had any bearing on them in a negative way. Ultimately, I stayed in community with folks.

The people that had the strongest reaction to my transition were a couple of exes. Ironically, one was the one who was the first to call me "boy." Recently, we reconnected, and I was like, "Yes, the last conversation I remember is telling you I was going to transition, and you being upset about it, and dismissive."

And she was like, "Oh, my God, I was such an asshole. That was very selfish of me, and I don't feel that way. I'm really sorry."

It was just a very sweet exchange. People grow. Their understanding grows.

TUPILI LEA ARELLANO: When I lived in Tucson as a lesbian, white lesbians used to tell me, "You are emulating a man, you're behaving like a man."

And there they are in their damn flannel shirts and their hiking boots and shit and everything. I go, "What?"

It was also a lot of racism. From their entitlement, they were saying, "You make us uncomfortable."

NELSON D'ALERTA PÉREZ: It's really interesting, the dynamic with gay
men. I've had many problems. There's a certain distrust of feminine
people, or people who are calling themselves women and are going by
a woman's name.

Once, in Cuba, there was this guy who was my lover, and during
a conversation after making love, he said to me, "There's somebody I
never want to meet. Somebody called Catherine."

He didn't know that Catherine was me. But he'd heard stories. He
said, "I've heard she dances and has a show. It seems scandalous to
me. Why do things like that?"

I thought, "Oh my god." I saw myself as transexual, then. As a
woman. But I didn't say anything to him. No. I should have said
something, but I didn't. Over my dead body.

Even the gay men here in the US are distrustful of transsexuality.
It's a problem of not accepting other people for what they are. It seems
incredibly strange to me. A terrible thing. I've pondered this, and
drawn my own conclusions. It's sexism. There's a lot of sexism among
gay men, too. Trousers have a lot of power. And when you trade
your pants for a skirt, you're becoming something that doesn't have
power—or that the world doesn't want to have power.

But we do have it: we women are stronger than men.

TINA VALENTÍN AGUIRRE: If people want to focus on what you are or what
you're not by their own definitions, that's their business. And it's okay
to tell them no, that you don't get the right to tell me what I am.

We should not give ourselves hassles and problems. There are
plenty of people who are going to do that for us, we don't need to do
that to each other.

CRYSTAL MASON: There came a time, after I was out, when kids would be
like, "Is that a man or a woman?"

I always thought, "Well, both."

Kids always understood that. Gender is about markers, and certain markers hold more sway than others. At that time, I had a bald head. I had sideburns, dressed quite masculine, and was also moving in ways that people see as masculine. I mean, I have big tits, and they're easy to see! But people still kept seeing me as possibly male. Literally, people didn't see my breasts. They just saw this male-presenting person.

ANDRÉS OZZUNA: I started by saying I was nonbinary. I was in my forties. That's when the new concepts started, these new terms. They helped me question what was inside me. I didn't really feel nonbinary, but for me it was a kind of transition, a way of saying, "Okay, I'm getting closer."

Then I had friends who started to transition. And that's when I realized, "Oh, maybe that's me."

A friend of mine had top surgery, and it was the first I saw. That blew my mind. I started to think, "I want that," to imagine it in myself. I saw myself reflected in that possibility.

FRESH "LEV" WHITE: I actually had top surgery before I even identified as trans. My breasts weren't working for me. I went to a doctor's office to get a physical, this is maybe 2004 or 2005, and the assistant says, "Oh, I bet you want to get rid of those, right?" Only in San Francisco. Because they can see how butch I am. And I'm like, "Oh!" I had no idea that I could make that happen.

So he writes something, and the doctor writes something, and I end up at the surgeon, and he's like, "No. I can't take them all off. I can only give you a reduction."

I'm like, "Are you sure? Because this is what I want. This is what the doctor asked for." "No, I can't do it. You might want to have kids."

I'm like, "No, that's not what I want to do."

He gave me a reduction. And I remember going back to the doctor and she goes, "What happened?"

"This is what I was allowed to get."

It was transphobia, absolutely. I probably could have used some guidance, and counseling, and support along the way.

I was glad to be able to wear a T-shirt and not have double Ds. I love breasts, people, so don't—you know! I'm not anti-breast. It just didn't work for my body.

ANDRÉS OZZUNA: I was forty-five when I had top surgery. I felt so guilty. I didn't want to tell anyone. Not my mother, no one, except my ex. I said, "Don't tell anyone. I don't want the judgement, 'Why are they taking your tits off?'"

I just wanted to keep myself within my own desire.

In the time leading up, I'd look at myself in the mirror, in a binder. It was hard to breathe. I was scared, I don't know why. It wasn't regret. I never regretted it, I loved it, I enjoyed it. And now, I'm more connected to my partners, because they can touch me. I used to hate for them to touch my breasts. Now, when they touch my chest, I love it. I love for them to lean on it, touch me, grab me, whatever they want to do.

Later, I started some testosterone. Just a little. I stopped, then started again. After a long time, I realized people were perceiving me as male. "Here, sir, there sir." I liked it. It's still hard for me because I'm not sure exactly how I'm supposed to respond. And sometimes, I'd forget.

Once, I was at the airport in Argentina and I went right to the woman for a pat down. There I was, surrendering my body to her. And she said, "No sir!"

A couple of times in Argentina, I used the women's bathroom and they said, "Sir, no!" And I thought, they're going to kill me.

But then, if I went to the men's room, I was afraid. Because you have to wait to not use the urinal. And I'd think, "I don't want to wait with them staring at me." So I couldn't pee there.

Using the men's room was a problem. Using the women's room was a problem.

CHINO SCOTT-CHUNG: When I was identifying as butch, but passing as a man a lot of the time, I used the men's bathroom primarily. I was really nervous when I went in there. I would do all kinds of things to make sure that nobody heard me or suspected me.

I was getting kicked out of the women's bathroom. They weren't allowing me in. Women would be really scared, sometimes, and I was like, "Okay, I've got to do something about this." There were times where I came out of the women's bathroom, and men would go into the women's bathroom because they thought it was the men's room. So I transitioned over. Sometimes, I would still go to the women's if there weren't a lot of women around, but I still felt scared and nervous to go in there.

ANDRÉS OZZUNA: I'm handling that better now. I love it when there are gender-neutral bathrooms. You take a piss, and you leave. You don't have to think about who's staring at you, what they might do to you when all you want to do is pee.

LANDA LAKES: My relationship with pronouns has changed over time. In the Chickasaw language, we don't really have gendered pronouns. So it doesn't really matter in Chickasaw, you can be whatever.

I used to go clearly by he/him. Over time, because I do drag so much, I'm in female persona a lot, she/her is okay with me. In the drag community in general, back in the eighties, we started with the she/her and never really let it go. Everybody is a she/her, no matter what. Which can be problematic when you're dealing with somebody who's a drag king.

But lately, I've really latched onto they/them. I've really appreciated that.

Language is constantly changing. Maybe they/them is going to fade away over time. But for now, I really like the use of they/them. At work, I changed my pronouns to they/them, because I feel that it's more appropriate for me.

Every now and then, I don't know why, but when somebody calls me he/him, I sort of go, "What? Are you talking to me?" I think that I've moved away from it. I won't say I'm offended by it, but I definitely feel like they/them describes me more. She/her is fine, but to be honest with you, I'm not always dressed as a woman. So they/them fits me better than anything else.

JOAN BENOIT: Pronouns are interesting, when you have a seven-year-old ask you what your pronouns are! Which I get a lot. And I love that they have that language at such a young age.

I volunteer at my son's school on the second graders' library day. I get to see all the second graders, and yes, I've gotten that question from little ones. They'll ask my son Otis, "What's your mom's pronouns?" Or they'll ask me directly.

What a great thing, to be able to see people in that way.

My trajectory has been interesting. My tagline on my emails is "she/her/they/them." I'm still coming to the they/them, I think. In a lot of meetings I will make sure that I use they/them just to give face to that for people. To represent. Make room for and allow others to identify that way if they choose to.

It's empowering. This is who I am. There's no hiding anymore. There used to be a lot of hiding. I'm not timid anymore. I'm too old for that shit, I don't care what people think of me as long as they don't hit me.

DONNA PERSONNA: When people in my own community proclaim their pronouns, well, I don't talk about it a lot, but I would say, "We just didn't want to be kicked in the head. Call me anything, just don't punch me or knock me to the gutter and have people walk by and laugh because I'm getting beat up."

CHINO SCOTT-CHUNG: For a while, I still didn't identify as trans. I felt like a fake. It was my own internalized transphobia. Especially when I was with other trans guys who had gone through the journey, who had walked the walk and done what was necessary to be trans, which was, in my opinion, having top surgery, bottom surgery, taking T, going through what that means, all the wonderful outcomes but also the really hard parts. I have a friend who had bottom surgery in Syria and is still going through having to go back there for surgery, and it's been years.

I felt like I hadn't done what it took to identify as trans, to have what I felt was the most wonderful identity in the world.

I helped organize the first Asian trans retreat in 2017, called API TransFusion, and I still felt like a fake, like other trans people would judge me and think I hadn't done enough, wasn't trans enough. Of course, nobody judged me. I mean, other trans guys. No one ever felt that way. It was just my own fears.

FRESH "LEV" WHITE: At thirty-eight, I'm questioning. Every day, I asked myself questions. Am I butch enough? Does it mean I'm not butch enough if I transition?

Finally, ten years later, I'm forty-eight years old, people are already identifying me as trans. I turn to my then-partner: "I think I want to try being a man now."

That was the last straw in this particular relationship. I was already masculine enough that it was pulling her away from her identity as a lesbian. She wanted to be seen in the world as queer. I totally get that. I honor that. But then, also, we were in an interracial relationship where she was already having a problem being seen as dating a Black man, getting dirty looks from Black women or at least feeling like she was. She's white. I wasn't reading well enough that her family was racist. She appeared not to be racist, but she wasn't doing any work around it. So that started showing up.

STORMMIGUEL FLOREZ: For a long time, it felt like transition was not going to be an option for me. I'm meeting people. I'm intrigued. I want to get close to them, even physically, just to be like, "What? How does this look on you?" But I also wanted to be respectful, not some weird gawker. Some of the people I was doing drag with, we would talk about it. We started talking about testosterone more, and thinking about it together. It got to a point where I started thinking about it all the time.

I didn't want to lose dyke community. That was very scary, to think about losing that, losing being a butch person, being a butch performer. But something was pulling and pulling at me.

I'm like, "Okay, no, I am genderqueer, I can be genderqueer, I can express myself however I want."

But it was that question: "Do I want to take testosterone?" What's going to happen to my voice? My family, what's my family going to think? And what's going to happen in dyke community? Every day, thinking about these things. Still the drive was there.

Once I decided, something just lifted. That was it. I was done stressing out every single day. "I am going to do this."

FRESH "LEV" WHITE: I decided to take testosterone. It was an amazing year. 2008.

I chose the cream, because my understanding was, if you take the shots, it could shut down your vocal chords really fast.

As soon as I started taking testosterone, the first time I put the cream on my belly, I'm like, "I'm trans!" When I'm out in the world, of course, I haven't changed.

STORMMIGUEL FLOREZ: I started testosterone in 2005. I was in my early thirties.

Coming out to my family was hard. My transitioning felt like a big imposition on my family. When I told them I was trans and that I wanted them to start using he/him pronouns with me, they continued using she/her pronouns. They said, "Why do you have to do that? Can't you just be who you are?"

It was so hard to get my mom to talk about how she felt. On the phone, after I started testosterone, I was like, "We're going to see each other soon, you'll notice some changes, how are you feeling about it?"

She's like, "Well, I'm afraid I'm going to run screaming."

That just hurt me so much.

I had a nephew, who my brother adopted when I was starting to transition. He was little, about four. Everybody was so excited about him. I just wasn't being mentioned to him. I was like, "Does he even know who I am?"

I had a conversation with my brother: "Hey, I would love for him to meet me as his uncle—"

And my brother was like, "No, that's just going to confuse him."

"Kids are not the ones that are confused about this. Kids pick up on gender, they know what's going on."

"No."

I said, "So what's he going to know me as? Is he going to know me at all?"

I was told that I'm being selfish. It was awful. The first time I met my nephew, he had no idea who I was. I was that guy who played guitar, because he had a little guitar and I was showing him some stuff on it. It was very hurtful. He didn't know I was family.

KB BOYCE: I was in my forties when I decided to breathe in, breathe out, and say, "You know what? I am going to own who I am. I'm going to see what happens if I actually make this physical transition and start testosterone. Just see how that goes."

I had this way of being able to pass for most of my life. I was able to dress and carry my body in such a way that I could pass, at least peripherally, as male. And I was happy with that. But as I started to hit my later forties, I'd go into a store, and they'd be like, "Oh, thank you, ma'am."

And I was like, "What the heck is that?" I had to figure out how to deal with that.

Part of this was as a performer on stage. I felt that confusion coming from the audience, like, "Is that a man or a woman up there? I can't tell." I didn't mind confusing folks, but I also kind of wanted to be seen for myself.

I've always fought just to be me.

I feel comfortable with calling myself transmasculine. If you must label me, I think that is the most apt: a transmasculine being.

I'm absolutely fine with the amount of physical transitioning that I've done in my life. I feel pretty at ease in my own skin these days. A lot of things happened that I was not anticipating, that I had no frame of reference for before transitioning, before starting testosterone, before growing a beard.

I have a beard. It's not much of a beard, but I have some peach fuzz on my chin. I actually joke around often and say, "Yeah, I got my mom's beard." Because my dad, he didn't have facial hair. My mom did. So I feel like I got this from Mom. My mom was a farm woman. She was very strong. When I was little, I wanted her biceps. It's like that. My dad on the other hand was, like, the bandleader kind of guy. He was always in a suit, and a Stetson hat, you know? My mom was very butch and my dad was a bit effeminate. It's like, my butch mom and my kind of nelly dad got together, and hey, here I am, this transmasculine being.

It just makes sense to me. That's my story. I'm sticking to it.

C. NJOUBE DUGAS: There were two times in my life when I really considered transitioning. One is when I was thirty. This was '90, '91. Transitioning then was a different thing, y'all. You had to dress like a male, you had to cut your hair, you had to do all these things, and you had to live as a male for a year before you ever even got hormones. Before they were granted. You had to go through therapy. They needed to check in to see how male you looked. All these conditions. It was so uncomfortable. I was like, "Wait a minute, is this really what this is about?"

I knew three other people who'd transitioned. Two of them disappeared. They hid themselves, I'm assuming in the straight communities, right? The other person, I actually worked with, and they were transitioning, and their parents found out about them transitioning, and they up and quit their job and just went into hiding.

I thought, "Man, that's what this is? No, I can't. How am I going to talk to eight sisters and brothers and my mother?"

I just didn't feel seeded, comfortable enough in that space. Me and my mother were starting to have a relationship again. We had completely stopped talking for about eight years. I was really trying to have a relationship with her, and she was doing the best she could to try to have a relationship with me. "Okay, well, I get it, let me just put this on pause."

I thought about it one other time.

I'm going to say this, y'all.

I had a spiritual journey with a shaman. After that spiritual journey and being renamed, the shaman asked me, "Why do you think you came back as a female in this lifetime?"

I said, "I don't know, I'll have to think about that."

I was just so energized by this experience I had. I mean, I was on a high-flying kite for a long time. And I thought to myself, "There is a particular reason why I came back the way I am." I told myself, "It's time you start getting comfortable in who you are and what you are. It's time to stop worrying about people who judge me, who may say negative things about me. There is a definite reason why I'm here the way I am, and I'm okay with that today." So I didn't physically transition.

That's it, that's just me. This is just for me, y'all.

It's a spiritual journey, it really is.

CHINO SCOTT-CHUNG: I've had top surgery, but I don't want any other surgeries, and I don't want to take testosterone.

How do you actually make that decision? It's a huge decision.

Surgeries are one thing. But changing every part of your body through taking testosterone . . . what we all want is a deeper voice and facial hair and a more masculine-looking body, including your bone structure. But how do you start that transition? How do you make that decision? I mean, that's big. I've thought about that through my life. And years ago, I decided that I don't want to take T.

One of the big things for me is my health. I have several autoimmune disorders, and lupus. These are some pretty serious conditions. I'm in total remission, and I'm doing great. I'm very grateful for that. But I don't want to jeopardize my health any more than I already have.

That's one of the big reasons why I decided not to take T. And that's my decision. Everybody has their own process.

It's about clearly accepting myself, first of all. Being comfortable with myself as masculine and trans and in my own skin. And not being afraid that people wouldn't accept me, specifically the trans community. How do I accept myself?

It was a journey. I'm still on it.

KB BOYCE: I'll tell you: being seen as a Black man has been challenging.

It's not necessarily a change in the way people treat me. It's more my feeling, as I get older and look more like an older Black gentleman out in the world. I am feeling a different kind being in the world, realizing that as I'm walking down the street at night, and a cop car drives by, I am seen as a Black man now. I felt like before, cops would maybe look at me and go, "Oh, weirdo. Gay person. Whatever," and not give me a second glance. Now, I can be perceived as a heterosexual Black man. And it's giving me pause, you know? It's changed the way that I move through the world.

Sometimes I feel like I am seen as kind of a pretty boy. I get treated by Black men sometimes as, like, a little guy who might be a faggot or something. It's some energies that I had not experienced earlier in life, coming into play now. I mean, I have been called a faggot. That didn't used to happen. Those are the visceral things I'm feeling now, walking around.

FRESH "LEV" WHITE: Once I was being seen as masculine, I remember having a white trans male friend of mine say to me, "Isn't the privilege amazing?"

My immediate response was, "If you mean I'm even more likely to get pulled over and shot, I'm not feeling it."

It's different to choose to transition as a person of color, particularly Black and Brown folks, than it is as white. I'm just naming that.

MS BILLIE COOPER: Can't nobody tell me how to be Black. Can't nobody tell me how to live my life as a Black person. You know, before I was queer or homosexual or faggot, I was a Black person. I've always been Black.

I've been through many transitions, but I've always been Black. Even when I tried to shake it! It was still there.

FRESH "LEV" WHITE: When I decided to come out, I remember thinking to myself—still in this young, naïve mind of mine—that now I'm going to be part of this trans community who's oppressed by everybody, and we're going to be a force to be reckoned with.

And I was just slapped in the face with racism almost immediately.

I was like, "Oh, yeah. That's right: People. Still humans."
Still humans.

DONNA PERSONNA: I didn't don a dress until I was fifty-nine years old. The reason I waited so long was: I wanted to live, I wanted to live. I saw what went down for other people that were more daring. It wasn't good. I wanted to get an education, graduate from college, and I did that. So I waited a long time.

Both my mother and father passed away. After all those years, I finally was comfortable with the idea that I wasn't going to ruin anybody else's life.

I don't have a deadname because I have a living family today, and I'm not going to make them dead by anything that I want. There's nothing about me that's dead.

ADELA VÁZQUEZ: I have no breast implants. These are my tits that I grew from scratch, with hormones. I started that in 1992. I'm a size 44DD, which I'm totally proud of. A little bit too big for what I wanted, but . . . they're there, you know?

NELSON D'ALERTA PÉREZ: Thankfully, before my mother died, I had the chance to see her become very close with my housemate Adela Vázquez. Adela was just starting hormones, and my mother would say, "Be very careful with this girl's breasts!" Adela was in her transition, and my mother was fascinated by her.

One day I said, "Wow, you're really something. You made my life hell, and now you're friends with Adela. I love that you and Adela are friends, but why did you do that to me?"

"Oh, but I didn't know, then," she said.

And I said, "I forgive you. I forgive you."

That was hard work. But I was always showing her the truth. The truth, I believe, is where the light is.

ADELA VÁZQUEZ: Right now, I'm about to make a decision of having a sex change. I'm in that process. That part of myself is not something that I want to share. I don't want to sleep around anymore. This time, it's not for sex; it's for me.

They already approved me. I can really go and make the phone call.

I'm very healthy—I might be a unicorn! I'm sixty-four years old and I've never been operated on, never been in the hospital overnight. So what will this imply for me?

But that's an excuse. Really, I'm insecure at the moment, about the surgery. I do want to have a pussy. There's no question about it.

It would mean completion. Completion, you know? I'm not a perfect woman. I'm a great transgender woman. Do I need a pussy? I don't need it. Do I want it? Yes, I do. I'm afraid, yes. I'm afraid. It's a big decision. An important decision. I have other friends who are very successful, happy and all that. Like I said, it's not sexual. It's not that, "Oh, I'm going to fuck my pussy." None of that. Although my dick doesn't work anymore, because I'm too old, and that is one of the reasons I want to have a pussy.

It's just: the day that I die, whenever I die, I want to have a pussy. When I get there, God is going to be confused. "Oh, wait a minute, she has a pussy!" You know what I mean?

Yes, I think it would complete me.

You know: it's my pussy. For me. For me. That's it.

NELSON D'ALERTA PÉREZ: I don't need to change my body to see myself as a woman.

When I was very young, I had a great desire for surgery. But then, I realized something: if I get gender surgery, I'll have a man and that man will tell me what to do. I don't want that. I don't want to be that kind of woman. I'm going to keep going the way I am, which is that I'm a woman. Whoever understands me, great. Whoever doesn't, fine. So I decided not to have surgery.

After I arrived in San Francisco in 1983, I had the good luck to meet many girls who'd already had surgery, or were in the process. I was fascinated. I supported them wholeheartedly. They all said, "So when are you starting the process?"

And I'd say, "Well, I'm already in the process."

"The physical transition?"

"I'm already there, I'm going great this way, don't worry about me."

All my life, I've wondered: how did I get like this? Who taught me to think this way? It's a gift of life. An ability I've had, and maintain. There was nothing like this in my home. It all sprang from my own mind. I came to live this way, divinely. Happily.

Many people have asked me, "Why don't you complete your transition?"

I have a lot of hair. I've had to fight against all those parts of my natural state. I lived as a woman for many years when I was younger. Now that I'm aging, I'm more focused on making art, things like that. But I feel transsexual. I love women's clothing, dressing as a woman, looking like a woman. For a party, socially, I like to present that way. But at work, it has felt too difficult for me to contend with all that.

All my life, I've had this kind of double personality. There are people I've started to love: how do I tell him I'm transgender? How will he understand? What happens when he learns I've got women's shoes under my bed? It's been hard to live my life the way I have.

I'm happy with myself. I know what I am, where I come from, what I've done. Just the other day, I said, "Okay, let's give it a try." I put on a wig, dressed as a lady, and took the dogs for a walk. I said, "Uy, how delicious, what a liberating feeling."

But am I going to do that every day? No. And I say, "When I'm like this, looking male on the outside, I'm a lady anyway." Whether you like it or not.

TINA VALENTÍN AGUIRRE: In 2018 or 2019, the state of California agreed to let people go to the DMV and change their gender marker to nonbinary. The first week that was possible, I did that. On my ID, under gender, it now said "X."

I said, "Oh, society has caught up to what I've always been."

Society has caught up with me and my peers. Younger people now definitely understand what I am, who I am.

ANDRÉS OZZUNA: I like my body a lot. Much more than I used to. I have a better and better relationship with my body. It's a beautiful thing, to accept myself, to have that inner peace. That's essentially what I like most about being trans.

MS BILLIE COOPER: I'm still on a journey. We're always in transition, no matter who you are, what you are, how much money you have, or how much money you don't.

Transition is everywhere. Everybody transitions. I would say my transition has so far been for sixty-four years, and I'm still transitioning.

In my life, I have the right to transition any way I want. I have the right to live my life any way I want, as long as I'm not hurting myself or anyone else. You know? Just to move in the key of life. Like Stevie Wonder says: moving on in the key of life.

SEVEN

* *

Chosen Family

DONNA PERSONNA: In the LGBTQ community, since time immemorial, we've made a family of each other. Because in a lot of cases, you can't stay with the family that you were born into. So we choose each other. We choose to bolster each other, to lift each other the way you do with your loved ones.

To me, that is very, very important.

FRESH "LEV" WHITE: Yeah. Beautiful chosen family. Finding people that love and respect you for who you are, which comes from loving and respecting ourselves. I feel like I make more and more all the time.

NELSON D'ALERTA PÉREZ: Oh my God, chosen family is so dear. I appreciate my friends so much. I adore them. To me, they are up on an altar. I understand what they're going through because I've felt it myself.

Back in Cuba, all my friends were transsexual. I didn't seek that out; they appeared on their own, a blessing from God. They've been my family. The family I couldn't otherwise have.

In the moments when I most needed them, as a teenager, these people were there for me. When I was jailed for holding drag shows, they said to me, "It doesn't matter. We'll put on another show. Put on more makeup."

We'd play at seeing who was the strongest, the most fabulous. What a miracle. A wonderful thing.

ADELA VÁZQUEZ: I take people under my wings and I talk about my life, continuously.

It's a queer family.

The whole children thing came without me knowing that I was going to be a mother.

It started in the early nineties. Alejandra was eighteen years old when I met her. She was a fresh drag queen, fresh transgender, Puerto Rican, very cute. I loved her. She said, "You're my mom." So I took her under my wing, and she was my daughter.

That's my first daughter. And then I had another one, and another, and before I know it I have a lot of them. I didn't want to be a mother, but how can I deny that?

Until now, transgender people didn't get married and have kids and all that stuff. Family—for transgender people it was almost impossible. I mean, hello?—to this day, a lot of people confuse or mix pedophilia with being queer, which is so far away from the truth. Before HIV came along, transgenders were underground, completely underground. We were showgirls and prostitutes. That was it. And the two or three that went to work, they had to pass, people didn't know that they were transgender at work. That lie, that big lie.

I have gotten to savor a little bit that part of life that was forbidden for me.

And I think it's needed. I think it's needed to have a family.

They become your family.

I also have a lot of straight people in my chosen family. I have friends that I may have fucked, and they're still my friends, they're my family, we communicate all the time.

From a very young age, I learned how to live without a family. Every time I went to bed, nobody came to say goodnight and ask me if I had something to eat that day, how are you doing? I have made it on my own all the way through. And to be an immigrant and make a decent life, considering that, I've done well. So now, what I have is a plus. It's beautiful that I can have that in my life.

You have to have a group of people that is your support emotionally, and that knows you, you can be yourself, you don't have to lie. That's important in anybody's life.

TINA VALENTÍN AGUIRRE: There were lots of families, where we had room-mates, lovers, best friends, sisters. We lived, and worked, and had fun on Sixteenth Street. For me, Esta Noche and La India Bonita especially were the ones that really brought that out through music, and parties, and also times when we were really sad because somebody was sick or dying. There might be a benefit before they died. Or there might be many benefits for somebody who we knew was sick and wasn't able to pay their rent, or wasn't able to bring their family from wherever they're from.

It was really important for us to be able to come together and share that love when we're alive, and then, if somebody passed, to mark that in the bars.

Some of the people that I met early on at Esta Noche were Mahogany and Ronnie Salazar and Teresita la Campesina, who all did drag on Sixteenth Street in San Francisco. Teresita was our trans mother. She was older than us and had an operatic voice. She sang rancheras, and she was a sex worker, and a loud, loud person who took up lots of space. She was Mexican-American, but she spoke mostly Spanish. Teresita la Campesina was what she adopted, but she was never a campesina, that was her persona. She had breast augmentation and she maybe was on hormones, but it was not a constant for her. She was pretty. She adopted me as one of her children, along with Ronnie and Mahogany. We were her children, in a chosen family, that was part of a bigger community and chosen family. But we, in particular, were the very tight family. We supported each other and went to each other's shows.

LANDA LAKES: In drag families, we realize that we're all different, and we accept those differences in each other.

Mine is called the House of Glitter. First, we started with the Brush Arbor Gurlz, which was the first-ever Native American drag troupe. Then, being at Trannyshack created the House of Glitter. Suddenly people wanted to be my drag children. I was very resistant

at first. I was like, "No, no, I don't want any children." And then I had
Holy McGrail, one of my best drag friends, and then I slowly started
collecting children. Kenya Pfister, Pollo Del Mar, Euphoria. We would
meet almost every Monday night. We would just have a family dinner, and maybe watch *RuPaul's Drag Race*. We have a really great
family dynamic.

And my drag children come over for Thanksgiving. My drag children and some grandchildren, I guess you could say, they all come
over, a lot of people. Christmas, too, we'll do a kind of gift exchange,
and then everybody will complain about the gift they get. And so,
that'll be fun. But you know what? There are real family dynamics
that happen within drag houses. There were times where, like children, they were trying to vie for my attention, pulling me this way
and that. It's like a real, true family dynamic. Everybody's like, "I
want Mom's attention now."

When I started off in drag, I didn't have a drag mother. But I sort
of had a drag sister each time. Fast forward to the House of Glitter:
we've created some beautiful pieces on stage, but more than that, I've
tried to also help them. Most of the people in the House of Glitter are
clean and sober. I've just never touched the stuff. That's one of the reasons why some of them came to me early on. I've been able to assist
them in a lot of different ways. When it's happened that they've gotten
sick and have ended up in the hospital, it's this whole family dynamic
where you get together with the rest of the family and decide: how
can we help this person? What are we going to do? Are we going to go
over and take care of his dog?

I think that one of the things that nonqueer people could learn
from us is the true definition of family. I think it's important that
when you are from the same house, you support each other. That's
how we say it in Chickasaw: family, from the same house.

MS BILLIE COOPER: I'm a community mother. I am community.

I have been a mother figure to many, many people. To gay people, lesbians, gender-nonconforming people, nonbinary people, especially trans people, people that are not under the trans umbrella, straight people, queer people, Black people, white people. I'm just so grateful that I have that appeal. I'm approachable. I will always be approachable; I will never let myself be unapproachable. We have to be kind and gentle.

I'm good at seeing something, whether it's negative or positive, in other people that they don't see in themselves. I see people for who they are. I have one eye. I lost my left eye to cancer. I have squamous cell carcinoma cancers, aggressively growing cancers that have been dormant for five years, thank god. I see many people for who they really are, with one eye more so than when I had two eyes. I can really read people now, being a mother figure.

I'm so happy to say I have many, many chosen family members, who sometimes feel like they're blood family, like we're from the same mother, the same father. I'm grateful for my chosen family. It's meant so much to me, helped me stay on the right path, stay on my chosen path, be who I authentically am, be my authentic self, you know? Not cower down. Be a better voice, a better face—for I am one of the many, many voices and faces of my communities, and I stand on the shoulders of many, many, many, many, many people.

DONNA PERSONNA: I have a biological family. That's not one that I chose, but it's fully mine. I'm not alienated from my biological family. Actually, we all adore each other. I'm kind of an elder in my family that everyone looks to.

But I want a family every day of my life. And as an activist, I want to be family to my LGBTQ community, too. So I have a chosen family.

One of my boys—he is gay—when I talk to him on the phone, he says, "I want to be with you always. I want you to think about me."

I say, "I think about you all the time." That's part of it. He's my son, and he wants that from me. That brings me such joy.

He said this to me before, years ago: "You are my favorite person in the universe."

I said, "Baby."

"Oh," he said, "You're my mother, you're my mother."

And I said, "You know you have a mom in Scotland."

But he just wanted to say that to me.

It makes me feel good. I am really, really his mother. The world has given me what I always wanted, but in a different way. When he looks at me and he knows I'm in the world, he knows he's going to be okay. There's been times when he needed me, and I got in the car, and I drove up, and I was with him. I do that, too, for my kids. I get to fill the role. The universe and the world and life has given me everything. It's everything.

SHARYN GRAYSON: In later years, my mother became a surrogate mom to a lot of my friends whose parents were not as accepting and supporting as she was. I remember times I'd go to my mom's house and there'd be all these cars in the driveway. I'm like, "What is going on?"

I'd go in there, and there'd be a lot of my friends.

I said, "This is *my* mom. She's not you guys' mom!"

Trans and LGBTQ friends. Everybody. A lot of whom didn't have family acceptance. The concept of family is so important, particularly to trans people. I mean, I don't know if you could imagine your parent telling you, "I don't want to see you. I don't want you around me. I don't care if you live or die." I just couldn't imagine that.

With the stories that I've heard from so many people I've encountered over the years, I'm like, "How could a parent do that? How could they do that to a child?" I mean, these are young people. Young adults, at the most formative portions of their lives, knowing that these people don't care if they live or die.

And my mom, bless her heart, was able to take those little shells that were left and bring them into the fold. There were other people there who had experienced the same thing, and they would all talk.

It was just that sense of family. She did that. I just watched it. I was so proud that that was my mom, that she saw that need in people. I mean, there was no hesitation. She did not care how you dressed. She didn't care how you looked. None of that. It was: "Baby, have you eaten? Where are you staying? You're welcome here any time."

I was very proud of that. To be adopted into a family that accepts you for who you are, that is something that makes or breaks a person. It is everything.

A lot of the people that my mom was surrogate mom to have said that, had it not been for her, they don't believe they would still be here.

FRESH "LEV" WHITE: Unfortunately, many of us can say the most harm we've received in the world is from our families.

ADELA VÁZQUEZ: Your family can make you or destroy you. There are families that don't have an open mind and they don't want to have it. They decided that you are wrong, for whatever reason.

NICKY CALMA: Me and my dad never really had a relationship, ever since I moved here to the United States. He always says, "Well, you wanted to go there. Then you do what you need to do." He was not being vicious. But I feel like he was also hurt.

Every time I talk to my mom now on Facebook, she always asks, "Do you still wear women's clothes? Do you buy women's clothes?"

It's like, "Mom, what am I going to wear?"

"What about your underwear, do you now buy women's underwear?"

"Yes, Ma, what do you want me to wear? Fruit of the Looms?"

She's adorable. She's just like that. She still calls me my dead nickname, and it's fine, because I can say that she's always been there for me. Even though she has nothing to give, she's just there to listen.

Even if we fight, after a week she will call me, "How are you doing?" And she'll check in and everything. I feel like she never lost hope for me. Being away from your family was unconventional. Not normal for a Filipino family. She wanted to support the things that I wanted to do, but she couldn't, because my dad was always there. There was a time that I hated them. I didn't want to talk to them, I was just on my own. That was also when I was starting to use drugs.

It took a book for me to realize that they do love me, how they knew how to love. All the screaming, cussing: that was the love that they were giving me.

The book is called *All About Love*, by bell hooks. It's so funny: when I was finishing the book, I was on a plane. When I was finishing the book, on the flight, oh my god, I started crying. I started bawling. I wanted to call my parents, I wanted to call my sister, I wanted to shout at the world. Then this gentleman next to me was like, "Are you okay?"

I was like, "Yes, yes, no, this book is really moving me."

He offered what he was eating, he had chips.

I said, "No, I'm good."

He said, "Must be a pretty interesting book."

"It is," I said. "It really is."

CRYSTAL MASON: In DC, in the eighties, a lot of the people I knew were artists. I had a group of queer people that I mostly hung out with.

It was my first experience of feeling like I had a family that didn't think I was odd. That first time of feeling not othered. Like I belonged there, like people were willing to see me as I was and as I might be, could see this change and transformation and was all right with it. As we know, when you're growing up someplace, it's difficult sometimes for people to give you that space. Most of the time, people prefer you in the role that they're used to seeing you in.

This was an opportunity for me to really grow and to start to try on different things, but also to be free of the expectations of other people, of family members. The people I was hanging out with, fortunately for me, really just loved me.

ADELA VÁZQUEZ : Since 1982, Nelson and I have been friends. We still live together. Oh, my God, I'm so happy that I have Nelson in my life. We have each other, you know?

NELSON D'ALERTA PÉREZ: Adela Vázquez! Yes. I've been living with her since 1983, and from that moment on, we've had an incredible friendship. She's supported me a lot, and I her.

JOAN BENOIT: Yes, chosen family. Clearly, I am in Oakland because this is where my people are. These are the people I feel a heart connection to. My biological family isn't here. But these are the people who I am aligned with politically, I'm aligned with community-wise in that we're all queer in some way or another—there's this queer kinship— and it's largely a community of color. Chosen family. We are here in a way for each other that our biological families can't be, whether by distance or because they're not as connected to our hearts in the same way as these people are. I would do anything for my family here that needed to be done. I was bailing water in the pouring rain last week. It wasn't my house, but we just showed up to do it.

I am raising a young Black boy in Oakland. I should say an Indigenous Black boy, because he's also Blackfeet. That's a little scary. It makes me want to change the systems that are in place that really brutalize our young, Black and Brown boys, in particular, and girls. I'm really committed to changing those systems so that he grows up in a world that's safe for him and his peers. And also, giving him that language and knowledge, to be empowered instead of squashed.

CHINO SCOTT-CHUNG: Before my daughter Luna was born, my wife Maya and I talked about what we thought she should call us. Dad, Mom, Baba. It's pretty incredible because I, as the male-identified parent, wasn't out as trans then, and I didn't feel like I could ask my daughter to call me Daddy or Dad or any of the more male-identified terms. I didn't feel like I had earned that. I didn't feel like I was good enough to be called dad. So I thought, Okay, I'll have Luna call me Baba, which is more male-identified. In the Chinese language and Chinese culture, the dads are called Baba, so I thought, that's good, that fits me. But it's not Dad or Daddy, which to me was the ultimate, the best of all, you know?

So when Luna was born, and as she started talking, I asked her to call me that.

One day, she just came home from day care and called me Daddy.

At first, I didn't feel like I deserved that or I could own that, so I ignored her. I didn't say anything, I didn't act like I was that person. She kept calling me Daddy, and just insisted. I was her dad. That's just what she called me. So one day I started responding, answering back to her. That's how it happened.

As a little girl who was just finding language herself, she helped me to accept my own identity. At the time she was born, in 2004, the members of my community who were having kids in the more masculine butch roles, their kids weren't calling them Daddy. My friends were coming to me and asking me how I was able to take on that name. My daughter helped me to be that. Who I wanted to be.

C. NJOUBE DUGAS: There have been stages of my life where I've had different chosen families. They've provided me with safety. They've provided me with knowledge and stories. I choose family wherever I go. I have a small group of friends that we're really, really close. I believe in uplifting community members wherever I can.

I love that idea: chosen family. They choose me, they literally choose me. I'll never forget it: I was going to Mills College—I went back to college when I was forty-eight or something. It's orientation day, I got the paperwork, I'm trying to figure out where I'm going, and there's these two queer women, they're like: "Where are you going?"

I said, "Well, I think I'm going to—"

"Okay, then we're going with you, we're family, come on, let's go."
They're still my ride or dies.

TINA VALENTÍN AGUIRRE: Somebody who I remember is Cindy Liu. She
was a trans Latina drag performer at La India Bonita. She did Cyndi
Lauper songs. That's how she got her name. She was really pretty, and
nice. She worked at the bar sometimes as a bartender, but mostly as a
performer.

She had this really hot cholo boyfriend for a few years, but he was
struggling with his identity. I don't know that it was easy for him; he
really was a cholo and straight. At the time, there was not the vocab-
ulary to say, okay, obviously you can still be straight. At the time,
unless you had an operation, many operations, you couldn't say you
were a trans woman. So, that was a struggle that they had within their
own relationship. We all were close with Cindy. And it just got really
bad. He cheated on her. He would sometimes taunt her. She ended up
deciding to kill herself on Valentine's Day. I think it was in '89. She
just went to the top of her building and jumped.

For us, it was really awful, because we couldn't help her. We were
not able to prevent that. We did try. We were young, in our early
twenties. We were going through a lot of challenges from outside the
community, and even inside.

I'm happy to remember Cindy Liu. Cindy Liu was awesome and
one of us.

We loved each other.

CHINO SCOTT-CHUNG: I had a best friend. His name was Christopher Lee.
He was a lovely person. Very generous. If he was your friend, he was
your friend all the way. He was very loyal, just a beautiful person. He
also was very annoying: once he got an idea in his head, he would not
let it go.

Oh my God, he just impressed me from the beginning. I had a
girlfriend who moved here from New York. It was her birthday, and

she wanted to meet more people, so I had a big birthday party for her at her house in Bernal Heights, in San Francisco. Christopher came, and that was the first time I ever met him. This was the early nineties, and he hadn't transitioned yet. He was Chris Lee. We were up on the balcony because my girlfriend lived on the second floor, and he came in and started singing *Grease* songs in the backyard up to the birthday girl on the balcony, on his knees.

I was like: what an incredible person!

He had *love, hate* tattooed on his fingers—you know: L-O-V-E, H-A-T-E. He showed it to me. I was like, how could somebody be so bold, to do something like that?

To me, at the time, he was a woman. A butch woman, a butch Asian. He was half Polish, half Chinese. I've met both his parents since. Clearly a butch woman, butcher than me, which I really respected. But he insisted that we call him "he" at a time when nobody ever said that. Nobody. I had never heard that before. At the time, I couldn't accept it. I was never going to call him "he" because he was clearly a "she." We had discussions in the community about it. This was all part of trans inclusion, my first introduction to it.

Some people were like, "Yes, if that's what he wants, then okay."

I was like, "No way, I'm not going to do that."

At that time, I couldn't see beyond the gender binary, even though I was a butch masculine-presenting person and was starting to get kicked out of the women's bathroom. That was at the very beginning of my journey. Just think about that! He, Christopher, was introducing our community to what it meant to be trans.

We were friends from that moment—from the moment I saw him on his knees singing *Grease* songs—until he killed himself in 2012.

Two decades.

Sometimes we wouldn't talk for periods of time, because I was mad at him for something or another, or he was mad at me, but we were fast and furious.

I'll just tell you about when he started on T.

It was a big decision for him, and I was with him through it all. He had CFIDS, chronic fatigue immune deficiency syndrome, which made him very tired, and lupus also makes me tired, so we really had some things in common. He also didn't want to affect his health, so he started taking testosterone really slowly. He took micro doses at first. He slowly started changing. He would show me. Like when he started growing a little bit of peach fuzz, and when his voice was starting to get a little deeper. I remember particularly when his supraorbital ridge started growing, his—basically, the bone in his forehead—we were both really impressed with that. It's like, wow, how could that happen?

That's when I started realizing how deeply testosterone changed a person, how deeply and all-inclusively it changed you, down to your bone structure. That was incredible. He didn't seem like he changed that much to me, like his body structure changed that much, but he went from wearing a small men's shirt, I believe, to a large. Even though he didn't grow taller, he became more muscular, more dense.

He was on Social Security disability for his CFIDS. He lived on a boat in the San Leandro Marina. I used to go visit him all the time. He'd have barbecues and stuff. And when he started really changing, his sex drive got so high. He was having guys over, I swear, sometimes three a night. It was like, whoa! I think he was doing craigslist of all places, and guys would come over. He'd have a quickie, they'd leave, someone else would come over. Incredible, what this hormone was doing. But then of course, I was always worried about whether he was practicing safe sex. That was a big thing,

Now that I look back, he was just having so much fun, just living his life large, in this huge way. That's who he was.

He was trying so hard to live life. He was just trying to live his life.

Thing is, he was living on that boat for many years, but he was getting seasick. He couldn't live on it anymore. He was homeless at some points. He was trying so hard to get on his feet again. Because of his mental health issues, it just wasn't going to happen. And there were no resources for him.

It's so tragic, and so sad. His last year was just so intense. He was suffering a major mental health crisis. He was having hallucinations, he was very paranoid. He was in a mental health institution, he just was having a really, really hard time. You would think in San Francisco, they would have resources for him, but they didn't. I was trying to help him. There was no place for him to go, because he was trans, because he was disabled, and he had chemical sensitivity. There was one shelter for trans people, but it was mostly trans women, and trans women—at least at that shelter—wore a lot of perfume and scents. He couldn't stay there because it would make him sick. That was the only place where he could go other than the psychiatric institutions where he ended up.

We ended up having to take him to John George Psychiatric Hospital when he was having really major hallucinations. We had to sit there and educate the doctors and the woman at the desk about him being trans, who he was and what he needed.

I couldn't take care of him. I couldn't have him in my home. I had a young daughter, and I didn't have the capacity to help him myself.

He took his life in my house.

It was horrible.

I went to Hawaii with my family, he was here taking care of the cats, and he took his life in my room.

I still feel so much grief over Christopher. It's still hard to talk about him.

When I think about Christopher and the way he just was who he was in all his glory, all his beauty and all his differences, I think: he was one of the trailblazers. He was one of the first people who said, "Call me he." That made such a big, huge impression on me. It's like, be who you are, in all your glory and all your beauty and all your identities and all your genders.

NICKY CALMA: I have a few chosen families. My family's in the Philippines, so it's nice to have a chosen family here. I think these are folks that provide validation, comfort, especially when the world is being vicious towards you.

To give it that definition, that they are chosen family: it's revolutionary.

TINA VALENTÍN AGUIRRE: I was in a new writing group, and I said, "Okay, I'm going to do a spell."

We held hands, and I said the poem: "For this moment, you are my family. I need family. We all need family. This is the spell."

I can do that wherever I am, whenever I am. I need that. I need to be able to continually make connections, keep connections. It's okay if some of these connections don't stay. If they're not permanent. That's not the point. I can't control that. What I can control is that I hope to connect, and I can enjoy that connection.

We find ways to connect with each other, even in the midst of great political turmoil and discrimination.

FRESH "LEV" WHITE: For me, we're all family.

That might come from being separated from my birth parents at birth, one of the ways I cope with it, I don't know. Might be. But we're all fucking humans—excuse my French, or New York, you can't have that in France—and we're all breathing each other's breath. Supposedly, it takes about, I don't know, 247 days for our breath to come back to where we first breathed it. We're all breathing each other's breath. We're not that different. We're all drinking the same water. We're all breathing in each other's skin flakes. You know what I mean?

That's family. Yeah.

JOAN BENOIT: There are Indigenous teachings on how to build community that are really important. And one of them is that no one's left behind. Everybody is worthy. You don't lock them up, and you don't push them away, and you don't shove them out. You bring them in and you try to work with them to make a community. The circle's whole then. When you have missing pieces, it's not whole.

That's one of the courageous things.

DONNA PERSONNA: You're all my kids. Everyone is.

I feel like I am Earth mother. I'm Earth mother. In my particular life, I did not have the wherewithal to have children of my own. A child did not come out of my body.

So you're all my kids. What you need, I'm going to try to give you.

JOAN BENOIT: There's no paper that can define a real family. It's just who you're with. The people you make a commitment to.

People try to put us in a box. We defy the box.

PART THREE

* * * * * * * * * *

BEING THE CHANGE

* * * * * * * * ** *

EIGHT

Activism

YOSEÑIO LEWIS: I became an activist at a very early age.

DONNA PERSONNA: I've been an activist all my life.

I'm a full-on activist. I'm here to try to change things that I see need to be changed.

TUPILI LEA ARELLANO: I've been a social justice activist from a very early age. The first time I went to the streets was in 1968 to fight against the Vietnam War, and that was in Silver City, New Mexico, a very small, conservative town. But there were people who said, "You're coming with us." I've been very active since then.

MS. BILLIE Cooper: I am a forty-year-plus activist, a forty-year-plus advocate, not only for Black rights in the early days, but for trans rights.

We have been called many names by many people. But we have been called transgendered, I would say, for maybe the last ten to fifteen years.

We have been fighting for trans rights, transgender rights, since long before we were transgender.

SHARYN GRAYSON: I became an advocate of civil rights, trans rights, LGBT rights. Well, let me back up. There was no trans rights then: it was gay rights. Then it became LGBT. Then we had trans rights.

At first, when the only movement was for gay rights, I was a part of it on the periphery. I had friends that identified as gay. That's not who I identified as. But I supported my friends who were gay.

Black trans women have always been a part of the movement. Stonewall, in New York—that's a perfect example. Stonewall replicated what had happened so many times before, and people just never knew, but trans women were at the forefront.

TINA VALENTÍN AGUIRRE: We know how liberation movements, the Civil Rights Movement, were built on the backs of women. And we know that the queer movement was built on the backs of trans women.

SHARYN GRAYSON: It was us out there, Black trans women, advocating, standing up against police barriers, and a lot of times, being pushed out front by Black gay men. But we were there. We were a part of the fight. We were a part of that movement, and even in that, we were not equally supported. That was hurtful. Very hurtful. So, we have always, as a community, had no other alternative but to take care of ourselves. And that's what we did. We could not always get jobs. We couldn't always get educations, particularly if we were comfortable in who we were as a human being. If I said, "No, I'm not putting on a pair of slacks. That's not who I am. I am a Black trans woman," or, "I am a Black woman of trans experience." If my survival means that I have to deny who I am, I don't want that. I'll die first.

You had the people in New York, like Sylvia Rivera and Marsha P. Johnson, women like those two that said, "No. Absolutely not. You are not going to ignore us anymore. Enough is enough." And other trans women around the country began to speak out and stand up against the system.

MS BILLIE COOPER: The person who started me in my lifelong work as an activist, advocate, and community liaison was Miss Major Griffin-Gracie. When I met her, in San Francisco in '79, I was AWOL from the Navy. I told her I wasn't going back. She told me, "Queen, go back, do what you got to do, get your discharge, and then come back to San Francisco."

For the few weeks I was with her, I saw how she reached out to the community. She never threw anyone under the bus. She always gave her last to someone who didn't have anything. I wanted to be like that. I hung around her each and every day.

TUPILI LEA ARELLANO: In the Bay Area, in the 1980s, I was one of the visionaries and founders of Mujerio.

I just want to shout out appreciation so deep, deep, deep for the founders of Mujerio and the ones who organized it and ran it. The commitment there, to give ourselves space, a space as Latinas, as queer women of color with origins in the Americas. We had meetings, we'd have food, we danced, we'd meet new people, we'd hear people's stories. Isolation kills, it kills, so that was the big medicine. That was some social justice.

We had a newsletter, and I was "Ask Doña Marimacha." I was the secret Ann Landers of Latinx queer women. I had my column in that newsletter. They'd write to me—we didn't have email then, folks, believe it or not—and send me questions I would answer. That was so much fun. That newsletter was really a connector.

In those years, like the early eighties, the mid eighties, people were not talking about trans stuff. Trans people already existed, we've existed for millenniums, but we weren't talking about it.

YOSEÑIO LEWIS: In the mid nineties, I was part of a group that would go to Washington, DC, to lobby for trans inclusion. In anything, but especially around medical care. Unfortunately, one of the things that we had to do was convince the people who were supposedly there to represent us that we were worthy of being represented.

The amount of times I had to go to the Human Rights Campaign office! To try to convince the people in charge that trans people were a part of the queer community.

That we did need to be represented. That we were not asking for "special rights."

How dare you tell us that we're asking for special rights, when that is exactly what you grew up hearing all of your life? When you said, "I just want to be able to rent an apartment, I want to be able to have a job, marry the person I care about, have children and not worry about custody issues."

And dealing with the backlash from cis gay people. "Oh, you guys are freaks, we're just at the point where straight people are beginning to understand that we're normal, that we're just like them, we can't have you come in, you're going to mess everything up."

There was a bill, ENDA, the Employment Non-Discrimination Act, that was supposedly to support the "normalization" of LG. It wasn't B and T, it was LG. "We're getting accepted. People like us now." ENDA was on tap, but it never passed.

And some of us were saying, "Look, if you're going to be coming to DC every year and lobbying for this, and you're raising all this money for it, why can't you include the B and T? We're here. We've been here. We've been here forever. We've been in the back rooms, doing the grunt work. Why are you ignoring us? You're a part of us, we're a part of you. You don't recall Stonewall, and what really happened there. We're getting killed by the dozens, and you don't want us here because we will make you unpalatable. You were unpalatable just a few years ago. But because you decided to start dressing preppy, and move to places where there was a lot of money, you think that's going to make people accept you, and that it also makes it okay for you to treat other people poorly."

So then all my years of hearing "You're not Latin enough, you're not Black enough, you're not woman enough, you're not man enough"—all of those things came up for me to say, "No, not again. This is not going to be yet another place where I get told I don't count."

So I made it my mission. For years, a bunch of us would go to Human Rights Campaign meetings and talk to them, to get them to be more inclusive of trans people. Well, now they are, and now they fight for us.

STORMMIGUEL FLOREZ: In the early 2000s, the queer community was shifting. People would get together and have these conversations, sparked by the presence of transitioning—the guys who were transitioning in the dyke community, and the tensions that were there. It got a little weird. I was noticing that the spaces were often mostly white, and just feeling less and less comfortable.

There were moments where it felt sad. Just sad. Because of what people were going through around transition, the fear and loss.

Now, the majority of us get it. The majority of us have come to an understanding that gender is not about genitalia. It's more complicated than that. And that inclusive space shouldn't be about genitalia either. At the time, the loudest conversations were happening among white people, or the pushback was coming from white people. So this idea of women being the ultimate oppressed people—it was white women who were saying that and creating space based on that, not considering the dynamics in those spaces around race and ethnicity, class and disability.

I think that, now, the community is really understanding about intersections and who is actually being targeted, who is the most vulnerable. That's who we need to center and bring into leadership. I don't think that's happening across the board, but I do think that we are headed in the right direction in the queer community. There are still very vocal people who are toeing that TERF [trans-exclusionary radical feminists] line of, like, no penises in women's space, which is just ridiculous.

White cis men still have the ultimate power in this country. Right? White cis women can align with that, and also be harmed by that— that's real, I acknowledge that, but they have more to gain from it than anybody else. If you think about police and who police target, it is not cis white women. And who's getting the better paying jobs? Who actually has privilege?

CRYSTAL MASON: In the dyke community, for a long time there were these arguments about who's a dyke and gold star dykes. I remember in ACT UP—this is not a highlight, this is a lowlight—having to meet for two and a half hours because there were some women who wanted to call themselves bi dykes and others who didn't want to accept them in dyke space. I was so mad. I can't tell you how mad I was. But I hung in there. I was like, "Really? These people are out there doing the work every day, but we're going to have this conversation?"

In general, I support people calling themselves whatever the fuck they want, and I will call you that too if that's what you want, because it's no skin off my nose. That was my thing back then, and it still is. It doesn't bother my conception of myself if these people want to call themselves bi dykes.

As much as people in this country go around screaming "Freedom," people don't really like it. They don't really want to have choices. I think that's what's disturbing to straight people, even to gay and lesbian people who are straight-adjacent: that we say we have choices of how we want to be in our bodies, how we want to move in the world. And all of the pain and sorrow comes from how other people want to treat you. Their refusal to see us the way we want to be seen.

JOAN BENOIT: I don't identify with the LGBT community so much, as they put it out there in the media. As the Castro District portrays it to be. This white, rich, wealthy movement that moved the whole marriage thing forward and all of that. That feels very commercial, capitalistic, very money-based. It's not the same as Indigiqueer. I care about people in the way that Indigenous communities cared about people. I want the people to be whole, I want my community to be whole. I don't care about the money. Marriage was never a thing. My wife Andreana and I have said it over and over: marriage was not our fight. This is not our thing. Our thing is people of color, young people, not gay marriage.

I benefited from that, and I am grateful, but we were married before it ever became legal. And that's our wedding date. It's not when the laws changed. It was when we stood in front of our people. That day. When we signed papers and got legal status, that was extra. That wasn't the commitment.

That said, I was part of the first lesbian couple to be declared a family, if not a married couple, by a federal court of law in the United States. This was in 1991. Long before gay marriage.

My then wife was undocumented. They were raiding establishments, and picking up undocumented people, just shipping them off. So she started a suspension of deportation hearing. And at that time, the only way to get a suspension of deportation was by showing that the harm would be on your family, not you as an individual. Like your own harm didn't matter. Being shipped back to a country that was homophobic, it didn't matter, because it was just an individual harm. You had to prove that your family would be harmed. And because the only family that she had here was me and my family, we had to testify on her behalf. The judge declared us a family in the court of law, granted suspension of deportation, and she got a green card. Then, a year later, we broke up.

It was stressful and quite an ordeal. But it was historic. A federal court recognized us as a family.

CHINO SCOTT-CHUNG: It's incredible how things can change.

I went to go pick up my best friend Christopher's ashes. When he died by suicide, his mom wasn't talking to him. His dad was very sick and having a hard time himself. His half-sisters had totally distanced themselves because he was trans, because of their transphobia. Christopher had come out as trans, and he was somebody who would not hide. He would not act like he was anyone he wasn't. He was always out as trans.

The woman at the Neptune Society gave me his death certificate. It said "female" on there. When the coroner came to pick his body up at our house, we gave him all of Christopher's documents that showed he had transitioned, that he had changed all his documents to reflect his true gender identity. We gave that all to the coroner. The fire department was the first on the scene, and one of the firefighters was the dad of one of the kids at my daughter's school, so I knew him, and I told him, too. I said to him and the coroner, "Christopher is trans, these are his documents, these are his wishes, I was his power of attorney, please respect that." And even then, when I went to go pick up his death certificate, it said "female."

I said, "He is a man, he is trans—here's his documents."

The woman said, "It's all based on genitalia. That's how the coroners make that decision."

Christopher had never had surgery. In fact, this was another thing I just totally respected and loved him for. He had never had top surgery. He didn't have much of a chest, but he did have big nipples, women's nipples, and he didn't care. He'd go swimming in trunks, and if guys would look at him, sometimes look at his chest, he just stared back at them, and they would stop staring. That's how he handled it. He was just such a role model to me, a vision of being in his whole self. With no surgery, this was him. He wasn't going to take any shit from anybody about it. I respected and loved him for that.

When the woman told me that, I was shocked and just couldn't believe it. I was so upset. How can this institution define him? This is who he was in all his glory, all his body, his gender identities, this is him, you can't say anything else. You can't take that away from him. You can't define him the way you want to define him. That's bullshit, total bullshit.

This was in 2012, in California.

So I flipped that. I'm not going to accept that, Christopher would not accept that. That is not who he was. My ex and I went to the Transgender Law Center, and we worked with this beautiful, wonderful trans woman. Sasha. A white trans woman and a beautiful person. I loved her. She was a great lawyer. She was my friend after that.

We're like, "We're going to change this."

We went up to Sacramento, to the California capital. I testified twice.

It was Assembly Bill 1577. The Christopher Lee Bill. I had to go in front of the senate. I had to go up there twice to testify, and I remember, oh my god, I was so nervous because you can't even sit down. You have to stand there. It's like you're standing in this low pit, and the whole senate is up there. It was a half-round of seats, and there's three tiers of senators all just looking down at you. Talk about nervous! They're all sitting there looking down at you and it's, "Okay, now I have to testify." When I get nervous, I sweat. I was just pouring sweat down. I read my testimony. I was too nervous to try to speak it.

The head of the senate was this Japanese guy, I don't remember his name. Sasha said, "When you're nervous, find somebody that looks like an ally, like they agree with you or support you." So he was the one. He was the head of the senate. He was the senate president or whatever they call it, he looked really friendly. He was nodding. I don't think he was smiling, but I could tell he agreed with the bill. So I focused on him when I read my testimony.

I had written in my testimony about who Christopher was and what a lovely person he was, how much he gave to the community and how he was, in every way, a man. How it really hurt to see "female" in his death certificate.

The bill got passed.

I helped change the law so transgender people can have their true gender stated on death certificates in California.

LANDA LAKES: Twelve years ago, we created the Two-Spirit Powwow, primarily to be really welcoming.

Because we found that having a powwow is great, but not everybody feels welcome, at least in my experience, especially if you're LGBT or two-spirit. You may not necessarily feel at home. Me and one of my best friends, Russell Big Horse, we used to go to the Red Earth Powwow, which at the time was one of the largest, a huge thing in Oklahoma. It started in the eighties, and everybody was really excited about it. But so much snickering, and looks, and everything, just made us feel less welcome. However, after a powwow, sometimes they have these things called a 49, which is sort of like the after-powwow powwow. Everyone was happy to see us there, but not at the powwow. It reminded me of how sometimes, people want you to shrink or disappear in a big public setting, but when it's private then it's okay to be however you want to be.

I kept pushing to do a powwow, while I was chairperson of BAAITS, the Bay Area American Indian Two-Spirits. Everybody was like, "No, we can't do it, we don't have the people power."

So after I stepped down, and Ruth Villaseñor became the chairperson, she was like, "What do we want to do?"

I said, "Let's have a powwow."

"Yes, let's do it!"

I was just like, "Oh my gosh!" After all these years of pushing for a powwow, now we're finally going to do it?

So we did.

The first Two-Spirit Powwow was in 2010. It's been pretty amazing. We get thousands of visitors each year now, coming to our powwow.

We wanted it to welcome all people. A lot of the dancers are two-spirit, but not all. It's just a powwow that's created by two-spirit people. We have children's categories all the way up to golden age. The focus is to be very welcoming and make sure everybody who comes feels like they belong. That was the core mission. We've kept that mission.

A lot of people who come have not necessarily been greeted in the most loving ways at their own powwows. We had someone come down from Canada named Gabriel who was a jingle dress dancer, and was never allowed to dance the grass dance. Gabriel came to our powwow, and for the first time was able to dance in what is considered a men's category. Shortly after having that experience,

Gabriel felt it was time to embrace his true identity, and transitioned. I thought that was beautiful in so many ways. It was the first time that Gabriel had the opportunity, outside of his own community, to dance. We didn't realize how transformational that was going to be, that his dancing meant more, that it was this opportunity for him to really embrace who he was inside. I mean, we saw the tears. He cried because he was finally able to do it, saying, "This is transformational. This is who I am. I'm going to dance, regardless."

We really didn't realize how big it was going to become. We started at the LGBT center. It's sort of a large room. We expected maybe 250 people—that would fill that room—but around 500 people showed up. We got a bigger space the next year, and it wasn't big enough again. We went to a third space the next year; it still wasn't big enough. We see around 3,000 to 5,000 people now.

Sometimes you put on an event and it's almost like a snowball. It can really grow. One of the things that we did at our very first powwow was we brought in our honor guard—you know, that's all the flags and everything—and we included the rainbow flag. Shortly thereafter, some of the other local powwows here in the Bay Area started carrying in the rainbow flag. We saw that change. We've seen other two-spirit powwows sprout up across the nation. That's really cool for us, that snowball effect.

CRYSTAL MASON: I am the cofounder of a nonprofit called Queering Dreams. I started that a little over a year ago. We're sort of an incubator. We incubate relationships, projects, things like that, and cultivate spaces of belonging.

MS BILLIE COOPER: I will always fight for the underdog, and underserved people. I have always challenged authority, and I have always questioned authority, because for many, many, many decades, we as Black people have been forgotten about in so many facets of life. When it comes to giving Black people their roses—not only Black people but

Brown people, too—give us our roses while we're here. While we're still here.

TUPILI LEA ARELLANO: Oh, the PTSD of racism.

Anyone who hears this that says, "Oh God, do they have to harp on racism?"

I say, "I have to harp on it because it harped on me. I wake up into it every day."

NICKY CALMA: In this field, you know, I think there's so much hate going on when you're not white. I mean, I feel that way. They don't want to see an Asian transgender woman up there commanding, or talking. I still get it, even from folks in the transgender community, sometimes. We have internalized transphobia. When you're doing good, some people don't want to see that, they want to see you fail.

Suddenly, you have all these organizations popping up, wanting to serve transgender people, and yet they just take the money. They'll hire a transgender person, but they won't invest in that person. They want someone with a degree in public health. Well, I have twenty-five years of experience working with my community, and I think that's good enough. Because you probably haven't experienced things that I've experienced. I say that, and I come from a place of love, but give us a break.

BAMBY SALCEDO: I have the pleasure of being the president and executive director of the TransLatin@ Coalition. It's one of the largest organizations led by a trans person in the United States.

The idea came to me in 2009. At that time, there were two national organizations led by trans people. But, unfortunately, they were not including the needs of trans Latina immigrant women. There was a conference here in California. I decided to gather a contingent of trans Latinas. Thirty-seven trans Latinas from different parts of the US. That's how the dialogue began. "What are we going to do?"

Specifically, about the violence that was happening in Puerto Rico, and, obviously, the violence we were facing in immigration detention centers. I'm someone who's personally experienced those things, I was assaulted at a migration center, they broke my nose. Of course, I was in a different situation by then: no longer using drugs, I was working, involved in activism. But I knew things like that were still happening to my companions.

So that's how we started. Talking about what we were going to do for our people.

We started writing letters to the girls in immigration detention centers. We sent money. We raised funds to put money in people's commissary. We would pick them up and take them to other organizations that were providing services. That's what we were doing. And we were also thinking: how do we influence change in institutions that continue to marginalize us?

Everything was volunteer. All of the leaders were organizing locally. Some were not working, or were doing sex work, or other things. All of us coming together to plan strategies that would help us have a better quality of life.

We got our first official grant in January of 2016. We hired case managers. Then I quit my job. I had a beautiful, amazing job that I loved, that was well paid with great benefits, but I left to dedicate myself to building this organization. I just left with a leap of faith. It was very painful. But it was beautiful.

That's exactly why you exist, right? I have been a privileged trans woman. I'm one of the chosen few who was able to get into treatment, reform my life, move up in the social ladder. Many of my friends haven't. I believe that with my privilege also comes a responsibility: to do the best that I can to support my people, just as they supported me when I was in need.

SHARYN GRAYSON: I am currently working as the executive director of TGIJP: Transgender Gender-Variant & Intersex Justice Project. TGI is greatly involved in abolitionist-type work, but even more than that, we work with people inside prisons and jails, and we offer services, resources, and support.

I know it may be hard to consider, but a lot of times, trans and gender-nonconforming people are confined due to reasons that they didn't have a lot of control over. In many, many cases, the circumstances that led to their incarceration were what the rest of us would consider simple survival. It's not heinous crimes. It's mostly shoplifting of food, maybe clothing, things like that. But where the normal person would probably get probation, or community service, the system punishes our trans and gender-nonconforming community in ways that are totally unjust. That's part of what we, as an organization, are fighting against.

One of the things that's always been my little soapbox focus is trans health. Because I have seen us discriminated against. I've seen so much lack of equitable services. So many abhorrent situations.

It's something people don't really think about. When you think about trans people, you don't think about the trauma. Being thrown out of your family, just thrown out in the streets. Nothing but what you have on. "I never want to see you again. I don't want you to call me. I don't care if you die." That's trauma. That's traumatic for anybody. People have to survive through that. They have to go out into the world, and act normal, as though that does not impact them, and be able to create a life for themselves, and just move forward. How do you do that? How is that even possible?

There are so many people that don't ever deal with that trauma because there aren't avenues to address it. So, that eventually evolves into mental health issues. That could manifest itself as suicide. A bipolar condition. And of course, we add in the socioeconomic factors. You've got a homeless person now. "I've given up on life. I've given up on the world. They've given up on me, so I'm just out here." That is so sad. But it is a reality for a lot of trans people, and particularly Black trans women.

That's been one of my focuses: to bring equitable practices and resources that support trans health and wellness.

CRYSTAL MASON: We have these big dreams, but they won't happen overnight. We have to create the pathways.

C. NJOUBE DUGAS: I believe we need to build systems where we create our own reparations. Regardless of whether this country ever does anything about the harm caused by American slavery. So the work I do as a business instructor and advisor—that's the paid work—helps entrepreneurs or those aspiring to be entrepreneurs to gain traction, so they can hire within their own communities, help build their own communities again.

My mom came from the South. She came from that. Black businesses, Black owned. They had a really viable business economics until, of course, things happened like the Klan, Jim Crow, you name it.

How we create our own reality cannot be based on what we see others doing, saying about us, trying to do about us. We need to stop focusing so much on "what white folks are doing," and focus on what it is we need to do for ourselves. We need to have control over our own economic realities.

FRESH "LEV" WHITE: Some of the wonderful connections I've made were when I was working with a group called Trans: Thrive. I was connecting with Black trans women, whether I was the leader or supporting their leadership, and then, of course, in Black trans male community, there were groups that I was involved in.

When I want to be in Black space, there's power. There's something about being in Black space.

I don't want to tell any other group that they can't have their space. How do we do that, and then come back together? That's the work. We're doing that work so we can be in community with others, not so we can isolate.

YOSEÑIO LEWIS: You know how you have, like, a gumball machine, but it's segmented? So there's this kind of gum here, and there's this kind of gum in the middle, and that kind of gum in the other silo, but down at the bottom, if you turn the buttons the right way, you can get something from all three silos, and it's all together at the bottom?

That's the analogy that I can utilize to best explain how I could recognize that kink liberation, sexual liberation, trans liberation—all of it was the same. Even though they were in different silos, once you turned a certain knob a certain way, all of the gumballs all mixed together at the bottom.

In order to get liberation for one, you ended up getting liberation for all three.

If I want to get Black liberation, I'm also going to get the kink liberation gumball, which is going to be close to the sexuality gumball, which is also going to be close to the Latinx gumball. And all of it comes out in one handful. That new taste that comes from all of them being together is a taste that I will go to the ends of the earth to achieve. It fulfills me. Because that allows me to be my whole self.

I spent so much time compartmentalizing myself. Because I knew if Group A knew about Part B of me, I would be cast aside. I would never be allowed to come back to anything that Group A did. So Group A never knew about Part B of me. And Group C never knew about Part A, and on and on and on. It's tiring. It zaps you of life, of strength. I finally had to say no, this is not authentic living. I had to recognize: do I want to keep living my life so compartmentalized? Or do I want to try and be whole? Walk into a room, and be myself.

FRESH "LEV" WHITE: Way back, Yoseñio Lewis was in a documentary. I think I saw it on PBS. I don't know if that was too early for me to catch what it meant to me, but I remember it. Him being on there! Talking about being trans.

YOSEÑIO LEWIS: The God that I know gave me that responsibility. And told me, "You know there is harm and hurt in the world. You have experienced it. Try and alleviate the pain that others are experiencing." So that's what I've been doing.

We recognize our gifts, we give the gifts, and somebody else can take from that, get the energy, and then move that energy on to someone else. I've known that forever. I've always known that I was supposed to do something to make the world better.

MS BILLIE COOPER: My DNA is my advocacy and my activism. It's embedded in who I am. Not one day do I wake up and live my life that I'm not helping someone, or being there for someone.
Because we have to.

NINE

* *

The AIDS Crisis

SHARYN GRAYSON: I remember when it first started. They were saying it was this pneumonia that was affecting gay white men. I remember that.

TINA VALENTÍN AGUIRRE: AIDS had a delayed impact on us, because it was initially amongst gay white men in San Francisco, and New York, and other metropolitan cities of the world. When I got here, my friends were like, "Oh, a protective measure is don't have sex with white people."

But it did get us after all. One by one, many of us started to become infected.

C. NJOUBE DUGAS: I remember the panic. It was just the panic. Going to get HIV tests and the fear. How do you know, how do you know, what did we do? And then the wait time for HIV tests back then. Three weeks, even a month. It was like, okay, now you're just sitting there waiting, do I have this thing that's potentially fatal or not? It was just a lot of fear. A conspiracy: "Oh, they're killing gay men."

No more one-night stands. People were partnering up if they could. If they were already partnered, they were staying partnered. I remember conspiracy theorists saying, "It's in the water." We just we didn't know. It was a scary time.

NELSON D'ALERTA PÉREZ: In the eighties, I experienced the first loss of someone I knew to AIDS, the lover of a friend. It was so painful. In the newspapers, they called it the "gay cancer," and I'd say, "So then, when is it going to happen to me? I'm sure I have it."

FRESH "LEV" WHITE: Okay, so I'm on college campus, actually, in 1983. One of my friends, the Boy George guy—he's always dressed as Boy George—comes back from New York City. There are three of us standing on the mall at SUNY Purchase and he says to the two of us, "There is a disease that's killing men in the Village." That was the first time I heard about AIDS.

That propelled me to DC. I started fundraising through performance. My first fundraiser was, I think, at a place called the Hung Jury in DC. That's how I started performing and raising money.

SHARYN GRAYSON: Some of our gay Black friends started becoming sick. I remember when it began in the Black community. Oh, my God. If a person coughed or sneezed, everybody would move away from them. It was horrible. Families were putting people out of their homes. We had a couple of friends who passed away in hotel rooms, alone. That was devastating.

My cousin was a very famous beautician. My adopted cousin. He had a shop in the Oakland area, and he was very popular, he had a big clientele. He did a lot of the baseball players' wives and so forth. And he became sick. His dad said, "No, no, no. Can't stay here. I'm not going to your house. I don't want to be around that." Also, his partner. It hit him, and just within weeks, he was incapacitated in bed, maybe weighed ninety pounds. I mean, it just went very fast with him. Of course, we had to close the shop. Clients were saying, "I'm not going in there." He became so sick and weak that I moved him out of his apartment, into my apartment. I was working, so I got someone to come in and take care of him during the day, another friend of ours. I paid him to come in and take care of my cousin.

We had a retreat, and I kept telling my boss, "I think I need to stay. I don't want to go." My boss said, "No, you really need to go to the retreat. You're presenting."

We left that Friday, and sure enough, I got a call Saturday evening that there was an emergency at my home. We couldn't get out until Sunday. When I got back home on Sunday, my cousin was gone. He had passed. The friend who was taking care of him had left. The whole scene was traumatic. I could still see some of the apparatus the emergency team used, on the living room floor.

That was my first personal experience losing someone close.

I had a friend, a trans woman. She was in the hospital, and when she was released, her family refused to come and get her. I brought her to my house, took care of her. She had a husband or partner, and he was just absolutely—oh, my God. I don't even have the words. He had no part of her care. This is a woman who had been with him through some really bad times. His family had disowned him because he had been in and out of prison and jail. But she really supported him, took care of him, and I watched him walk away. Just walk away. There were times that she would ask for him, and we'd have to make excuses. She passed. That was my first experience of a trans person close to me passing. So, now, I've had two people that I've taken into my home that have passed away. It was just a horrible experience. That's all I can say. Absolutely horrible.

After that, it just became one friend after another. It was happening so fast.

I think a lot of us became numb. I mean, honestly. We were going to like four or five funerals a week. It came to a point where I said, "I can't do it anymore." It was just unbelievable.

TINA VALENTÍN AGUIRRE: There was great turmoil in all levels of our community. There was lots of death, lots of attacks, emotional and political attacks.

SHARYN GRAYSON: You would have had to live through that time to understand how devastating that period was. I know a lot of people talk about it, and they try to explain it to other people, but you had to have lived it.

CRYSTAL MASON: I became a bit shut down because of all the death. There were people you might see out at a protest or at the bar, and then two days later, they would be dead.

DONNA PERSONNA: In the eighties, I took care of these guys that contracted AIDS. They were gay people. We took care of those people suffering from HIV.

I would take two or three men who had AIDS to a museum. I got the tickets and walked with them through there. Different things like that, just to have them be a part of life. I would go visit them in the hospitals. This, I'm going to say, was frightening for me, because when I would go, the nurses and doctors wore protective equipment. They had a mask on, and they were all covered up. And they said, "You go in there." I understood that they don't want to go in. But I'm going in there. Yes, I did. I'll say this, it sounds corny, but it really is who I am: "I would die for you." They needed that, they needed that.

So I'd go in there and get a list of what they wanted. I would go shopping for them, talk to them, shoot the breeze because they weren't getting phone calls from anybody, not their mother and father or their brother and sister and none of their friends in some cases. But I did it. I did that a lot.

JOAN BENOIT: When I moved to Seattle, that was a huge eye-opener for me. It was 1989. I'd never been in a community like that, so predominantly Native. It really made me more aware of the situation that Native Americans have throughout the country. So many homeless up there, I was so stunned. I started doing volunteer work there, HIV work and homeless work with Native American people up in Seattle.

My roommate had HIV at the time and was sick. My awareness of AIDS and HIV was pretty heightened during that time.

Once I got to the Bay Area, in 1989, I really started to get involved in a lot of different things. Like the Grandfather Project, through Shanti Project. Predominantly, they would do hospital visits, especially around the holidays, because so many of the HIV patients were alone. Their families weren't coming to see them. People were still afraid of seeing them and touching them, so we wanted to make sure that they were seen and held. We would go to hospitals during holidays and drop off gifts, and spend some time, and visit people who were there on the AIDS ward.

That was such a miserable place back in those days. It was big. Bigger than you would think. All men, young men dying of AIDS. Skinny, and lesions on them, and lonely, and so happy to see people who came through to see them, and remember them, and could queer it up with them. It was very flamboyant and gay. It was an interesting place. It was a hard place to go. There were a lot of hospices around San Francisco at the time, too, to help people who were dying. That experience led me to want to get involved and do HIV work.

LANDA LAKES: When I was in college, I belonged to the GLA, the Gay and Lesbian Alliance, at the University of Oklahoma. Back then it was just GL, that was the whole community at the time, it wasn't like all the acronyms that we have today. Just "gay" and "lesbian." Yes.

We were chalking the sidewalks all the time. "Are you gay? Call me." And then giving the number for the GLA office.

I remember us having like, a die-in. We went to Oklahoma City, to the legislature's building, and we all did a die-in on the steps. It was Silence Equals Death. This was to protest the silence around AIDS.

CRYSTAL MASON: I was actively involved with ACT UP for about four years.

I went to demonstrations and stuff in DC, and then when I came here, to San Francisco, ACT UP was one of the things I found and was drawn to.

A lot of the white gay men who came to that activism came for specific reasons, which were, they and their friends were dying. Some had been in liberation movements—feminist movements, clinic defense, stuff like that—and had a bit more political analysis, but it was difficult. These boys were gay, but they came from society, as we all have, really. This drove me to think deeply about my own internalized racism. I came to the understanding that I don't care how many Black people you fuck or love or live near: the system that we all live in and under, you can't exfoliate that away. There has to be actual intention and learning and work. It made it clear that being gay did not make you progressive or a warrior for justice.

At protests, I was often the target of police because I was big, Black. I was fat, I had piercings and purple hair. I think cops resented that, and resented that I would have the nerve to be out in the street, demanding something.

SHARYN GRAYSON: At first, everybody was focused on gay men. But then, as I began to look at my community, my friends, I'm like, "Wait a minute. We're losing Black trans women." For a lot of them, it was because of the men they were with—who were having relationships with cis women, with white men, with Black men. Once we began to realize that, we started support groups at the organization I was working for. We started trying to educate trans women. We started trying to get funding for Black trans women,

The organization I worked with was a Black-led nonprofit organization that began to acknowledge the fact that we were losing Black trans women—not only Black gay men—and no one's saying anything. No one's talking about this. They allowed me resources. We were one of the first organizations who began having support groups for trans women.

They began to recognize the fact that Black gay men were being impacted. And then, the government began to release funds for Black gay men. It was very specific that this funding was for Black gay men. So, some of the organizations came up with a twist to that, a creative twist which the trans women community didn't particularly care for, but it was a way to get funding. The organizations would say, "Well, the Black trans women were originally men, so that's how we're using funding to support them."

ADELA VÁZQUEZ: In the AIDS epidemic, transgender people were treated like shit by homosexuals in the community. Telling them, "Now you have to dress like a boy, you cannot really do this, what you're doing."

Women who already had the big silicone tits and stuff, to tone it down and become a boy so you can get your services.

I found that very wrong. Extremely wrong. Because if you now have a disease, and you're dying, who is anybody to say you have to die this way? No, my dear. I'm going to be a bitch till the day I die, I'm going to do my nails, I'm going to do my hair, whatever the fuck I want to do. Don't tell me to dress like a boy.

SHARYN GRAYSON: Oh, my gosh, it was so demeaning. It was demeaning, but it was a way that we initially began to get funding to support the Black trans women community. It was the only way. Only way. The government did not see trans women as a legitimate segment of the population that deserved funding, and there were no numbers. No one was tracking the numbers.

ADELA VÁZQUEZ: I started working for the community at Proyecto ContraSIDA por Vida. How beautiful that project was! It was an AIDS prevention agency. We prevented AIDS through art. It's incredible. It was an amazing concept. I worked on Proyecto Contra SIDA Por Vida for many years, until 2000. I'm still in touch with the people.

When I started working at Proyecto ContraSIDA, I did so as

transgender. It was my first time living as a woman. I gave all my boy clothes away, and I became a woman. I had a boyfriend: all that happened at the same time. Life was beautiful.

A lot of girls looked at me at the time. Young, queer, Latina—these new girls that were coming up, they wanted to have a boyfriend, to have a job. If you're a fresh immigrant in this country and you see that, then you know you can do it. You can be transgender and have a job like the one I have. I was a pillar for the community. I was interviewed by newspapers, I traveled. I loved it.

I was the first trans Latina to work on HIV prevention in San Francisco. There were a lot of protests. Some didn't want a transgender person to be making money. Berkeley had a Chicano group, and they were not happy about it.

I had a mentor, Diane Felix. She was involved from the very beginning. In many ways, Diane taught me how to be a woman. That dyke, that beautiful, beautiful person, taught me how to be a woman. She taught me about pride. She'd been an activist since the very first days. I'm a grassroots activist; I didn't take a class to become this, it's something that I felt. I came to save the world. I want to save the community and I'm going to give it all I got.

TINA VALENTÍN AGUIRRE: The Mission Neighborhood Health Center, and Instituto [Familiar de la Raza], all had remnants of homophobia, transphobia, even misogyny built into them. When I looked at how it was playing out, how limited strong women could be, for me, that's an aspect of how misogyny works. They can't be their full selves in those roles. My question was, "Well then how the hell can I be my full self here? I can do a lot of good, I can make a lot of change, but are they going to keep thinking I should tone things down?"

Later, I left Mission Neighborhood Health Center to work at CURAS, the Community United Responding to AIDS/SIDA, which was openly queer, openly trans, and openly feminist. Radical feminists with a Brown and Black people-of-color blend. We developed our own model. It was inclusive in terms of gender, and that was new.

I'm outrageous. I am eloquent. I am going to tell you what I think. Life is short; I don't have time to do otherwise.

SHARYN GRAYSON: Black gay men were much more organized. I remember going to a meeting here in San Francisco, and this big organization over here was going after funding directly from the CDC, the Centers for Disease Control and Prevention. And what was said at the meeting was, "Okay, we're not going to include Black trans women in this proposal, we're going to use Black gay men, but this is a promise: once we get the funding, we'll come back and get you all."

Okay? Never happened. Never happened.

That was the first time I had ever known an organization to get a million dollars in funding. The Black trans women community did not get a dime of that money. They lied, and we were right there, supporting them. That's kind of how things were back then.

It took us another ten years to really begin to get funding, services, resources, and support, specifically for Black trans women. In the nineties, I was hired at GLIDE, a nationally recognized church and organization in the San Francisco community. We had people like Oprah Winfrey who came and gave a million dollars at the service. It was a very prominent community-based organization. It was a pillar in the community. It still is. I was able to capitalize off that momentum. I wrote a grant for our HIV program, specifically for Black trans women. We were funded. I think that was maybe three hundred thousand dollars.

Our program became a focal point, a center, for Black trans women in the Tenderloin area. The money was coming in now. That began to open things up. I didn't know of anybody else that had done anything like that. I don't want to toot my own horn. It wasn't just me. It was others, too, people that worked there that helped me put that together.

JOAN BENOIT: I started over at GLIDE. They did all kinds of stuff:

prevention, HIV testing/outreach, syringe exchange. I first got hired there as a program assistant. Sharyn Grayson came in, and she also was really helpful in showing me everything I wanted to learn about how to administer these programs. When Sharon left, I was the interim director for a short amount of time.

SHARYN GRAYSON: We began to see other organizations becoming funded. The San Francisco Health Department now had funding for Black trans populations. That was in the mid nineties, when that began to happen.

But all of those things that other populations received funding and support for, the Black trans community was always left out of. We didn't exist. And even now, with the funding that we do receive, believe me, it is not significant enough to match the services needed.

TINA VALENTÍN AGUIRRE: In 1990, '91, and '92, there were just so many people coming down with AIDS.

I ended up becoming the chair of the Latino Coalition on AIDS in 1991. I was twenty-three, twenty-four. I was so heavily recruited. It was, "Oh, we're dying, if I'm the one that can easily stand up and speak and write, there's not really a good response other than yes."

It makes sense in retrospect: we just needed it. Nobody really cared how old I was if I was going to do the work. And I could do it well.

I would show up as me in these meetings. I would use my gender, honestly, as a way to confuse people. What I found is, "Oh, somebody wants to focus on how pretty I am and what kind of lipstick I'm using or whatever. Good. Because I'm going to follow it up with, 'Why have you done such a poor job distributing millions of dollars and that's resulting in our deaths? Let's get to the point now.' I'm going to use this as the entrée where you're disarmed by me using Lancôme or Chanel lipstick, and then I'm going to go for the throat and get what I came here for."

What I learned was, yes, gender is part of what I bring to all this work. It can also be a tool. People are confused by gender? That's okay, I can use that.

NICKY CALMA: I was looking for community, and that's where I found Asian AIDS Project.

Mostly, at the time, I was presenting as male. But I was looking for community. I wanted to volunteer. And they took me in. This was in 1993.

I went to the Filipino Task Force on AIDS. They were all Filipino, so we ate the same thing, we spoke the same language, and everything. During that time, they were really having a challenge on how to reach out to highest-risk Filipinos for HIV infection. Because there's this thing about Filipinos, like, "Oh, no, we're not that. We won't get infected." But at San Francisco General Hospital, Ward 86, the highest incidents of HIV infection for the Asian community was Filipinos. That's why they were able to get some money specifically for Filipino Task Force on AIDS.

The executive director and I had dinner one time. I was volunteering. And the ED was like, "This is really what we're experiencing. I wonder what we can do."

I was like, "Well, did you ever think about, maybe, having a spokesperson, or somebody who will talk to the community? They don't want to talk to you all, because you're preaching."

. So we thought about it, and then the idea of Tita Aida came around.

There was this famous actress in the Philippines who was a stand-up comic, and her thing was that she was nouveau riche. She suddenly became rich, and started to act like she had good breeding. She was just so funny. It was fun, it was slapstick comedy. And someone suggested, "Well, how about a character like that one? Someone who, instead of all this comedy, maybe gives advice."

We started toying around with the ideas.

I said, "I think that's good, let's try it."

They took care of it. They had this search for Tita Aida: "Tita," as we call our aunties in the Philippines. "Aida" was the gay lingo for AIDS in the Filipino community. At that time, Filipinos had a way of talking to each other, how to say someone has AIDS or HIV, they'll say, "This person has Tita Aida." So, if they're talking about it and they use it, they're familiar with it, let's use that.

So they had this search for Tita Aida. There was a prize. It was $300 if you get chosen to be Tita Aida. And I won.

We developed the Tita Aida character. There was going to be someone who sends a letter asking advice on certain sexual issues. About condom use, or things like that. I would reply live and give advice. We were kind of like, "This might work."

Asian AIDS Project put on this guerilla theater called Rubber Club. I would have a segment of the show. There's this grandioso piano music. "Oh, hola mis amigos, mis amigas! My name is Tita Aida, and I am your hostess with the moistest tonight."

People were buying it, people were getting it.

"Well, I am here to help a fellow Filipino man with issues in condom use." I would say things like that. I would read the letter, a mockup letter, we would address the issue and I would reply. One thing a lot of people remember was when I was demonstrating how you should use water-based lubricants versus oil-based on latex products. "I love using Vaseline, petroleum jelly, versus lubricant. But it's really not good. So, here's two balloons." Blowing the balloons. "Condoms. And my hand is a glove, latex. Here I'm going to use lubricant, and here I'm going to use the petroleum jelly." And I would rub it. And then, suddenly, the petroleum jelly balloon, pop! People saw that immediately, and they were like, "Oh. Okay." Very educational, yet funny.

It was really becoming a hit. I mean, it was every fourth Sunday of the month, and we would go to this club, the N'Touch club, which is an Asian club, and do the thing there. That's what started things rolling for Tita Aida. Everybody was like, "Oh, Tita Aida, can you emcee the show? Oh, Tita Aida, can you be here and do one of your standups? Can you do this, this, and this?" I wish I had an agent at that time! I was doing shows in gay clubs. We had Tita Aida's dating game. I mean, when I sent out postcards like, "Hey, we have this show," bam, three hundred people would show up. I was doing something that was rewarding, that was helping people out. I mean, all of these things to promote, really, first, positive images, positive representations of API gay men.

We would go to Ward 86, for clients who were already at their deathbed and just needed support. People who were dying of AIDS. I would go as Tita Aida. Just to comfort them, to hold their hand, because no one wants to hold them.

That was a big, significant thing in my life.

TINA VALENTÍN AGUIRRE: I was a part of coalitions, and coalition building. We formed a coalition with Gay Asian Pacific Alliance, American Indian AIDS Institute, Black Coalition on AIDS, and us, the Latino Coalition on AIDS.

We were all forming new community responses to AIDS, but AIDS was just one of many things including poverty, crack, discrimination, and all of the traumas that have impacted us. White AIDS movement building really didn't have to deal with any of that stuff. At least not on the levels that we did.

We were the experts.

So we helped each other.

We would see each other at Ward 86, when we would go see our clients who were dying of AIDS.

NICKY CALMA: I was in the behind-the-scenes, the trenches, the ugliness of HIV. We had to visit folks in SROs, single-room occupancies. Their rooms were cockroach-infested. They didn't clean it because they had already lost hope in life. We were the ones who would bring them out.

Every day, there was an obituary of someone who died. And

sometimes, we would see an Asian name. It was just sad, really sad. And when we would go to Ward 86—I would go with the case managers—I would always say, "This is it for them? This is the way you're going to go?" I mean, there was no dignity. There was no dignity, dying of AIDS. They couldn't do anything, they were just lying there. There was no medication, they were just waiting. It was hard. It was so hard. Something had to be done. And, at the same time, you feel helpless, because you couldn't do anything anymore, no matter how much comfort you want to give somebody.

TINA VALENTÍN AGUIRRE: All our clients, really, were Latinos from other countries. So, often, when they got sick, it meant the work we had to do was also family-oriented. We needed to case manage the entire family, not just the one person. And it also meant that it was international, that it included the legal logistics and financial logistics of, like, how does a family respond to one of their members being sick and dying of AIDS? How does the mother come from Peru, and where is she going to stay?

It was really complicated. There were often unresolved issues. People coming from other countries because there were more opportunities, you could be yourself, you didn't have to fix other people's homophobia, transphobia, or whatever. For a lot of the Latinos who came from other countries to San Francisco, it was because of their gender and sexual orientation that they'd migrated. They continued to face these problems when they got sick with AIDS.

I think for me, doing that work, it meant, how can I show up with humanity? How can I show up as my full self, when families come and are trying to very quickly resolve stuff that really was not going to get resolved as part of the dying process? Like, there's not enough time. What I've learned is if, say, you've inflicted trauma and transphobia on somebody for ten years, the undoing of that is probably going to take an equal amount of time. It may never actually get undone. And yet this is what you're bringing up to your child. Your child is a grown adult who is dying right now. You can count the hours that you have left, is this really what you want to focus on? Your unresolved issues with your child, before they die?

For me, that became a major frame for how I look at life. Like, how much do I need to fix somebody, in terms of their transphobia? How much do I need to fix them in terms of their internalized traumas? Not much, is my answer. I'm going to focus on the people who I love and love me back, and the rest can get on board or not.

All of that would get into the mix right at the very end of a dying process. It was tough.

There were many of us doing this work, as case managers, and we had to take care of each other.

NICKY CALMA: HIV had a whole different face at that time. Even the doctors were just hopeless. "We are just waiting for this person to do their last breath and whisk them away." That was the intensity of it. The finger-pointing of why this happened, like shooting bullets in a dark room. How did we get here? It felt like limbo. The way I interpret limbo is that you're just floating, you're not able to do anything. I liked going there, to Ward 86, because I just wanted to contribute, but I also hated going there. When the FX series *Pose* came out, I cried, because that was what was happening, I remembered. You could feel that. *Pose* really did a good job in looking into how it was before. That scene where the room wasn't decorated, it was kind of yellowish? That was the scene of Ward 86. There were, like, ten beds. And the stigma. Oh, my god, the stigma. Stigma is still the strongest enemy here. Especially for marginalized populations. If you're not white, you're on that island. You will be at risk, you will be degraded, you will be berated. I mean, you are shit, basically. And if you're not loud enough, you really will not get anything.

NELSON D'ALERTA PÉREZ: I saw it with my friends. I had friends whose legs came apart from their hips. I witnessed horrible things. I closed the eyes of so many beloved friends, I can't even tell you. It took away friends of my soul. Took them from me at thirty, at twenty-something years old. I still think: if only those friends were here, what a joy it would be to talk to them, to have them visit me. What would their evolutions have been like? What would life have been like if I had as many friends now as I did then?

I don't have them with me anymore.

I still weep for them.

MS BILLIE COOPER: In 1985, I tested HIV positive. I've been living with HIV since the eighties. I probably got it when I was in the military in Hawaii.

I tested positive here in San Francisco, on May 15, 1985. I was deep in my addiction, so I really didn't grieve. I also fell into prostitution. My T-cells went down to under 200, and my viral load would sky-rocket up into the millions. I was still in my addiction, like from '82, to 2002, for twenty years. I didn't know I was dysfunctional. I didn't know I had PTSD from the military, and from all my trauma. Hear this, people! We not only go through life trauma, we go through other people's trauma; we go through other people's *drama*. Some of us just pick up other people's shit. And we go through life dealing with it the best we can.

NICKY CALMA: I found out I was HIV-positive in 1997. I preached preven-tion. But did I do what I was preaching? Everything became dark. I mean, everything. But you've got to have a good support system. I mean, that's what I tell folks who test positive now: "Who's your sup-port system? Who can you talk to when you wake up at two o'clock in the morning and question and cry and say, 'Why did this shit happen to me?'"

NELSON D'ALERTA PÉREZ: Oh, my God. It's been so hard, my whole prob-lem with AIDS. Really hard.

I've been HIV positive since 1990. My lover at the time said, "I tested positive. I want you to get tested because I'm sure you're positive, too."

When they gave me the news, it was as if I'd been doused with a bucket of cold water.

After I was diagnosed, I started losing friends. They fell like flies. "Carlitos died." "El Chabuca died." "So-and-so died"—oh my God. And being positive, it was really hard, because I'd say, "When is it my turn? Any moment. Will this be my last shower? When is my last day?" It was all so stressful.

When I received the news, I had a problem with the owner of the hair salon where I worked. He threw me out of the salon. I've lost my job, and I'm HIV positive. It was a terrible thing. For a week, I couldn't sleep. I was placed in a psychiatric hospital for another week. When I got out, I looked in the mirror and said, "Oh my God, look at you, you're crazy." I didn't look good. I hadn't brushed my hair, hadn't wanted to eat. A total depression. And a terror; terror of death. Of death.

My lover happened to have a friend who was studying medicine, and he said, "I want you to go see this doctor."

He was insistent. He said the doctor wanted me to cut her hair—that was how he got me to go.

I said, "Fine. Tell her to go to the salon." Because, you know, it's a little uncomfortable to cut hair in people's homes. "The salon has all the supplies, have her go there and I'll attend to her."

"No, no, she wants you to go to her house."

I go to her house. She starts to cry. She tells me, "I've got a problem. I've had a terrible divorce, and since my divorce, I've neglected my hair."

She had a great deal of hair, in tangled clusters.

I said to her, "Get in the bath."

It was such an interesting thing. I'd just met this woman who would later become my doctor. We had this intimate experience where she was almost naked, crying, while I worked on gently detangling her hair so I could cut and style it. Today, I still adore her. She later gave me a spiritual opening, teaching me about yoga and meditation. She said to me, "You're not going to die. If you want, think that you're going to die. But if you don't want to die, you won't. When the dark spirits come, tell them, 'No! I'm not going to die. Get out of here, it's not my time.'"

I learned how to send positive energy to the television, the bed where I sleep. All of that I learned from her. I immediately wanted to share it all with my friends. My friends took to laughing at me. They'd say, "Nelson has gone off the deep end. He wants us to send love to the refrigerator."

And I'd say, "My God, you don't understand the meaning here: that you have to live with love. It's a strong thing. It's the only way we're going to survive."

Because we were fighting so much propaganda. People dying and dying.

And here I am today.

JOAN BENOIT: In 1999, I got hired at the Native American AIDS Project, as the director. At the time, we were a program of the Native American Health Center.

There was a series of funding issues while I was director. Our rent had tripled. It was during the first dot-com boom. The health center was going to incorporate us into their medical model, and I thought, oh no, that's never going to work. They're an abstinence-based program. We're a social service model, a harm-reduction model. I had an advisory board at the time, and they were like, "Let's go, let's go out on our own."

I was like, "Oh Lord. I'm not ready for this, but okay! Let's do it!"

The idea around a lot of our services is the homelessness that I saw in San Francisco, especially among the Native population there. It was such an underserved community. Nobody was reaching out to them. The health center just wanted to tell them to stop drinking and get into a program. I was like, "That is not going to work with a lot of

these folks we're seeing that are multiply diagnosed." All of our programs were based on the idea of harm reduction: everybody needs to
be part of the circle, they all need to be brought back in.

So we started bringing people back into the cultural stuff. We used
the city's money so frugally that we were able to do much more. We
had a food bank, we had traditional healing, we got San Francisco
Department of Public Health mental health dollars to pay for traditional healers, and they had the drum there, and talking circles, and
the sweat lodge, the tipi ceremony, all paid for by city dollars, because
we argued that that was traditional mental health services and they
couldn't deny us. Because they didn't have anything to say it wasn't.

It was amazing. It was an amazing time. We really worked hard
to create a safety net. And then we went back to the Native American
Health Center, and we went to BAIITS, and we got a contract that
made all of the organizations work together, doing our best to create a
safety net for all these people. It was really a magical time.

Then the Department of Public Health in San Francisco started
to change their funding policies. The money from the CDC was
getting tighter for prevention. They wanted it all to be a medical
model. They were trying to cut their budget. They put the health
centers at the lead. Three years later, they said the health centers
could do it on their own. They took all of the money. And all of
these social service organizations—the smaller ones—we were left
with nothing. That's when we went out of business. We weren't the
only ones. I think we might have been one of the first to drop. But
all of the smaller HIV organizations—especially the ones that were
community-of-color-based—had their contracts eliminated.

Now most of the communities of color are serviced by the San
Francisco AIDS Foundation. And they're all white.

So that's the story of Native HIV services in the nineties and in
the 2000s.

I got a Circle of Harmony Award. Circle of Harmony is a conference held biannually, usually in New Mexico, for Native American

HIV providers. I got an award from them for all that work. They gave me a blanket. It's beautiful.

And then I just kind of walked away from HIV services.

TINA VALENTÍN AGUIRRE: I got burnt out. I'm happy that I was a part of all of that. But direct service was all about death and dying, and it got to be too much.

I decided I needed to leave CURAS, the organization where I was working. I thought, I need some distance from all of this, I have to take care of myself. I have to repair myself and this grief that I have, it's much bigger than I'm able to hold.

ADELA VÁZQUEZ: In 2000, I got laid off. I learned how to get a job as a transgender person. It's not easy. To go for an interview with women's clothes and to be taken seriously is not easy. I give it to any transgender that goes to do that. When you show up, a lot of people are not happy. But if I have the skills and I can prove to you that I can do this job, you have to give it to me. That's what the law is for.

I became the transgender coordinator for TARC, Tenderloin AIDS Resource Center. I wanted to serve the transgender community. I knew in my heart that they needed it.

The last thing I did, I worked for Instituto Familiar de la Raza. I was a clinical case manager, working with mental health. I did it until I couldn't no more.

I discovered that I suffered from PTSD because of work. Working with the transgender community is a beautiful place to be: it's amazing, attractive, obscure, mysterious, blah, blah, blah, so on and so on, but it's very cruel and it's very real. Working for the transgender community takes certain cojones, because it's the never-ending story. Problem after problem after problem.

NICKY CALMA: Since 1998, I've been with API Wellness, now San Francisco Community Health Center.

Nowadays, HIV's a manageable disease. As long as you're making sure that you're healthy. I'm in a different state right now, of my career. I try to get contracts for HIV programs to happen. I write reports. Sometimes I ask myself, maybe I should jump into another career, or do something different. But I go back to that time. And say, "Why am I doing this?" I remember that people suffered. These were innocent people. They didn't want to get AIDS. They just wanted to live life, and it was taken away from them. So, much as it's very painful to think about it, I also use it as a grounding exercise, to help me continue the work I'm doing right now.

NELSON D'ALERTA PÉREZ: It seemed marvelous to me, that people created so much support for people who practically had no resources. Simply to say, "I am here, I'm here with you. I'm positive too, but we're here together, we'll go through this together."

That was a gift, for me. A gift I'll appreciate all my life. It was something really, really wonderful that's given me great memories of very good people. Such good people.

The community opened, and was not afraid to embrace us, to give us a hand. It was a beautiful thing, really beautiful.

ADELA VÁZQUEZ: We are pioneers. We conquered things, difficult things. AIDS was not easy. People still die from AIDS to this day. But the eighties and nineties? That was ridiculous. It was a very depressing time. And among all that depression, we had beautiful people who were there doing drag, and being transgender, and being oppressed. We saw the life, we took a good look at it, and we learned. With pain, with a lot of sorrow, but we learned.

And that cannot be forgotten.

TEN

* *

Art and Expression

KB BOYCE: Queerness and art, they're really together in me. I can't think of one without the other.

NELSON D'ALERTA PÉREZ: I'm a generalist. I paint, but I've also directed theater and cabarets. I've done a bit of almost every kind of art.

TINA VALENTÍN AGUIRRE: I looked to art to come up with a different way we could live. How can we just put it out in the open? I really thought our stuff needed to be in museums, in galleries, in theaters. There was nothing wrong with what we were doing. It didn't need to stay behind the scenes or in private. We're not bad. We're just humans.

TUPILI LEA ARELLANO: I came from a family of creativity. That was encouraged, that was made space for. I always knew I had creative gifts. I'm just very turned on by creativity, and I'm very turned on by performance and learning through the arts.

CRYSTAL MASON: Ever since I was a kid, I've been doing art. I always liked being creative and making stuff.

I feel like my art-making follows the Black tradition of making do with what you have. My art is a lot like that. I started with spoken word because all I needed was a pencil and paper, right?

KB BOYCE: Because we're queer, we have already gone through trying to find ways to be ourselves against all odds—people calling you derogatory terms, all the things that you go through as a queer person, a trans person, a member of the LGBTQ+ community. That strength, and that willingness to just say, "I'm going to be me no matter what," that fierceness is so engrained in being queer in my mind.

And that's the same kind of energy it takes to move forward as an artist.

That bravery that it takes to be an artist—period. And then, to be an artist who is openly out and queer?

Those two things go hand in hand, and always have in my life. Being in the world is challenging as a queer person, as a queer person of color, as an artist, as a queer artist of color who is transmasculine.

That bravery, that willingness to just do you. Just do what is coming out of you. Maybe folks are not going to understand, or even get it, or be able to see it, but that doesn't matter. You just keep going. You do that thing.

STORMMIGUEL FLOREZ: Most of my high school years happened away from the actual school. I was never in class. People were finding out about us being queer, and we were getting bullied. It was not a fun place to be. I graduated by the skin of my teeth.

One of the things that I started doing in high school was playing music, out in Albuquerque. The year after I came out, I went to my first National Women's Music Festival in Albuquerque, called WomenFest. This is where I started veering away from my more Latina-based queer high school crew who were my age, and moving into this other world of lesbian feminism. I started getting introduced to this other culture that was mostly white-centered, or at least white-led, in a lot of ways.

At WomanFest, I was just blown away. I'd been playing music since I was a kid, writing songs, playing instruments. I'd learned to play the guitar. I was already playing music and doing some performing that I really enjoyed. But I went to this music festival and something opened up in me. I was so inspired, I was so excited, I knew what I was going to do with my life. I was going to be one of those women playing on those stages and traveling and touring across the country and around the world. That was my plan.

I started writing songs. At that point, I would only play them for my friends at the park if I was a little bit drunk. That was how I would get up the courage to play. But then I played an open mic, and they brought me back as a feature. It was really exciting. People were interested in my music. I was snuck into my first dyke or queer bar ever to play a gig. One of the older dykes, who was white, and looked nothing like me—which of course, this is totally possible, there's many ways of being family—told the manager that I was her daughter so that I could get in.

I was just like, "I can't believe he believed her, clearly I am not her daughter." Looking back with a deeper understanding of queer culture, I get that he was probably thinking, "Oh, that's your gay daughter, and of course." That made sense to him. Me, I'm thinking we're pulling one over on him, but it was a much bigger historical context that I wasn't quite privy to at the time.

So yes, I played this show, and then I just started to play a lot of different places, whether bars or open mics or coffee houses. I would bring my guitar to parties. I was playing music all the time and writing all the time.

When I was around twenty years old, I met some other musicians and started playing in a band called Too F.I.N.E. Minds. We were an all-dyke band, and we were really popular in Albuquerque. We would basically turn the straight biker bar into a queer bar whenever we played. It was a really exciting time.

KB BOYCE: I am an African American transmasculine being. And I am a lifelong musician. I delve into a lot of projects. I've made films. I love experimental filmmaking. I am an audio engineer and producer.

I've been a musician all my life. My mom and my father were both musicians, and very, very supportive of me as a kid any time I was interested in anything musical. Growing up in New York, when I was a young'un—you know, preteen, teenager, we're talking 1970s—a thing called punk rock happened. I happened to be in New York, going to a school where I met some other weirdo kids, and we formed a band called Nastyfacts. Strangely enough, as kids, we got signed by a record label. We put out a punk record. We started playing night-clubs in New York. So I've been getting paid as a working musician since I was about fifteen.

The bravery it took just to be a Black punk rocker in the seventies in Brooklyn, New York, went hand in hand with trying to be myself as an androgynous person. Those two things married, and they just became me, you know? And yeah, punk rock saved my life. Coming out and realizing who I am saved my life. And those two things have fortified each other for the rest of my life.

I have kept that musical part of me going throughout my life. It brings me joy to make music, and I feel it's a blessing to have. I don't take that for granted at all. I've somehow managed to be a working musician throughout most of my life.

I still play all types of music, and that will never stop.

ANDRÉS OZZUNA: Dancing tango is my passion. I started dancing here, in the United States. I was about thirty-five years old when I started really taking classes. Before that, the class I went to was: you're a woman, so you follow, never lead. I didn't want that. It didn't feel good to me. When I went to straight places, there was physical repulsion toward me. When I was perceived as a butch woman, they wouldn't want to dance with me. I went to a couple of classes and dropped out.

At that time, I had no concept of transness. That was in 2005. I had relationships with women, but I had masculine qualities in me that I didn't feel able to express. Or better put, I had repressed them, for various reasons. It took a lot for me to express those parts of me.

Many years later, I learned about queer tango. I went to my first queer tango class and that's where I stayed. I wanted to lead, and it was welcomed there. There was no problem. It was a completely queer environment. An entirely different atmosphere.

I'd lived all things tango since I was little. Because we lived with my grandfather, and he listened to tangos all the time. He was insufferable! In the house where I grew up, we listened to tango, sang it, danced it. It was part of the family atmosphere. Part of the family. My grandfather danced tango at home, with my mother. And sometimes he sang tangos, grabbed his guitar and sang. I mean, he had a few glasses of wine, and started singing—it wasn't anything sophisticated. But it was very common in my house.

So when I heard the music, I liked it a lot, it felt so familiar. My first queer tango classes were at the White Horse, a queer bar in Oakland. It was maybe ten people or so. But for me, it was pure magic. Because you didn't just listen to tango: you were dancing with a woman who identified as lesbian or queer. Beautiful sensations. The sensation of having someone close to you like that, in your arms, feeling an intimate connection with someone without speaking, letting the music and your bodies communicate without speech. For me, it was magical. Incredible.

I'm part of the queer tango community today.

The beautiful thing about queer tango is the people. They're accepting of all kinds of bodies and presentations. If you're tall, short, not skinny, you have a mohawk, whatever. It's all good. In places that aren't queer, it is not all good. Women have to wear a dress, high heels, that kind of thing.

I try to explain the culture to people in the queer tango community. To help them understand where tango comes from, to know the history, because it's tremendous. It has roots with enslaved people from Africa. Sometimes I try to help them understand the meaning of the songs. Because a lot of the songs have to do with being an immigrant, the experience of missing another land, the relationships and struggles of a new life.

For me, the dance is full of emotion, flowing between three things:

the person you're dancing with, you, and the music. That's the trinity contained in the dance. Sometimes people here see it very mathematically, as a kind of exercise. "Oh, I put this foot here, then there, then over there." Well, it's not about your foot, it's everybody's feet and the music all moving together. Everything together: that's what makes it magical. To me, it's a deeply cultural thing.

There are different ways of dancing tango. I like the close embrace. There are people who like it more open, who don't want to feel the other person's body as much. To me, it's like, "Give me the whole body"—you know? I love it. Some people say, "No, the sweat!" I love that people sweat. Hair, breath, let it all be there. It doesn't bother me. But, you know, in Argentina, when we dance, when we share yerba maté, we share space. We live close together. For me, that's normal. I love to feel the other person's heartbeat. You dance a thousand times and you hear "Boom, boom, boom"—I love that.

CRYSTAL MASON: There was a moment after I got out of the San Francisco AIDS Foundation where I really didn't know who I was or what I was doing. If I wasn't an activist, if I wasn't doing AIDS work, if I wasn't working with women in prison, what am I doing?

But I came to believe that giving people spaces to tell their stories, to be loved on and accepted by their communities, was also political.

Art has the possibility of creating vision, empathy, and seeing. I think activism in a lot of ways is about the same things. It's about persuasion. It's about seeing. It's about vision. It's about shifts, small and big, and also the idea of who is talking or being seen or representing in both activism and art is political stuff, right? If your intention with your art or your activism is really to be involved in creating something that moves things forward, it's a political act.

In '91 or '92, one of my best and oldest friends Miriam and I had been doing some performance and organizing shows. People kept asking us if we knew any women performers, or any Black performers, or any people of color, and we would always be like, "Yes, this person." But then, every show, they'd come back to us and act like they didn't know any people of color or any women. So we created a women's performance space, to give women a space where they could feel like they were professional performers. We found this space. We put in a floor. We put in a lighting deck and a sound booth.

It was called LunaSea Women's Performance Project.

We were young and didn't really know what we were doing, which probably made it possible.

I started to see myself again as an activist. Mostly art-making on the face of it, but it was also about politics because of the way we tried to run the space. We came up with the idea that even though we owned the space, we weren't going to censor anybody's performance.

The highlight was how often we had really full houses, and how hungry people were for what we were doing. For me, it was really exciting to fill a niche, especially in the queer community. That was really exciting, the fact that we did so much of what we wanted to do. Over half of our performers and the people who used the space were women of color—poor women, girls. It was intergenerational. It was just everything, right?

Jewelle Gomez performed there, Eileen Myles several times, Harry Dodge—just a bunch of people. It was really exciting.

NELSON D'ALERTA PÉREZ: I built a career, here in the United States, in cosmetology. It gave me joy to learn something new. It was so satisfying, to go to school without being bullied.

I graduated in 1987. It was magical, a magical story, to practice cosmetology.

When I put on makeup, I become another person. Spiritually, that fills a lot of little holes in me. I feel good, I feel fully in my skin, in my body. It's a really interesting thing. And it's all thanks to makeup.

Makeup.

It's an exquisite art.

You have to learn it. Otherwise, it's not the same. I mean, it's all good, I imagine each person is at their own stage of learning. But when it's fabulous, it's something magical.

TINA VALENTÍN AGUIRRE: Finding community through art was really important to me.

I also was a writer, a reporter. I would do readings, and that was fruitful and awesome and fun, but also very limited to who was there. Though I love live performance, there wasn't a means for it to be preserved. With people dying, I thought I needed that. So, I decided I would get into movies.

I started interning with Osa Hidalgo de la Riva on her movie *Me and Mr. Mauri.* I also interned with Electric City, which was a public access cable queer and trans program. I started to learn how to make movies. .

I decided that I would shoot *Viva 16* about the people I love and care for, and that it would include complexity around gender and how we build hope despite so many challenges. I envisioned collecting a lot of people's stories through interviews, and then events, and putting it together to tell the story of how the community came together in San Francisco, how LGBTQ Latinx people came together, especially on Sixteenth Street, and also how the community was at risk because of displacement and gentrification.

I interviewed lots of people. Many lives were at risk. Cancer, crack, poverty, hopelessness, and AIDS were all impacting us in very real ways. I was starting to feel better about at least having documentation. It really was, like, "This is who we are. We're special, and here's a little tiny bit about where we're headed." There's a lot of resilience in that. Amongst ourselves as subgroups—trans women, let's say darker Latinx people, lighter-skinned Latinx people, immigrants, people who are from San Francisco, Chicano, and otherwise—we have a lot of differences. We also have a lot of commonalities. In the movie, I put that together.

What is in *Viva 16* was not anywhere else. There weren't depictions of us telling our own stories in terms of gender and race, and Sixteenth Street—so I'm really, really happy about that. And it's been really appreciated. It means a lot.

DONNA PERSONNA: Recently, in 2018, I cowrote a play about the Compton's Cafeteria Riot of 1966.

I first happened on Compton's Cafeteria in the 1960s. This was in the Tenderloin District of San Francisco. It was like an Edward Hopper painting. It was nighttime, and I'm walking, and it was really lit up that night. The sky is all dark, but Compton's is bright and lit. Outside, I saw these beautiful women, overdressed for ten o'clock at night on the street. They had their eyebrows arched and plucked. I wanted more. I went in there with them.

I'd go back home every weekend, and this was my place, my second home. I met these trans women. There were many of them. I would sit in a booth with them and hear their stories, their existence. I heard things like, "I was born in the South, in Georgia, and the preacher at our church forced me into sex with him." This girl, she left when she was fourteen, she's now living as a transgender woman in San Francisco at twenty years old. She ended up there at Compton's, with other girls.

I'm just a kid. I'm in my late teens. I'd sit with them, and I'm listening to these stories, like, "Oh, my God, this is unbelievable. They're brave. This is too much."

I remember a girl named Sandy. She said she was with a man. They found ways to be validated as a woman, and having a man was one of them. He wasn't gay, he was straight, and she supported him through sex work. He kept pushing her. We're having toast and coffee, and she's saying, "Oh, my God, he wants me to get bigger breasts. I'm afraid. I have to go get a kitchen-sink operation." There were no hospitals or anything like that. She was afraid, but she would do it. He was always wanting more, for her to do more to be the woman that he wanted. She would say, "Oh, my God, I get up at five a.m., I go in the bathroom, I get fully turned into a woman, then I get back in bed, so he can wake up and see Loretta Young." Bullshit. He finally left her for somebody else that was more developed, he left her in the lurch, but I was glad because she was pushing against that.

I heard a lot of these different stories, and I was all ears.

There were such beautiful women. And they were so nice. These women were wonderful people, they were so sweet, they watched out for each other like you would not believe. We'd be in Compton's, and one of the girls would come back, and they'd keep looking at her: "Okay, her mascara is running, what happened?" And they needed to know, how did it go? Friendships aren't always like that. I was seeing super friendships.

They did drugs, they slammed drugs, they did shoplifting. They shoplifted because it was against the law to buy women's clothes, can you imagine?

They never offered me any drugs, never suggested that I do sex work, they never suggested that I paint my face, they just took care of me like a little family. I wanted as much time as I could have with them.

I used to go to their hotels. They would have a hotel room in the Tenderloin, one of those where they had a washbasin in the bedroom. I saw how they lived. And I have this image: the washbasin was full with a bunch of makeup, and they would use each other's makeup. Like maybe seven of them, six of them, they rented the place together, and would take turns. Like from two to four, Ramona and Jessica slept there. They were able to sleep while the rest of us were there.

I wasn't absorbed into the Compton's girls. I'm not so much a joiner.

The magical part of that is, in 2005, in the news, I learned about that history at Compton's Cafeteria. That they rioted and they pushed back against police brutality in 1966 before Stonewall.

I'm proud to say this: we cowrote and produced *The Compton's Cafeteria Riot* and I brought my memories to the writing process. Things happened as we imagined them. I wasn't there, at the historic Compton's Cafeteria riot, but I knew these women's stories.

I was invited to City Hall and given an award, in front of senators and the mayor, for my work on this play. I was telling them: this story was buried and hidden for almost fifty years. What if it had never emerged? It impassions me now. This story is not going to die. Every word I wrote, and we wrote, in the play, is the truth.

I cried, at City Hall. Sometimes you have to cry a little. I got raped many times, and no one ever did anything for me. I went to the police, and the police laughed at me and said, "We're not going to make a police report, that was a hookup that didn't work out for you, ha, ha, ha." I needed someone to hug me or whatever, but that's what I got.

After City Hall, I went home, and I talked to the girls. "I'm sorry that you died, and you never found out that you were doing nothing wrong—nothing. And that actually, you're heroes, absolute heroes, not to be kicked around. You laid the foundations for what transgender people need today."

We need health care, we need legal advice and protection, we need police protection, we need jobs, we need homes, we need a voice.

And now their story, it's going around the world. Those ladies are going to be validated now. They weren't then, but I'm helping to make it happen now. I love that.

STORMMIGUEL FLOREZ: So much of my life is based in performing, and some kind of activism. That's where a lot of my freedom has happened, my liberation and my expression.

A performance I did that was really fun: at one point, I had a girlfriend who was not into BDSM at all, but knew I was. She respected that, but we weren't going to be doing that. She was like, "I want to do a performance where I feed you vanilla ice cream."

I was just like, "Ha ha, that's cute, but no."

But then there was this whole leather-and-lace show, with no SM, and I was like, "Aha!"

We had this idea where basically we were just going to ride the edge of their thing. In the performance, I have a table and I walk into the room. I'm singing "Master and Servant," and I'm in my leathers.

I start placing out my whips. It's like I'm getting ready for a date. I'm just placing out all my gear, and I'm like, "Master and servant, oh, this is going to be a hot night." I'm just going out there, laying all the stuff out. I swear to God, I can see people coming down the aisles just like, "What the hell?"—like about to stop something.

And then from the wings, my girlfriend says, "Ahem, ahem, Miss Conduct? Miss Conduct!" That's my name in the scene. She whispers out, "Ahem, they said no S/M, they said no S/M."

And I'm just like, "Oh, I hate this!" I start going off on a rant. "Nobody tells me no S/M." I'm just like, "Blah, blah, blah."

Some people in the audience are whooping and hollering. I swear people from the group are about to get on the stage and pounce on me. And then at that point, my girlfriend comes out fully laced and backs me into a chair and feeds me vanilla ice cream.

That was the whole scene. There was no S/M. It was just this really fun, powerful moment of kind of taking the wind out of their sails and making a big statement at the same time.

CRYSTAL MASON: Lately, I've done a little bit more performance and more visual art.

I've done a series of videos about identity. I am centered in my videos—all three of them—sometimes naked. One of the reasons I made that decision was, basically, the lack of representation of fat Black queer folk. If I want that representation, then maybe I need to have the courage to make that art. So for me, the message wasn't necessarily political, but the act of taking up that space and being on this big screen was a political act.

STORMMIGUEL FLOREZ: In 2004, I had an idea for a performance piece I wanted to do. I was talking to a friend about it. This person was also genderqueer, and we decided we're going to do this show. We were like, "We can do this."

It was going to be called "Trans as Fuck," and it was a live tranny sex show. That is how we called it. At the time we use the word *tranny*. Everybody was using the word *tranny*, it was not a problem to use the word. I knew a lot of people from all over the place who were using it. Trans women. That was a very affectionate term among Black trans women I was friends with. It was just being used, like, "Oh, this tranny," or "Yes, she's a tranny," or "Oh, the trannies are going to go do this."

ADELA VÁZQUEZ: I'm very good with my hands, I can fix things. I'm very handy. I call myself a handy tranny.

STORMMIGUEL FLOREZ: It was really just an endearing term we used together. I was very sad when it became not okay to use. I respect that in my life, in everyday conversation, but it's important for me to talk about it in this time frame.

There was Tranny Fest, which was the first-ever trans film festival. It happened in San Francisco.

TINA VALENTÍN AGUIRRE: After *Viva 16* came out, I did do a short on Teresita la Campesina that came out in 1996 as part of the first Tranny Fest, at the Roxie Theater. I'm really happy about that.

STORMMIGUEL FLOREZ: It's now called the San Francisco Transgender Film Festival. So, yes, that was a celebratory term we used back then.

Our performance was "Trans as Fuck: a Live Tranny Sex Show." It was at 848 Divisadero. Which is this place where there were a lot of play parties and a lot of performances. A lot of anything-goes type stuff happened at this place. It was great. So we did the show there, and it was super scrappy. We just reached out to people: "You want to be in our show? Great, come do something." Not even like, "What are you going to do?" Not even like, "Tell us the nature of this performance." I learned some things from that.

Somebody did a beer enema as a part of the show, which is

apparently very dangerous and you shouldn't do, so that was a one-time deal. They were fine, and had clearly done it before. There was this whole scene of getting caught in the school bathroom by the principal, and they end up giving the principal a beer enema. They were actually doing that, it was real.

There was a performance that included ejaculation, masturbating while praying the Hail Mary. Just a lot of great performances. Beautiful performances. Body piercing. Fetishes like puppy play. It was a raunchy and raucous and wonderful night of performance. A lot of people were really uncomfortable in the audience. We gave them a heads-up: "There will be explicit sexual performance, bodily fluids, a lot going on." Overall, it was a success. People were very excited about it. It was such an exciting night.

You know what, I'm just going to be explicit, why the hell not?

I did it live. I played Reverend Rex, this priest who finds a dildo and is having feelings about it, gets very upset, but then ends up masturbating while praying for forgiveness. Then there's another scene where I fist myself and read poetry.

That was a very liberating thing for me, to show my body as a person who hadn't started transitioning yet. Knowing that testosterone was the thing that was going to bring me home in my body, or feeling that that was the case, yet still trying to love my body all the way through regardless of where I was. It was uncomfortable to be naked and to be sexual in front of people. And that was something that felt also important to me, because I wanted to express that it's okay to honor all parts of ourselves at all times. It was a very powerful experience for me, and I think it was powerful for people who saw it.

We did it again in LA, and then we did it at Queer Arts Festival, on a big stage in front of a crowd of people. The piece I did that night was called, "My First Year on T." I had been on testosterone for a good year at that point, and in the performance, I sang a couple of songs I wrote during that first year on T. My voice had started to settle, but I wanted to perform the awkwardness of my body and my voice changing while I was starting testosterone. Because I was performing while my voice was changing, sometimes, it was kind of funny. Early on, I would sing, and my voice would crack, and it would be like, "Am I going to hit this note? We don't know, let's see," and I'd play the song. Everybody was very supportive and wonderful; it was all very awkward.

So in my performance "My First Year on T," I wanted to simulate that experience of what it was like to go through what I was going through emotionally, through with my body, and in my singing. So in the scene, I was topless, and I had my guitar, and my partner came from behind me and pierced a corset into my back while I was singing and playing guitar. She'd be piercing me, and occasionally it would hurt, and I would yelp in the middle of the song. It was just a way of simulating, like, we don't know how this is going to go. Let's see what happens when I sing while this wild thing is happening to my body.

At the end the scene, she turns me around, and I have this beautiful—just—needles across from each other in a corset, kind of like I'm strung throughout them, so it looks like there's a corset sewn into my back. Really beautiful work, she did. That was my scene in that year's "Trans as Fuck." Again, it was just allowing people to share the experience of what was going on in my body, and celebrating it.

KB BOYCE: I am almost sixty, and I'm still a working musician. I'm able to pick and choose now, and I decided in the 2000s that I no longer would play in bands or musical projects or any kind of projects that were not headed by queers. And then later I refined that to, "I'd rather work with queers of color."

It was important for me to work in the queer sphere, and to try to create community for artists of color. I needed those folks in my life, these incredibly strong artists.

And here I am now, almost sixty, a working drummer in a punk band that gigs and tours, as an afro punk OG. The lead singer, Lynn Breedlove, was in a band called Tribe 8, whom I call the queer grandmamas of punk. We're called the Homobiles.

I was just asked to be in a production called *The Red Shades*, which is a trans superhero rock opera that took place in San Francisco, written by Adrienne Price. It was incredible. There were so many incredible actors, performers, and I was able to be in the stage band for this musical. So I got to work in the theater with these incredible queer and trans performers, and play to sold-out shows. We got beautiful write-ups in the press. Audience members who came two and three times and were singing along. It was insane. That is my life.

TINA VALENTÍN AGUIRRE: For me, art is about hope and love. Without hope and love, a revolution—or let's say social movement—is bereft of soul, of humanity. I crave art for us that is more complex. I believe in fine art. I privilege great art, and I encourage that in others. Like, life is so short, who has time for shitty art? What is that doing for us? Practice. Learn your stuff. Do it. And then, make some mistakes, but maybe not everything has to get shared. Ultimately, I want people to be moved, and I want to feel good as an artist. Not that everything is going to be great, but I can try.

KB BOYCE: I cofounded and I continue to run an all-queer-and-trans-artists-of-color production company based in the Bay Area called Queer Rebel Productions. Its mission is to create a space for queer and trans artists of color to be commissioned to create new works. It's grant funded. We're an intergenerational production company, so it's about the emerging artists working with artists who have been around the block a time or two, and creating a space to build community for queer and trans artists of color.

I hope that that is helpful to the community. I certainly didn't have that kind of backup when I was coming up as a young kid.

That is probably the most important thing going on in my life right now, one of a bazillion things. I feel that I still have a lot of energy, and it's important for me to do all the things that call to me, and put my hands in a lot of different things. A lot of things on my plate! But it all brings me joy. It keeps me young, and it keeps me doing what I love to do.

NELSON D'ALERTA PÉREZ: I'm a true artist. It's very spiritual. I love art. Art has helped me deal with so many things in life, and helped me be happy.

I had a therapist who was a real gem. May god bless her for me, wherever she is. I had an incredible journey with her, she taught me so many things, and she'd always say to me, "Focus on your art, focus on your art, that's your salvation." And that's how it's been. Through art, I learned to be happy.

* *

ELEVEN

The Art and Power of Drag

TUPILI LEA ARELLANO: I mean, I was doing Elvis Presley impersonations when I was in first grade. My parents would ask me to do them when company came over. I'd comb my hair like that and everything. That was part of my gender.

LANDA LAKES: The first times I started doing drag, I did it to get into the clubs. I wasn't performing at all. I just wanted to look like I was one of the performers. That's how I would get in.

There's a big difference between passing as a cis woman and drag, you know?

For instance, when I'd go to Bricktown, in Oklahoma City, I would basically dress like my sister. I would put on eyeliner, and eyeshadow, but I usually did not put on any base. I didn't have any facial hair at the time, even though I was in my teenage years, so I didn't even put on foundation. Just eyeshadow and eyeliner. And I ratted my hair. I would use my sister's clothes. My friends and I would go to the clubs, and we'd easily get in.

But when I started doing drag to get into those clubs, I wanted to look like a drag queen. That meant lots of foundation. It meant false eyelashes. I went all the way out. And the clothes had to be more ridiculous, it had to be way over the top, because I wanted to have this look as if I was there to perform, even though I wasn't, I was just there to have a good time.

So me and my friend Russell, we would go to these thrift stores in Oklahoma City, and we would find beaded dresses, and we'd be like, "Oh, this is perfect!" We would wear these beaded dresses and stuff to get in. Me and Russell started going to the Rec Room. The first time I went there, the MC was Patty Melt. That was her name, Patty Melt. When I went in, she was like, "Where's your music?"

And I was like, "Oh, I have this cassette tape."

So that was my first drag thing. I went in, dressed in drag, and Patty Melt just put me in the show.

Then she started booking me. That's how I started doing it.

I used Autumn Westbrook as my stage name back then, because it was like a nice, pretty name. That was what was really popular in Oklahoma. We also had Patty Melt, of course, a big camp name. But at the time, I just wanted to be pretty. That was my thing. It wasn't until years later that I changed my name to Landa Lakes, in about 2004.

It was fun! It was just so much fun. I mean, it was the eighties. Really a good time.

Even when I do drag now, sometimes, when I get dressed and everything, I pull back up those memories of the eighties, of just having fun with my friends. Good, positive memories.

NELSON D'ALERTA PÉREZ: I was part of a group of artists, about five people, who put on shows during the winters in Cuba—a forbidden thing, because it was all drag. This was in the seventies, until 1980, in Havana. For ten years.

It was very, very, very hard. Very hard. I've been through so many things in life because of the way I am. Abuses, the police. I was arrested ten times on a single night. I was taken to the same police station, until finally the officer said, "Don't bring her here anymore!"

Our cabaret was underground. I'd rent a house on the beach, one of the big mansions that could fit a lot of people. I'd always make sure it had a staircase, to make things as theatrical as possible. And that's where I'd hold my shows. It first came to mind when a friend said to me, "I dance ballet on point." And I said, "Me too." I'd studied a bit of ballet behind my family's back, because they hadn't wanted me to.

There were other people doing drag shows on the beach, using towels for hair, sheets as dresses. They were all gay. I wanted to create something a little fancier. And I was really lucky to meet these five people who had all these talents in addition to performance: one sewed, another was a hair stylist, there was a pianist in the group. We all became close with each other. We started out dancing ballet, and people said they wanted a cabaret. So we started singing.

I didn't charge an entrance fee because the police could have accused me of running a private business. In my time, that was illegal. Now it's accepted: you can do it, in Cuba. But back then it was impossible.

So I said, "No. This is free. This is for the people."

I put up the money from my own earnings. I was working in construction then.

I'd rent a private house, and then we'd say to people on the street, "You're invited to such and such address, on Saturday." There would be just one show, on a Saturday. So we'd arrive on Friday and rehearse. I was a real fanatic about rehearsals. I thought they were extremely important. And they are.

So we'd be about five guys—or girls!—and we'd have the pianist, and a small music player for us to sing to. I'd hang sheets, and we had a little projector, and one person worked in the film industry and got us movie scenes we could project as a background. The artists would be in front, singing. We did ballet, first. We did one ballet that my friend choreographed that was called "Life Itself." It started as two straight couples dancing, but then I'd arrive and it turned into trios, all very erotic. People liked that one a lot.

The first part used classical music, and the second part was modern. We sang numbers, songs that were popular in those times, by female singers in Cuba. I loved watching those shows, I really loved them.

Many people came. Many gay people—many. Gay women, lesbians, gay men, guys and girls. Straight people, too. There was a lot of approval in the community.

It felt so important. We were offering art, which is something for the spirit. It's like food for your soul. And aside from that, you're creating community. You're taking a group of people who are marginalized and saying, "This is your place. You can be yourself in here." That's the importance it had for me.

And we were very alert, because in those days, if the police caught you, it was six months to a year of prison. For dressing as a different gender. I was arrested many times, for walking the street with makeup on, in women's jewelry, women's clothes.

It was also forbidden to gather in homes, and I was gathering up to two hundred people. But it gave me so much satisfaction. It still does. I know what I've done. I was seventeen, eighteen years old, I knew exactly what I wanted to do, and I was a force of nature to do it. It was all I cared about. Little by little, I discovered that world. Nobody took me there. I got there on my own. I was proud of myself then—and I still am now—for being who I am.

I became something of a famous person, through the cabarets. I had a reputation in the communities of Havana. I was like a diva. My name was Catherine White.

FRESH "LEV" WHITE: I started drag king performing in the eighties. Supposedly I was the first DC drag king.

LANDA LAKES: When I first started doing drag, many years ago, there weren't a lot of drag kings. Years ago, I think there was like one person who became pretty well known as a drag king. And this was like, back in the eighties, one person, get it? Just one person. And people were talking about it. They were just like, "I can't believe that! Blah, blah, blah."

FRESH "LEV" WHITE: Oh my God, it was playful freedom, right? And this was about doing it for a good cause, raising money to fight AIDS. One of my last shows was in like 1989, and [the bookstore] Lambda

Rising had a pair of boxers that were white with confetti, and then something says, "the gay nineties," because we're going into the nineties. I remember stripping down to a tank top and my boxers, doing "I Wanna Be Your Sugar Mama." And then doing so on other stages in DC and joining in some competitions. I did Lionel Richie. Freddie Mercury. I could do the ballads, I did some Luther Vandross and stuff like that. Frank Sinatra, Rob Base. And then, I brought in the Mary Watkins, who was a female lesbian, but still, it was music to strip to. Billy Idol at the Mint in San Francisco, really out-of-the-box stuff with my energy.

I remember when I first saw drag kings, it was like romantic. I always thought of drag kings as gentlemen. Oh, I remember, I saw them in New York City. They were wooing women. It was a balance. And I came in and did the silly crazy stuff, but always, yeah, just creating joy.

It was sexy. Playful sexy.

Later on, I was known as Barry White. I earned my drag king name at the 1999 San Francisco Drag King Contest, where I won as Barry White. It's me, I've got three white backup dancers—they're femmes in gowns and dresses. It was hysterical. I had a whole thing, me and my people.

STORMMIGUEL FLOREZ: Early on, I did a little bit of drag in Albuquerque, just a little. That was very titillating, when I first started. I'm like, "Oh, I'm putting facial hair on!"

I had a girlfriend who was butch and liked to do drag, and I started exploring that with her in the early nineties. Getting to do drag performance was really fun. It felt good to get to look a way that I would have liked to look. It was also a little frustrating, because spirit gum and facial hair is just not quite it, right? It is, and it isn't. You want it to look real and then you're just itchy all night. There's always a level of discomfort, and not being completely satisfied, because that was something I actually wanted. But it was still another place to get to play in those masculine spaces, express myself that way, and connect with other people who were expressing themselves that way.

When I got out here to San Francisco, I tried to get connected with queer community, with dyke community, dyke musicians and artists. That was a hard community to get into. It was the mid nineties, and it was very kind of edgy, punk, leathery, rough. I'm an acoustic, mostly folk kind of rock player. At some point, my self-esteem was just out.

Then I started meeting other people who were transitioning, more trans people—those things were happening simultaneously—and some of these people were doing drag.

I started accompanying a person who was doing a drag show. I was playing guitar, but I was in drag. My drag name was Gordon Leadfoot. I was a seventies kind of cowboy, polyester shirts unbuttoned, facial hair and cowboy hat. I just kept my head down. It was fun. To be able to do drag felt like a fun way of being.

So I said, "Well, maybe I'll just do drag." Occasionally, just for going out, I would put mascara on my peach fuzz to fill in my sideburns, just masculinizing myself more. Drag allowed me to start playing with that more, presenting myself more that way. So that was great. It was a very natural place to start getting to present more masculine in my daily life, and even at work sometimes. Once, I had a job where we had a Christmas party, and I just put on sideburns and a beard and went that way. It was no big deal. It was mostly a straight organization, but I could still do it because it was San Francisco.

KB BOYCE: I went through a phase where I decided to become the Drag King of the Blues, as a performer. I took on converting Delta Blues songs and queering them up, you know?

Drag King TuffNStuff. Tuffy, the Drag King of the Blues.

That was me for ten years.

I would put on a fake soul patch and some sideburns that I would cut from my hair. I used to have long dreads. And I would cut from my dreads and create my facial fur.

I was queering the Delta Blues, and writing songs in that vein, queer songs in the Delta Blues style. I think I was a little ahead of my time. I don't think the young queers were really ready for Delta Blues. But I did it anyway. I played colleges and festivals and museums, wherever.

When you're a drag king, people are expecting you to come out and lip sync to whatever popular songs. And I wasn't doing that. I would come out with a guitar, and I would need a real microphone because I actually sing.

I was playing a venue in LA, for a Transgiving performance. It was just me and my guitar and my voice. I was really worried about playing this show because the audience was used to, you know, the sound system bumping, and the drag king or queen or whatever dancing and doing all that stuff. And then I come out with my guitar, and I start singing my Delta Blues. And in the back of the room, I saw people get up and start dancing. That just—I'm choking up right now. I did not expect that kind of warmth. That's not what I had been getting from young audiences. But somehow, I got people to dance to an acoustic guitar, and that meant a lot to me.

For the most part, I got good reception as the Drag King of the Blues, don't get me wrong. I was able to do it for about ten years, and get paid. But I always felt kind of out of the loop. I didn't fit in with drag performers. And I later realized that's because I wasn't really a drag performer. I was transmasculine, just trying to be myself onstage, to perform in a comfortable way that made me happy.

I still bust out some Delta Blues here and there, but the character of Tuffy, I kind of laid that to rest as I physically decided to transition, and things changed with my body.

ADELA VÁZQUEZ: I became Miss Gay Latina in 1992.

So I come to San Francisco from LA, and I start my hairdressing thing. Every time that I went out after I moved here, I would go out in drag, as a woman. The first few times that I walked around the streets as a woman, I was terrified. But at night, I was a girl. I always wanted to wear women's clothes to go out. There's so much variety, you can wear dresses, you can wear combinations, you can wear whatever. I had all these beautiful night clothes and sexy, beautiful dresses at night. I had long, black hair, my own hair, to my waist. I was that person.

At the Latino hair salon, Victor's, somebody came and said, "Hey, you know, I work for this place called Instituto Familiar de la Raza and every year we have a contest at the bar Esta Noche." They asked me to participate in this contest.

I was like, "Okay." I haven't done no drag shows till then; I was just a girl at night. It was fun, it was a lot of fun.

I was discovering that I was not very successful as a gay man. I've never really been a gay man. I was really weird looking. I was into goth for a while, trying to break the traditional man look, and it was not me. So, this was another way. At this point, I wasn't really thinking of tits or anything like that, I was just having fun. I looked very convincing. The body, the hair, the allure, the glitter, the sequins, the beading, the designs, all those things. I learned to live that way, go out that way. When the opportunity came to become Miss Gay Latina, I entered, and won.

This was at Esta Noche. A beautiful bar. In the Mission. The only Latino gay bar for many years. It was a whole thing. Many of the community's problems were resolved there. If you were a member of the gay Latino community, and you arrived in San Francisco and went there, you could find a roommate, you could find work, you could find a husband, you could find anything. That's where it all started.

How many friendships do I have from there? Many.

LANDA LAKES: In the early nineties, I did drag at Esta Noche. There were a few drag queens there that would put me in their shows. There was Lola Lust, and Francine. They had shows on different nights, and they would put me in their drag shows. Because I was performing there, and I was doing songs in Spanish, they thought I could speak Spanish. That happened a lot. I'd memorize the Spanish songs, because in the cassettes, they would often have the lyrics. I would just memorize the lyrics, so I got a good idea of what was being said.

ADELA VÁZQUEZ: That's where I know Tina Valentín Aguirre from. Esta Noche.

TINA VALENTÍN AGUIRRE: Esta Noche was really important to us.

ADELA VÁZQUEZ: I went there looking for fun. Looking for dicks. And I found a set of social problems and issues that I got involved with without even knowing it. Then all of a sudden, I'm representing this community. You know, when you're a Miss, you go places to do volunteer work, you do shows here and there. I knew the responsibility that came with being a Miss. I was parading in Gay Pride, in a Cadillac. It felt great. It felt great.

That's how it started. Then the idea of doing shows came. I went and talked to the owner of Esta Noche, and I said, "Listen, I want you to let me have a show here." They had a license to stay open on Saturdays until four o'clock in the morning. So, I said, "If you let me do a show at one forty-five, people have half an hour to get drinks, I can fill the bar up."

They gave it to me.

"I keep the door, you keep the bar."

He agreed to that. He was very happy about it because he was making tons of money. People would come to see me because I've been around, I have a bunch of friends who are queens, too, and people love me. During this time, in the AIDS epidemic, there was no

Latina queen out there. That was me. I filled all those blanks. And people were loving it. People would come to see me perform. And I was a good performer.

I'd perform a lot of "Eclipse Total del Amor," Annia Linares, Cuban singers nobody here had heard of. Amanda Miguel. Those eighties songs. I'd do La Lupe. I had my songs. But not in character; I'd just borrow those artists' voices, and bring my own style.

I formed a group: AtreDivas. It was two drag queens and two transgender women. We had a show every Saturday at 1:45 a.m. I would give the money that was collected to Proyecto ContraSIDA, for the transgender community, because I was still working there.

"AtreDivas." Because the act of dressing as a woman and working onstage makes you an "atrevida"—a daring woman.

It was so wonderful. We represented Proyecto, and we represented the community, the transgender Latino community. At Gay Pride, and here and there, we were present in the community at the time. Nobody had that before. We were pioneers in that. A group of transgenders that were out there in front of everybody, being who we are.

We gave a message of prevention: put a condom on the dick. We boiled it down. And, we were addressing the community in Spanish. All the programs were designed in English. So we provided that.

DONNA PERSONNA: I came to drag performance, and dressing like a woman, at a late age: fifty-nine years old.

Conventionally, in the entertainment world and in a lot of aspects, youth is honored and desired. Technically, I started as an older person. But—to circle back to "Donna Personna"—when I would "don" my "persona," it was welcomed by the world. I had beauty, I was ageless, I had this energy I really brought, I was successful in the drag world.

I don't compete. I just do my thing. I had no problem getting on a stage at this age. I was doing a lot of shows. I've been on more than a hundred stages in this country and beyond.

It took me fifty-nine years to get over stage fright. It was a learning moment. I had impostor syndrome, I learned that phrase. I used to have this inner dialogue: "That's what people who can do things do, that's what people who have talent can do, not me." I stopped saying that. Now my dialogue or my language is, "I have not yet attempted that." I've found a way.

I don't take myself seriously. But I'm desperately serious about what I do.

We all know academically that beauty is in the eye of the beholder. But everything that emanates from me is kind and funny. I'm not a threat to you. People love me, and they see beauty in me. It has nothing to do with me. It is what they are feeling when they look at me. They're feeling good, so they see beauty.

When I started seeing success as a drag queen, younger ones would say, "Oh, I want to be famous, can you help me with that?"

And I'd say, "No, I can't. Jeffrey Dahmer's famous. Watch out what you want."

"Don't you want to be famous?"

I said, "No, no, I'm not doing anything because I want to be famous, honey. I want to do something that reaches people, that puts me together with people. Something wonderful to do."

Just let me be. If the world lets you do that, gives you that, then you have the opportunity to be magnificent.

LANDA LAKES: When I decided to start doing drag again, here in San Francisco, I wanted it to be different. I wanted it to be politically charged in some way. And so I was like, I think I'm going to call myself Landa Lakes, after the mascot, the Land O'Lakes mascot. I wanted it to be very tongue-in-cheek and campy.

It just happened to coincide with the time when we, the Bay Area American Indian Two-Spirits, BAAITS, had decided to put on an International Gathering. And we were like oh, okay, well, we have to raise funds for it. BAAITS is clean and sober, but we knew that we could raise more money in bars than elsewhere. That led me to create a group called the Brush Arbor Gurlz. It was a Native American drag troupe here in San Francisco. It was the first all Native American drag troupe in the country. I created the first one without even realizing it.

Here's something I thought was really interesting: when we started preparing our first show, the first thing people told us was, "You Natives are not going to draw enough people. You're going to have to pull in a lot of other people."

So that first show, we did. We pulled in a lot of other people. They were great performers, and the first few shows had a diverse cast. Then by around the third show, I was like, "We have an audience. If we choose to be all Native American now, we can be all Native American."

We did an all Native American show, and people still showed up. Being able to say that we drew the crowd ourselves had this effect on me, I saw that we could do this. "Sorry, but you're wrong: Native Americans, we draw our own crowd."

FRESH "LEV" WHITE: There was serious racism. Oh my God. I'd go to a show, and there may or may not be drink tickets for us, there was no money or anything for us. Then we'd find out later that the white folks were getting all the drink tickets, and sometimes winning cash prizes. It was here in San Francisco where I experienced the racism in the drag community. It was insane.

I lived in a little bit of a bubble in my mind. My mom was really great at encouraging us to believe that everybody's equal. She never taught us about racism. I just didn't know it existed. And I didn't have to because, growing up, I was in this multicultural experience, in the Bronx, where it's West Indians, and Colombians, and really so rich. So what I ended up doing with my experiences around race was, A, being really naïve about it, and, B, learning how to navigate in ways that I didn't realize I was doing till later.

So, when I was performing that Black masculinity, for me, it's fucking amazing, and I'm feeling like everybody thinks it is, too. At that point, not having the analysis around how Black entertainers were part of what's acceptable. And then coming to San Francisco, I remember there were times when things were blatant, like at these events where people were going on stage and doing serious, redneck misogynist acts, and getting praised. I remember there was another troupe in town, and it was all masculine people of color, and they had a fantastic performance, but they sang live. And people tried to disqualify them. Right? And they were great. Their show was so amazing. And so, I would say, right: racism.

LANDA LAKES: It was a very crazy time. A lot of the girls, it was their first time doing drag. It was very experimental for them. There was this infamous place here in San Francisco called Trannyshack, and I went there. A lot of things happened at Trannyshack, a lot of shock drag. My name went right into it pretty well. You could expect something sick. And that's what would happen.

There's been a lot of political content. One of the very first things that I did when I came out as Landa Lakes, was with the song "Bury My Heart at Wounded Knee," by Buffy Sainte-Marie. I had all these Native mascots and Native mascot logos flashing behind me, my way of introducing the audience to the fact that a lot of times, Native people are made into cartoons, and basically slapped onto labels to give people this feeling of Americana. Like if they want you to buy their butter, they'll slap an Indian on it as though the Indian made this butter just for you, like it's really down-home because it's got this Indian on it. That was my first number as Landa Lakes: to push this idea of being more than just a mascot.

I can easily make drag political. At the same time, I can also do a drag number that has no politics to it. That drag number might be just something funny.

I've been doing this one number for many years. Actually, I

originated it at Trannyshack, back in 2005. It was called Duck and
Cover Night, and you had to do a cover song. I did "I'll Always Love
You." I've always had this battle with my weight. I'm thin sometimes,
then I'm fat, then I'm thin, then I'm fat, then I'm fat-fat-fat, and then
I'm thin. It's constant, just always going on. So I was singing to a
Twinkie, and then it goes on into like a low-carb diet that I'm trying
to do, and at the end, it all breaks, and I just start eating everything.
That's sort of fun, but at the same time, something that's very personal. Drag can be all that. That's what I appreciate about drag. I love
drag that can tell a story. I can also do drag that doesn't tell a story at
all, just me moving my mouth to somebody else's words. I think that's
fine. But I appreciate it more when it tells a story.

TUPILI LEA ARELLANO: La Chola Priest showed up all of a sudden. I had
this vision of dressing in Catholic priest drag to help others heal.
What I had been given in healing my damage from Catholicism, I
would pay it forward, share it.

So I ordered my clothes from a Catholic store in Utah. I ordered
hosts. I practiced at home first, wearing the whole drag, because it
was intense to put it in on and everything.

I really liked it. Oh, I liked it so much. It was euphoric. It was
almost like I was a priest at some time, in some life, and I was revisit-
ing something I already had inside of me. I had a great-grandmother
who was a full-blooded Rarámuri woman who was both invested
in Catholicism and in Indigenous medicine. She used to clean the
church in Silver City, New Mexico, where I was born, and she had
some things in her bedroom that were given to her by the church
and the priests. Fancy altar stuff. So that was in me. I knew a lot of
Catholic stuff, and I really studied the priests. I was more interested
in them than I was in the nuns. I really wanted one of those little col-
lars. I imagined wearing a collar secretly, but as a child I never did.

Back to Oakland: I had all of the support. The venues were

available. I'd pitch the performance, and people would say, "Oh, yes, how soon can you come?"

I said, "I do a sermon. As a performance artist. An actual sermon, I lift everybody, and I tell them the truth about themselves. I mention the lies that Catholicism has told about us as queers, and as women, and all of this."

So I started performing. People loved the performance. I'd give the service, and then I'd serve Necco Wafers, which are these little, round candy wafers, as communion. I'd say, "God is completely pleased with everything you are. Everything."

I went to Washington, DC. LLEGO which was a national Latinx political organization, had heard about me, and flew me to Washington to do a sermon with them. The majority of the people attending the LLEGO conference were gay men and trans women. Lots of trans women were at that. People really loved my sermon, and they were having catharsis right there during the communion serving when I was saying to them how pleased God is with everything you are. I'm apologizing for all the lies that Catholicism has told about you. And people were bursting out crying and having a breakthrough right there. I loved that, because that's my work. I loved being a priest.

Some of the people even wanted to meet privately with me in my room after my sermon. They said, "I really need your help."

I go, "You know what, you think you need my help. I want you to experience healing without thinking that you need more priestly support. There's nothing wrong with you. That's not true. It's not true, it's lies. And you deserve your own compassion." Things like that.

We were in a really beautiful hotel. When I was on the elevator going to do my sermon, people were addressing me as Father: "Good evening, Father, good evening, Father," and I would just give them a benevolent nod. I didn't say anything, because my voice is what it is, I wanted to be in character.

I really believe that healing is reciprocal, so that when we're giving medicine, we're getting medicine. It really helped me be bold, because later I promoted myself to pope! I had a pope dress in my closet, and a pope hat. "I'm the pope now, did you hear? I got promoted, and I'm in charge."

I loved it, I loved it, I loved it. It was euphoric.

NELSON D'ALERTA PÉREZ: When I came to the United States from Cuba, I performed professionally in Miami, and then in Dallas. That was my first work in the United States: performing in shows. I was paid to do drag, starting in 1980 in Miami.

I was still Catherine White.

The experience was incredible, because I'd be announced as having just arrived from Cuba. That was practically a political statement. I was welcomed in style. It really moved me, because I'd never dreamed I could experience such acceptance. The gay community came, and lesbians, and transsexuals, it was—oh, my God. There's a big Cuban community in Miami, and they'd come and say, "What? How is it possible you were doing this in Cuba?"

I'd say, "Well, I did it. It was important to me for the community to have a place to be comfortable. So I offered them that, even though my freedom was at risk."

I arrived in San Francisco in 1983. A few months later, someone came to me and said, "I've heard you do shows, that you know how. I've got a cabaret but I don't know what to do with it."

I said, "Oh, my God. You have a cabaret, and girl, you don't know what to do? How many artists have you got? Let's get started."

We formed a group. We went to the place. It was from the 1940s, just magnificent, with a whole stage, a greenroom, a bar and kitchen. Everything needed for a cabaret.

I went there and I made my dreams come true. Things I'd wanted to do: lights, costumes, music. All very professional. It was in San Francisco that I was able to do that.

I made myself a bodysuit covered in rhinestones. I dressed as a nun, because that was all the rage. I shaved my head and wore a wig, people thought it was my hair, because I'd dance and it wouldn't come off. I wore the bodysuit and wig onstage, with extravagant makeup, and the crowd went wild.

I did a number at one point to the song "The Party's Over." That was when AIDS was beginning. My friends were already dying. So it was a whole group performance, and then at the end they all started leaving, because the party was over, and I ended up alone at a table, crying and removing my makeup. That was an interesting one. I always had these vignettes I'd do, very theatrical. Very dramatic.

Everybody, all my friends, still call me that. "Catherine! Catherine—hey, tell me, how've you been?"

I say, "I'm doing great, darling."

They don't use my male name.

Adela calls me Catherine all the time.

It's part of me now.

LANDA LAKES: Things are constantly changing, and you see that even in the drag world.

Now when you go into a drag show here, you have all kinds of people. Gender has really geared up and changed. Our understanding of gender, our appreciation of gender as well. That's all changed. I would say that one of the things that drag has afforded me is to see the change, not only in society, but also within the drag world.

Because as it changed on the stage, so it began to change on the streets.

FRESH "LEV" WHITE: It was an interesting experience. It was so much fun. I think there's something about when we're joyful, how we help create joy in a space. So playful, carefree.

TUPILI LEA ARELLANO: A lot of trans people talk about how, when we're experiencing our true self, this euphoria comes. I believe it's sacred. I really do believe it's a sacred gift.

Performing in drag, I was euphoric. There's a power that comes with that, a hidden power we carry as two-spirit people, as people on the trans spectrum.

PART FOUR

* * * * * * * *

HORIZONS

* *

TWELVE

Later Evolutions

C. NJOUBE DUGAS: Yesterday was my sixtieth birthday, which is crazy.

Literally, I woke up in the morning yesterday, went in the bathroom, washed my face, and looked at myself. I said, "This is what sixty looks like? Weird. God, I never expected to make it past thirty."

I let fear rule me. I escaped in drugs and alcohol. At points of my life, I got really suicidal, because I isolated. And not until I opened my mouth and spoke the fears to my chosen family, could I laugh about it.

It's just amazing, being able to say I've been on this planet six decades. Part of me still feels like I'm twenty-one. My spirit is quite alive. I've got a lot of work to do here.

I made it past thirty! Now I'm sixty.

What the hell: I'm going to live.

SHARYN GRAYSON: I've had so many people tell me, "I've never seen a seventy-three-year-old trans woman. I never knew they existed. I can't even comprehend that."

I value myself. I know who I am. I know that I'm not going to accept anything less than what I think I'm entitled to. I don't want to take anything from anybody. I just want the opportunity to live my life, and that's it.

DONNA PERSONNA: I've made a lot of history. I'm here to make history. One example: there is a Spanish-language newspaper called *El Tecolote*. Two years ago, they featured me for International Women's Month. Donna Personna. They're seeing me not as a transgender person, but as a woman. I had this thing in my mind: how many Latinos are going to read this story? I just pray that I changed somebody's mind. Everything I do is like that.

It isn't over until it's over. It only gets better—or it should get better, and in my case, it is. I want people in their seventies and sixties to understand: you have less to lose by taking a chance on things, making an attempt. This is where you belong. Have that in your mind. Hone your confidence and know your worth. Right at this age.

It can happen for you if you're young at heart. Love what you do, and bring it. Bring it on. You can have anything in this life. I'm only beginning.

I'm seventy-six. My life is so splendid. I'm in love with it, I'm in love with life. It's a beautiful cocktail.

You can thrive, you can be magnificent at an old age.

TUPILI LEA ARELLANO: I'm still a street fighter. I thought by now I'd be so mellowed out. Oh, no, no, I still want to get in the street and kick ass, I still want to kick ass about racism—you know? I'm a peleonera, "Oh, I'm ready, I'm down." That surprises me because I really thought I wouldn't have this much fire for that still.

TINA VALENTÍN AGUIRRE: What strikes me about this current period of my life?

That I don't give a shit. I think I knew, learning from my elders, hearing it over and over again, that at a certain age, you just sort of stop—I don't know—giving too many cares about things.

I'm in these positions of leadership, in the last ten years, where I'm leading with that. That means you get all of me. A lot of times, organizations or collaborations want a part of me, but what they quickly learn is, ha ha, no, you don't get just part of me. You get all of me. You don't like all of me? I don't give a shit. It's too late!

I have a limited amount of time on this Earth. There's a max of how long I can be on this Earth in a way where I'm productive and healthy.

Whatever I'm doing, whatever job I'm in at the moment, it is finite, and if somebody pulls some babosadas—some nonsense—I do have empathy and compassion, but at the same time, it's not my job to fix somebody.

KB BOYCE: Now I don't care. I do not care. You get to a certain age, and you just don't care anymore. I no longer worry that people think I'm crazy, like back in the day when I was a kid, a punk rocker, and I thought, "People must think I'm insane." You can't change the way people see you. You can't change the way people think of you. We live in a society. We have to be seen by other people, and they're going to see you, with whatever biases they have. You can't do anything about that.

People are going to see me whatever way they see me, and it might have absolutely nothing to do with the way I see myself. That's okay. It has to be okay, because that's the way it is. Thinking like that is what makes it possible for me to simply try to exist in the world.

I have no regrets, you know? Here I am, almost sixty, no regrets. That's crazy to a lot of people.

ADELA VÁZQUEZ: It surprises me that I'm still alive, that I'm still healthy, that I'm having this conversation right now, that I understand life in this way that allows me to be free.

I'm a hippie. I'm old, with tremendous life experience. Happy by nature. Two of my therapists have told me I'm very intense! That makes me laugh.

Life has been very rich for me. I have had many experiences that I didn't know that I was going to be able to have. And that is a privilege.

This is my life. And that's all I have. So, why not live it how the fuck I want? It's my life. Nobody has the right to control it.

I have achieved freedom. I'm here in this life to be free. It's the only thing I crave in my life and I'm free. I'm free. It's amazing that I can say that.

This is one of the few times that I've said it, but it's true: I'm free. And that's amazing.

BAMBY SALCEDO: I am now knowledgeable about not just my own life, but the many issues that many of us encounter, we queer trans people within our society. I do have the privilege to be an academic now, as well. So I am able to understand certain things. I'm able to be a servant to my people. I am able to do what fills my soul, to just be a voice for many people who have not been able to speak.

It took me a long time to be where I am, today, feeling comfortable with myself, with my spirituality, with my sexuality, with other people, with my higher power, my Creator. It's taken me so much to become whole. I'm good, despite what it has taken for me to be where I am today. It has not been easy. But I also understand that everything that happened to me has allowed me to become the person that I am today. Like the multiple sexual assaults, both in prison and on the streets; the overdoses I was able to survive; the multiple suicide attempts; the violence that I experienced, physical and mental, not just by partners, but also by institutions, and just people in general. The hunger that I had to endure. The disgusting feeling like you're the lowest of the low because you had to exchange your body for food, or drugs, or even a place to stay. All of those things, like the tears when you're on the streets and just hoping that you're going to get some money for a place to stay, or some money to eat, or when you wake up in the morning at a park just thinking of what happened last night, what was I doing? Or when you are beat up by the police, or handcuffed to a bench for hours? Or when you're even assaulted by the very police, sexually abused by the police who are supposed to protect you, or when you're exploited as a minor for your body, or for work? All of those things. There are so many different things I can tell you, experiences that have shaped me to be who I am today.

And I am a whole person now. I'm a happy person. If I was going to die tonight, or tomorrow, I would die happy.

What surprises me most about this period of my life is that I'm living on cloud nine, as they say. My office here at TransLatina

Coalition is decorated with clouds. They're there to remind me that I'm in a beautiful place in my life, that I don't have to be tied down to what tortured me before, what hurt me before. Right now, for me, it's important to live in gratitude. As long as I live in gratitude every day, I am living my best life.

ANDRÉS OZZUNA: I live here in Oakland, and I own a company that makes alfajores, which are Argentinean cookies filled with dulce de leche. I've been growing this company for twelve years. This work is part of me. Cooking is my passion. I started because I missed the food from back home, I missed relatives or loved ones. So I started cooking out of nostalgia. I'd take what I made to many friends' parties, and they loved it. I'd always dreamed of having my own business, but I never had money to start one. I had no money back in Buenos Aires. Here, I had even less.

It took a lot. I came to the US when I was twenty-eight, and didn't start the company until I was forty. "I have this vision, I'm going to do this." It was hard for me to think that, that I could do it. I wasn't raised to believe in having dreams or seeking opportunities; I was raised in a manner where you keep your head down and do whatever you have to do. You don't envision anything. What vision? I had to learn to allow myself to think that way, to think that it's possible.

TUPILI LEA ARELLANO: Anything I do, I'm always wanting to bring value to my communities.

TINA VALENTÍN AGUIRRE: My day job is that I'm the director of the Castro LGBTQ Cultural District. For me, this work is tied together with how we support each other, how we support culture, homes, families, and businesses. That comes about through policies that are informed by people who lived lives like mine. Sometimes we have to fight for the right to just be happy where we live.

YOSEÑIO LEWIS: My latest thing right now is, I teach medical students at
Stanford University how to work with trans people and people of color,
so the patients are not exposed to that bias, or that ignorance. When
you encounter someone for the first time, if you are the doctor, you
have all the power. You make the decisions on whether or not this
person is sick, whether or not their symptoms deserve your attention,
and how much of your attention that person will get. And then on top
of it, this is the first time you've worked with a trans patient?
Your immediate questions can be full of bias. You start giving that to
the patient who's in pain and scared and unsure of what's happening
to them.

They're thinking they're dying, and you're here with, "So, when
did you know that you were trans? Have you started hormones? And
how many surgeries have you had?"

"I'm here because I can't breathe. Can we talk about how I can't
breathe?"

I wanted to eliminate that scenario occurring as much as possible.
It happened to me when I went to the doctor, many a time.

How do you think I feel when you don't even look at me?

When you read the note that says, "Identifies as"—and from then
on, it's just about that. It's not about: identifies as human being who
is having difficulty breathing. No putting oxygen on me, no nothing.
Just focusing on how many surgeries have I had, how much hormone
do I take.

I was so hurt by the way I was treated. I believed it was my responsibility not to allow others to go through that. So at least with some of
the Stanford medical students, I'm interrupting that process, of ignorance, of unintended cruelty.

I couldn't just be on the side of advocating for the patient. I had to
advocate for the doctor. I changed my attitude: I'm not doing this to
make life better for every trans patient. I'm doing it to make it better
for every doctor who encounters a trans patient. Because that doctor

is not being taught to see us as humans. We are specimens. We are test results. We are abnormalities. Not people. And I wanted that medical student to have the opportunity to see us as people.

And I didn't want trans people younger than myself, nonbinary younger people, to have to go through what I went through.

I've been doing it for almost ten years now, and it brings me such joy.

SHARYN GRAYSON: I am a senior trans woman, and I have lived in the San Francisco Bay Area for quite some time. I moved away, and I went back to the South, home to Dallas, Texas. I worked there with organizations and helped establish the first trans clinic that we'd ever had in Dallas. From there, I went on to Little Rock, Arkansas, to work with my dear friend, the original executive director here at the Transgender Gender-Variant & Intersex Justice Project, Miss Major Griffin-Gracy. I went there to set up her nonprofit organization and get it off the ground.

That was an interesting experience, being in Arkansas. I said, years ago, when people had asked me about Arkansas, "I'll never live there. You couldn't pay me enough." Well, I loved it! We lived in Little Rock, which is the state capital, and it was absolutely an amazing experience. Everything is downtown. I mean, all of the senators, all of the movers and shakers were right there. So, it was very easy access in terms of politically getting things done.

And not only that: surprisingly, there was a very united trans community there. Okay? And LGBTQ community. There were business owners. Professional people, doctors, lawyers. It was a very well-connected little community. That was surprising to me.

CRYSTAL MASON: I do dreaming workshops, trying to make time for us to dream again and make space to try to actually imagine the world that we want.

MS BILLIE COOPER: I am a sixty-four-year-old Black unapologetically transgendered woman. I'm a motivational speaker. I've been giving my story of hope and inspiration and encouragement, of being kind and honest. I tell my history. I tell the history I know about, about us being Black. You know, now we're transgender, but I remember when I was homosexual, when I was queer, when I was a faggot, when I was so many names, called everything but a child of God. Someone else, always labeling us. Some people are always going in a room, telling us what we should be called.

So many people don't want to fight, don't want to push against the establishment. But we have to; we really have to. Because we are oppressed, marginalized; white patriarchy holds us down; male misogyny holds us down. And you know, so many, many of my trans family don't get to use their voice because they're not asked their opinion and what they believe in. But I'm here, honey; I will speak until the lips fall off. And everything I say is true.

I've given speeches. I've talked to military professionals about what it's like being transgender, what it was like being gay, all the -isms. And recently, I finally stepped up to the plate, and wanted to be inside City Hall. After doing street politics for forty, forty-five years, I ran a campaign in San Francisco to be District 6 supervisor. It elevated me to a level that I could do anything. I went into it with my eyes wide open, my heart open, my ears open. I went to City Hall and did all the logistical paperwork, got on the ballot, and ran my campaign to the best of my ability. It was my first time, and there were some things I didn't know, but I saw it all the way through. I came in fourth place, but many people don't win on the first try. I'm going to run again if I'm alive in four years. I'm going to be more powerful and continue to tell my story. Because I am the community; I am District 6. I'm homegrown, forty years.

I would have been the city's first transgender supervisor. It's about time one of us is sitting in City Hall. I'm happy with my participation in the election. Oh, honey child, it wore me out.

I'm happy with where I am today. About thirty years ago, the life expectancy for a Black effeminate queer person was probably around twenty-eight, twenty-nine. And then as we moved forward, and forward, when we became trans, it got to like thirty-two.

I sit here: sixty-four! You know?

I have lived my life authentically. Out and proud.

KB BOYCE: You know, there are just so many layers to navigating the world, and trying to stay happy and productive. If I am sad and depressed, I don't get anything done. I realized that at a very young age. It was super important for me to find things that brought me joy so I could continue to do the things I needed to do. And I don't think I would be here as a trans elder running Queer Rebels had I not figured that out. I worked hard to find ways to have a little bit of happiness, just to keep the juices flowing, you know, keep that New York energy going.

I had no queer community of color as I was coming up. And here I am, all these years later. I feel like, "Wow. I created that. The kind of community I wished I had." Even though I'm poor, I am incredibly happy. I feel really fulfilled.

FRESH "LEV" WHITE: I think I could say I feel more comfortable just being seen for who I am. Sometimes it isn't about gender. It's about, when you're present, can you feel safe? Which, wow, has edges to it, growing up Black, being big. Mindfulness practice really helped me to get compassionate, to wake up. I'm waking up to so many things.

I was thinking about this the other day, too, working with a beautiful trans woman. She's about six-two, her shoulders are broad, and she's beautiful. Everything about her is beautiful. And she says, "Every time I walk down the street, there's people sneering at me, and giving me bad looks." So she's always looking down.

I said, "I know that that's happened, without a doubt. I'd like you to take on this challenge: to spend the next week assuming that everybody thinks you're beautiful."

She came back a week later, and it was amazing.

I've done this with other trans groups, and I do it with myself, when I go out. I mean, first of all, people are definitely following me in the store. But I'm looking for people who love, and connect. That's happening, too. So, how can I help create that experience for myself so that I'm more available to smile at some trans youth?

VIVIAN VARELA: Now, let me tell you something. There was a time when I was making fun and feeling embarrassed about butch, nonbinary, all these words. When people at church started talking about, I identify as queer, trans, nonbinary, whatever—I pooh-poohed it. I just put it off to the side. I'm like, "Oh my goodness, maybe I'm too old for this."

But in 2019, I was in the hospital because I was so ill, and I was awake at night. I would watch late-night programs. There was this program called *A Little Late with Lilly Singh*. And Lilly Singh was introducing Alok Vaid-Menon. And when Alok was talking about the nomenclature, how they were identifying themself, I began to understand differently. I began to question myself in a serious way.

I have felt, in my life, that I was never taken seriously. Who am I? Who is this little Mexican person? Even though my experiences are profound, anytime that I would try to give my opinion, share my story, no one would really listen.

I went up north to visit my siblings, in Redding, and I wasn't feeling well. I told my sister to take me to the hospital. In the ER, they had an electronic admission form. When it requested my signature, along with the signature, it said: "How do you identify: male, female, or nonbinary?"

And I'm thinking, "If I'm going to die, and this is going to be on my whatever the certificate is here, then I'm going to check off nonbinary, because truly when it comes down to the real nitty gritty, I am nonbinary. I'm going to take this seriously."

I was sixty-five years old.

TINA VALENTÍN AGUIRRE: We live in cycles of upheavals and progress, and regeneration is a big part of it.

LANDA LAKES: I already feel like I'm almost an ancestor. Almost. I have some niblings, two nieces and a nephew, and all of them are trans. I think it's a wonderful place to be, where you can help these younger people find themselves. My being the example within my family has helped to, I think, embolden them to become who they truly are. Sometimes, when you set precedents within your family, it makes that road easier. Because my road has been long and winding, and there's been lots of difficulty in it, especially with my family.

My sister did not like the fact that I came out, that I had a feminine persona. She was very hurtful about it. And now, she has two trans children, and she is super mindful of everything. She said to me that she didn't want them to have the same experience I had—which was really my experience with her. She wanted to make sure that she was supportive of them. I found that to be a really big win for them. It wasn't a win for me! She wasn't that nice. She wasn't that kind. But she has been super helpful for her children, and I think that's really remarkable. I'm very proud of that.

CHINO SCOTT-CHUNG: My dad died just last April. He was ninety-five when he died. He knew I was queer, he met my ex and my daughter, but I never came out to him as trans. That is the one thing I kept secret from him, that I'm trans.

I was with him right before he died. I spent his last week on earth with him. And as I was holding his hand, as he was on his deathbed, I came out to him as trans.

When I first went to Florida to see him as he was dying, I walked into his hospital room, and he looked at me and he said, "You look different."

I'd had top surgery. I love wearing V-neck T-shirts since having top surgery. I've always wanted to wear V-necks, but I couldn't because even if I wore a binder or really tight sports bras, my chest still really stuck out, especially in V-necks. Now I love them, and that's pretty much all I wear. These past thirty years, I've been very butch, very masculine-identified, and have passed as a man for the most part. Now it's a hundred percent of the time.

I was in my V-neck T-shirt when I walked in to see my dad. He looked at me and he goes, "You look different," and I'm thinking, "Yes, I look like a man."

I didn't come out to my dad when he said that, but I came out to everybody else in the hospital. I came out as trans to his friends' kids who came to visit him, because they remembered me as a little girl, a young girl.

It was hard. He'd been so critical. He's basically a traditional Chinese man. Traditional Chinese men want their kids to succeed, and the way they do it is through being critical. It's always what I'm doing wrong, rather than what I'm doing right, and trying to get me to do things right by telling me what I'm doing wrong. That's how I was raised, and I'm afraid of him. Even as this ninety-five-year-old man. I'm afraid to come out to him as trans even though it's so obvious, and he said right there, "You look so different." He's basically saying, "You look like a man," and I'm still afraid to come out to him.

I had been at his bedside every day since I had gotten to Florida, for two weeks. One day, I wasn't going to come in to see him, but the hospital called and said, "Your dad will be gone."

So I came in and held his hand. "The one thing that I haven't told you, and that I have had a really hard time telling you, is that I'm trans. I've had top surgery, I identify as a man and as masculine, and I pass as a man. I live as a man. I know you saw that." He was out of it. I think he heard me. I said that to him: "I think you hear me, and I think you see me. I just wanted to tell you this one last thing before you die."

I hadn't been close to my dad these past thirty years. I haven't been close to him since I was a kid. I forgave him for his abuse. He picked on me. I was the person he beat on more than my brother or sister. And it's so funny: I'm the person who's there with him as he's dying. My brother left him. My sister she said she wasn't going to go to his funeral. It was just my mom and I, and close family friends.

It meant that I could be my true self. I could tell him who my true self was even if he couldn't accept that. But I feel like he did. I feel like he could. In fact, in the last week of his life, he just seemed so accepting, of everything around him, including me.

YOSEÑIO LEWIS: Today in my journey, there's mostly looking back. I'm older. I'm disabled. For health reasons, I'm not able to be as involved as I used to be.

I want to be safe, physically safe. I want to have better healthcare than I'm currently receiving, and that means more advocacy work on my part. I want to know that wherever I move to next is the place that I can die comfortably.

STORMMIGUEL FLOREZ: Right now, I'm not a part of leather community. I'm too tired to do anything really, so I don't do that kind of performance anymore. But it has been such a big, important part of my life. Being leather or kinky, in a communal way, has been a continuous thread.

Part of it is, over the years, I've developed fibromyalgia. I have a lot of physical pain. My body does not do pain like it used to, it does not move like it used to. As I'm aging, I have a different relationship with my body. In some ways, I feel more protective of it.

My journey with my body has never been comfortable. I've never been comfortable with my body. I've tried. That ties in with my gender a bit. I started testosterone, and my body started doing certain things that I'd always wanted it to do. It started presenting in ways

I'd always wanted to present. I have facial hair, and my voice, I love my voice now. I love how I'm shaped, I love that basically I get to walk around in the world and be seen the way that I feel. That means I can go and explore other things. Testosterone in my body is a tether. It's a foundation. It keeps me safe in how I want to be, and feeling good, and that means now I can express in all kinds of ways.

NELSON D'ALERTA PÉREZ: In this period of my life, I've had a lot of health problems. I've had knee surgery, I'm currently recovering. But I'm always working with my spirituality, meditation, I return to art, art has been my healing and my focus. I keep learning to live with the people I'm with, and with myself. That's my present moment.

And if I had it all to live again, I'd do the same. I've had a glorious life journey. Incredible opportunities. There have been ups and downs, but in the end, it's been wonderful. And it's still full of colors, lots of makeup and dresses and feathers and hats and high heels. And laughter! So much laughter. So much joy in living. So much desire for life.

TUPILI LEA ARELLANO: I'm still on my journey of becoming my full self. It's lifelong, I don't care how old you are, I don't care how much you've studied and worked. Becoming ourselves is lifelong, and it's fluid. There's so much possibility in that.

CRYSTAL MASON: I see my life as a creation and a thing that creates. I feel like I'm in a constant state of creating myself still. If I'm lucky, I'll remain in that state until the moment I die.

* *

THIRTEEN

What Is Gender?

NELSON D'ALERTA PÉREZ: Who am I? Oh, a mix of many things. I'm a woman. I'm a man.

JOAN BENOIT: There's a spectrum.

MS BILLIE COOPER: I'm a much bigger, more intricate person than what people tell me I am, or what people see in me.

FRESH "LEV" WHITE: The term *dysphoria*, for me, means that our society has a dysphoric idea that there are only two genders. I've never taken that on. It's not mine.

DONNA PERSONNA: I'm my own universe.

C. NJOUBE DUGAS: Really, we're living in a nonbinary world.

VIVIAN VARELA: There is a queerdom. And we are part of it. All of us who are queer. Being in the queerdom is accepting yourself for who you are, loving who you love, and letting yourself be loved.

CHINO SCOTT-CHUNG: I have had multiple identities and still do. As far as my gender and sexuality, it has been a journey for me over the years and over time.

CRYSTAL MASON: When new things like they/them pronouns come up, new queer language, I get excited about it because I feel like that's a movement. I'm a forward looker. I know history, but I don't love history for the looking back. I like history for its implications for the future.

If you lay under a night sky, not in the city, out in the woods somewhere, you see the sky full of stars. So many. And you know there are so many more that are not even in your sight. I think about all those stars as possibilities. New words and new understandings also create possibility, which translates on a very micro level to, there might be one less person who feels alone. I think these words, these phrases, these pronouns, help create that space. You look up and you see a million stars. You know some of those stars are what's possible for your life. For me, it's like creating stars. We create possibilities when we create new words, and new understandings around those words.

FRESH "LEV" WHITE: When I do LGBTQ ally trainings, people are like, "What's with this alphabet, LGBTQIA?"

And I'm like, "We're just working our way back towards human."

C. NJOUBE DUGAS: They/them is not that hard. We say it all the time in the Black community. You say, "Where did Sheila go?"

"Oh, they went to the store."

We say that all the time, right? It's not that far of a jump.

KB BOYCE: My pronouns are they/them and he, and when I use *he*, it's not that often. It's usually because I'm in a situation out in Oakland where, you know, I'm with all these dudes, and of course they're going to see me as male, and they're going to call me *he*. And I'm fine with that. Otherwise, it's they/them, and he when it's needed.

I'm still learning. Everything changes all the time. But yes, I do now consider myself a transmasculine person.

My gender dysphoria is not around having to be a man, or feeling like I am a man. It's always been about being me, the person that I am.

CRYSTAL MASON: For me, the they/them recognizes that there's something more than the binary, that there are people who see themselves as either on a gender spectrum or not on any spectrum or outside the spectrum. Then also, I know that, again, this is not something brand new, the they pronoun. It's in historical use. I was discussing this with some friends the other day. One friend, she's my age, a straight lady, she was all mad about the they/them. She doesn't understand why. Why this, why that, and what's this all about?

And I basically said, "Well, it's evolution."

That's all it is. Because words are malleable and always have been.

I was trying to say to my old stuck-in-her-ways friend that this doesn't change anything about how you live your life or how you move in the world. It is simply the recognition that another person uses different pronouns or wants to be seen in a different way. It doesn't require anything from you except for empathy.

STORMMIGUEL FLOREZ: He/him pronouns are important to me, because there is no other alternative. If I spoke Spanish fluently, it would be "elle," you know? The nonbinary Spanish pronoun. I don't really relate to *they*, to me it feels vague, like it isn't about me. But *elle* would make sense to me. That said, in English, there's just no pronoun that makes perfect sense to me, so he/him is it.

FRESH "LEV" WHITE: My pronouns are he, they, and love. I identify as someone who is aspiring to live my life as fully as humanly possible, while also bringing experiences of love and compassion to the world.

Sometimes there's a part of me that feels male, but not quite man, because I identify the different challenges that younger cis men have to go through in our society that I got to step into but wasn't dragged into. There's a lot of trauma, especially around sexuality, that I didn't experience. So, I use the word *man* very loosely. But male. And so, honoring this masculine person that I am, *he* comes first, because that's the best tool that we have for identifying me as a masculine person in our world. And then, *they* is that gender expansive person who, I might not wear a dress—or I might, for a performance or something—but I'm not afraid of that like I was. I can throw a bow on and out-butch anyone, still. I'm talking to you, cis guys. So the *they* part is the human part, the expansive part, the "I don't need to have a gender" thing, call me Lev, or call me Fresh, just don't call me late for dinner kind of thing. Old joke. You've got to be older to get that one.

And then *love*. Ram Dass has a quote out there, it says, "No one knows your name until you take your last breath." And my response to that has always been, let mine be *love*. Right? When people talk about me, let them say that I was loving, that I was kind, and I was compassionate. That's my hope.

VIVIAN VARELA: I love the pronouns she/hers or he/his. And I have given myself my own label, which is a queerdo, in the queerdom. So, yes, I am considering myself to be male, female, two-spirit, a happy queerdo in queerdom.

ADELA VÁZQUEZ: I like the word *queer*. I don't really like the word *gay* that much. I like the word *faggot*, those words, because they are picante, because they're not nice. I like spicy things. And if I say "faggot," people think about it.

I understand that right now it's all about being politically correct, but I am not, really. At heart, I am not. I like to be a rebel, to provoke.

BAMBY SALCEDO: *Jotería*, for me—"faggotry"—it's just a beautiful word: all of us together. It's our strength. It's our beauty. It's our intelligence. It's our organizing. It's our love, our authenticity. It's just the colorful and beautiful people that we are. So, yeah. I guess to me, jotería is not just about one meaning, it's a compilation of beautiful and amazing things that makes me say: "We should own our jotería."

To me, it's power.

To me, it's just a beautiful, amazing, great thing.

DONNA PERSONNA: I endlessly am asked if I identify as transgender, and I say this. I look forward to a time when that's not a question and when that's not a thing. Can I just be a human being, magnificent? Just moving through life, being who you are and not having to explain it.

I'll say, "Well, when you find out how I identify or what my gender is, how is that going to change you or me? What are you going to do with that information?" I can tell you my shoe size or whatever, I hope you buy me some shoes.

CRYSTAL MASON: I favor labels. I know a lot of people are like, "Oh, I don't like labels," and stuff, but I feel like, for one, if you see labels as the beginning of a conversation rather than an end, then it gives you a door to the conversation. But also, the fact is, if you don't label yourself, other people will. And, for me, it's a matter of taking power back. And of being legible to other people who may be in alignment with your thoughts, or who are also genderqueer or also curious.

TINA VALENTÍN AGUIRRE: Yes. I am transgender. And genderqueer.

Now, that is expansive and inclusive. With the younger generation, it's not an issue. The older generation, we've had to negotiate with each other. With some of my trans mothers or tías—the ones who are still alive—we've had to have conversations.

In the eighties, with the club kids, the term was genderfuck. I did wear lipstick, and makeup, and lots of people knew me as Tina, and that's what I understood, "Oh yes, I am genderfuck." "Genderqueer" is now an acceptable version of "genderfuck," but ultimately, that's what I am.

For me, genderqueerness is different from being nonbinary. I am nonbinary. I am genderqueer. But the "queer" part of "genderqueer" is important, because it's me being upfront about the whole. Being genderqueer has always meant that. There's an aspect to the term that's countercultural, a radical element built into it. Genderqueer means you have to say the word *queer*, first of all. So if you have any hang-ups around the word *queer*, that's on you, but this is me, and that's it.

CRYSTAL MASON: I'm not quite sure where I first saw *genderqueer*, where that came up. Probably in the nineties. Yes, because in ACT UP, we were already starting to reclaim *fag* and *dyke*. It feels like *genderqueer* came out of Queer Nation. It just felt really right. I felt that word fit my feeling and my vision of myself. "That's the way I would like to describe myself."

One of the reasons why it fit was the words *gender* and *queer* together. To "queer" something is to question it, to break it down, to subvert. That's also a long-time definition of the word *queer*.

TINA VALENTÍN AGUIRRE: Gender can be art. We can be art. We are art. I am what I need to be in that moment, and if that includes my gender then I'm genderqueer.

YOSEÑIO LEWIS: We are given from Day One: "Oh, it's a boy!" "It's a girl!" And if it's a boy, oh, it's blue clothes, and it's trucks and cars, it's rough-and-tumble. And that's what we start from the beginning, so that that individual, who was just a newborn, begins to fashion themselves as a boy.

We are told, this is how a boy is. Any time you do anything that even remotely verifies that, or validates that, everybody and their mother is so happy.

"Ooh, he pooped!"

"Ooh, he hit that kid back when they said something about him!"

"Ooh, he knocked this down."

"Oh, he got a motorcycle and he just popped a wheelie—"

All things to reinforce that you are a man, you are a boy. You are masculine, you are real, you will conquer the world. As opposed to, "Look at him, he held the baby gently and kissed it on its forehead."

Or, "Look at him, he cried when he saw that play that was so amazing, just evoked so much emotion."

Or, "Look at him, he cooked a meal for his mommy because he loves her."

I was constantly in the "I kind of am, but I'm kind of not. I can claim this, but I can't claim that." There was always some part of me that wasn't enough, or was too much of something, so I couldn't be all of anything. And that led me to recognize: this is how I was made. If there's an overall label that I'm given, it doesn't mean I have to take on all of the connotations that came with that label. I don't have to conform and twist myself around to be something that other people can feel comfortable with. I can just go ahead and be who I am, weird as it may be to others, weird as it sometimes still is to me. It's still who I am. It's who my God has intended me to be. My higher power, my spirit, the universe—whatever the label might be—has given me this gift.

C. NJOUBE DUGAS: So my idea of gender today, and what I really truly believe in my heart—it may not be true, but I believe it to be true—is that given the freedom, people would just be like, "Oh, shit, I'm just nonbinary, man. Fuck, I got my mama, I got my daddy in me."

Femininity is beautiful. It's a way of gesturing, really. A way of celebrating. A lot of feminine women, like my mother, are badass. Kick-asses. It's a lot in the gesture, in the nurturing.

But on the other side of that coin, masculinity can be just as nurturing. In my father's time and in my brothers' times, they didn't get that. It's really changed over the years. Where masculinity is like, "I was born with this body, okay, but I'm still going to tell my kids I love them and play fairy with my daughter or whatever, or with my son, and that's okay."

There's this other thing, this hypermasculinity, that may not be true. There's a lot of fear associated with that, because there's no reason for you to be hyper-anything unless you need to hide or prove or show. Masculinity is simply a way of being, of gesturing, of feeling, being protected. I still have that thing, the provider; that's just who I am. It's also very nurturing, though.

There's some old-school hats that have certain beliefs. But it's just because we have these constructs of how you fit into a box. You start getting in that box in junior high, then high school. You go through your twenties and thirties swearing by that box, and you're going to protect that box. You get to your forties, and you're like, "Why am I in this box?"

In your fifties, you're like, "Oh, gee, I think everything I was taught, I need to relearn."

We all need to do so much healing.

Ah, it's such a complex question. It's a complex answer because it's all watery.

CRYSTAL MASON: I started, eventually, to understand that it was possible to see myself outside of the boxes that I knew.

TUPILI LEA ARELLANO: It is about being shape-shifters. We all do it in our own way, but we are shape-shifters. That's a medicine. It's very powerful if we know how to use it.

It's a medicine, it's for us, it's for our safety, it's for our development, it's for our well-being to be gender shape-shifters.

MS BILLIE COOPER: My gender is mine, personally. No one should ever come into anybody's space, or their life, and tell people their pronouns or their gender, what we should be called, what we need, or what they feel we need to be called. When I say *female*, or when I say she/her, it's my right.

It's my privilege to live my life as a senior Black trans woman, a woman of trans experience. I might not look like someone's mother, or their sister, or their aunt, but I will not let anyone come into my life and tell me I'm not a woman. Because I am a woman. I have always been a woman, even before I knew I was a girl back in the day. I don't have to look like what you perceive a woman to look like, America.

It's all about respect. If you want to be seen in an authentic, honest, true way, treat people with respect.

As I sit here today, my authentic self, I am a woman of loving and caring and honesty and truth. I'm unapologetically a Black trans woman, a Black woman of trans experience. And I won't ever let anyone take that away from me.

SHARYN GRAYSON: For Black trans women, there's something about the idea that you represent Black womanhood. Black femininity. All of those societal negative factors that come along with Black femininity, they come down to Black trans women, too. So now, you've got that layer that you have to deal with. It is hard. It has been hard for as many years as I can recall for Black trans women and Black women of trans experience to walk in their own power and light.

It's just—people don't understand. They don't have a clue. I just want to say that Black trans women are not the enemy. They're not. We're just people trying to be ourselves and live our lives, and that's it. We don't want anything but to be allowed to partake of the same things that everybody else wants. I don't want your husband. I don't. That's not my goal in life!

And certainly, I don't see Black women as a threat. Black women raised me. They were my models of femininity, and womanhood, and what I'm supposed to represent. I admire every Black woman that I see. I know it has not been easy for her. I understand that, so I support her.

But—I don't know. Somehow, a lot of Black women think that we're a threat. We're no threat to them. We're really your biggest supporters. We're not going to do the things to you that Black men do to you. They've done it to us, and many times, ten times more. So, why would I do that? I understand, and I support you. And all I ask of you is respect, like I respect you. You don't have to support me. Just respect who I am, and that's it.

I love so much about Black womanhood. The power and the strength. The innate power and strength that we have to have. We have no choice. It comes with the territory. You have to embrace that, and it makes you a very strong individual. There's a strength that comes with all of that—what do you call it?—gosh. All of that misery. I don't know. Again, I've been blessed, but I have seen it. I have seen the misery of life. I have seen people not accepted as human beings. I've seen all of that. But Black women have always had to . . . my mom, we can go back to my mom. After my dad died, my mom took care of us. And other Black women, you do what you have to do. Black womanhood is a source of power and strength. Even when you think you're weak, you have to have strength.

When you see a Black woman out here walking and looking good, smelling good, I admire that lady. I admire the hell out of her because I know that wasn't easy, to get there. The same thing for my trans women, my Black trans women, who I see out there. They're moving, and shaking, or they're in their careers. I admire that because I know that wasn't easy. I really know it wasn't easy for a Black trans woman. But that power, that strength, that sense of endurance that comes with—I don't know if it comes with it or if you're forced to do it—to me, that's what Black femininity is.

ADELA VÁZQUEZ: I have learned a lot about womanhood. I learned about respect, I learned about a place in the conversation, I learned how women get shut up. When there's a meeting and a woman is talking, then a guy comes and talks and is louder. I learned how to push society. I learned about humiliation. I learned about all that, and being humble. Being humble is far away from the male reality. "I'm the man, I'm the one in charge!" But humbleness is a beautiful quality in anybody.

Being a woman who is free means respect, means dedication. It means that you are going to do with your life whatever the fuck you

want. It means that you don't have to explain yourself for anything.
It's freedom of soul, of expression, of spirit. Free.

NELSON D'ALERTA PÉREZ: What it is to be a woman: a lot of strength, a
lot of spirituality, thoughtfulness, giving other people opportunities.
Women's intelligence strikes me as wonderful. Warmth, connection,
that's what I've learned. The warmth women have that's different from
men's energy.

What do I enjoy about being a woman? Everything. Everything,
everything, everything.

DONNA PERSONNA: I come preapproved. Are you looking for approval?
Do you want acceptance? If I would like to get a mortgage for a house,
then I might ask a bank for approval for a loan—but for you to like
me? No.

I feel at home. When I walk into a room, I own it, I own that
room. See, that's self-acceptance. Self-love. Self-acceptance is the sexi-
est thing going around, everybody wants it.

I don't compare to anybody else. I'm unique, and I'm very happy
with that. Gender, for me personally, is: who I am, that's the gender
that I am.

LANDA LAKES: I'm not going to say that some days I feel like a woman,
and some days I feel like a man, which is sometimes how some people
see gender. I don't feel that. I feel like I'm this crazy balance of masculine and feminine, and that's sort of where I'm at. Are all people
in that same spectrum? I don't know. Because my brothers are very,
very masculine, and they don't want to be confused with the feminine side. When people talk about gender fluidity, for some people it's
true, but for others, we end up being hardwired in some way. I think I
might be hardwired toward more feminine things.

These days, most of the time, I identify as being two-spirit.

Because two-spirit leads me to that balance of male and female energy that resides within me.

When I do things that are more ceremonial, I always find myself leaning more towards the feminine side. When I go to a powwow, I'll be in women's regalia. It's not the same as being in drag. Drag is putting on a show, and entertaining someone, whereas when you're doing something like a stomp dance, or you're doing powwow, it's about being a part of that community. There's a difference between the two.

It's a presentation of my spirit, I think, more than anything else.

When I have to tick something off, you know, when it asks for gender, I'll often say two-spirit.

JOAN BENOIT: So, two-spirit: it's a different kind of identity, and teaching. Ancient teaching. We have stories throughout the tribes of queer people. How many gender pronouns do they have in Diné Bizaad? It's got to be like thirteen. It's ridiculously high. In my tribe, there are stories of women who take on the role of men. They're always women, but they can be warriors, and they can take wives, and people will give them children to raise. That's their family, and that's their life. They're usually identified as male, but not always. It just is. That's just people.

I feel like I live in that kind of way. I've taken a wife and I just am. So there's this idea in two-spirit that you have the spirit of both a man and a woman. There's a masculine and a feminine. That's for sure true in my life. That's where I am. I'm in the in-between. I have both masculine and feminine: I'm both. It's interesting, because before I knew any of my own tribal history around two-spirit people or queer people, I was already in those places. We are the holders of history in the Ojibwe Tribe. We are the caretakers, and we are the ones who are there for people when they die. That's been my role, my trajectory, in so many different ways.

LANDA LAKES: When I first started hearing "two-spirit" used, it wasn't something that congealed with me very well. Because we already had terms and phrases back home. We have "hatukiklanna," which talks about somebody who's mixed, man and woman, you're a little bit of both. I was just like, "I don't know, is this two-spirit thing very Radical Faerie?"

Nothing against Radical Faeries, but they do have a tendency to take from Indigenous cultures, and it's cherry-picking, they pick and choose what they want to put into their stuff. I didn't want to fall into a trap like that, so I was very cautious. I knew where it was coined, at a two-spirit gathering in Winnipeg, I learned the history of it, but at the same time, it took me a year or two before I finally was like, "Okay, I think I can embrace this term."

JOAN BENOIT: I don't know that I have both spirits, per se. *Two-spirit*'s a little rough of a term for me, because I have one spirit. Just one.

LANDA LAKES: One of the key things, at least for me, when I think about two-spirit people, is that spirit part, the spirituality part. I think it's very important for a lot of Native people to have this spiritual part. A lot of times when you come to an urban setting—for me, I grew up in Oklahoma, so coming all the way out here—you lose some of that spiritual connection. Because back home, you have stomp grounds, and your family, and you do your stomp and everything, and it's all tied together. But you come out here to an urban setting, and that's all gone, so where is your spirituality? You sort of feel like you lose some of it. Embracing the term actually helped me think that I'm not losing my spirituality, I'm still able to hold onto it.

FRESH "LEV" WHITE: In the eighties, *nonbinary* was a term we didn't use. The closest I got to that term was when I was hanging out with some Black and Native women in DC, and the identity there was *two-spirit*. That was something everybody used in that space, people of color. It was so spiritual. I identified as two-spirit at one point, but I wasn't out blasting it everywhere.

C. NJOUBE DUGAS: The first time I encountered the term *two-spirit* was in 1993.

I was invited to a sweat in the Oakland Hills. Akiba—a really strong, beautiful, tall Black woman in the lesbian community who knew everyone—had built a sweat lodge. I had never sweat before. I thought it was for Native American people and their spiritual life. Charmaine held the sweat, she's native Lakota people. It was all women in the sweat, all women of color except for my partner at the time. Listen. I mean, it was just beautiful.

We went through this process and they would say, "Two-spirited, two-spirited, two-spirited."

I'm like, "What do you mean?"

"We carry both, we recognize both male and female energies."

I thought, I really like how that sounds, that's true.

At that time, in the early nineties, that idea of two-spirited—I don't know. I really liked the way that felt in my body.

FRESH "LEV" WHITE: Later, when I got to the Bay Area, it was totally different. *Two-spirit* was exclusively reserved for Native and Indigenous people. I try to be really respectful of that.

That's about who we are, too: culturally, regionally, ethnically, we all have different ways of identifying who we are, which is something that I find absolutely beautiful about our community.

LANDA LAKES: You know, at the organization I belong to, Bay Area American Indian Two-Spirits [BAAITS], we often say that we're here to restore and regain what two-spirit people once were. We'll never be able to attain that or anything, but I'll be darned if it isn't good to be included, you know what I mean? To finally be back as a part of our own people, and be back in that circle.

We'll constantly talk about our life, our family and our tribe, how it's all a part of this large hoop, or this large circle—and it's like: put your money where your mouth is. Because in the eighties,

it wasn't necessarily so. Some people who came up to the city, they
left the reservations to escape and be a part of the LGBT community.
Sometimes, when they passed, while they were still in the city, their
families back in the reservations didn't even want them to come back.
Didn't want them back in their pine boxes. They didn't really care. So,
we've seen a huge shift. I think it's beautiful that people don't feel like
they have to leave their family anymore.

VIVIAN VARELA: I am both male and female and the native language
expresses itself saying two-spirit. I am two-spirit. There is a synergy
within me that is both male and female. I can feel it.

It's sanity for me, because if I had to be one or the other, I would
be crazy. I would not be able to function as a human being.

TUPILI LEA ARELLANO: I definitely consider myself to be on the trans spectrum. I identify more as a two-spirited person, and I'm very happy to
be a transgender person. Trans people have helped me do my deeper
work in my gender. If nonbinary-ness had been an option, if trans had
been an option, as a child, I wouldn't have grown up with as much
trauma.

Some people will say, "Well, what are you?"

And I'll say, "I'm a lesbian, I'm a dyke, I'm two-spirited, and I definitely belong on the trans spectrum."

I hold all of those things sacred and dear, and I love them. I go
to the Dyke March, dance my ass off, I go to the Trans March, Gay
Pride. Those are mine. All of them are mine.

Whenever I need to shape-shift in and out of communities, I do it.
And I do it well. I do it respectfully. Unless somebody messes with me
with racism or something: then the respect is out the window.

JOAN BENOIT: There's just no one way of being. And you can't pin something down. I've transitioned through so many identities and gender
presentations throughout my life. I feel like I'm settling more and

more into my own skin, the older I get. In a lot of ways, I defy labels. I'm not just this or that thing.

I don't necessarily identify as trans, although I really get how young people, now especially, have more freedom to move in that direction. And I have no doubt, if we'd had that kind of language when I was coming out, things might have been very different for me. Maybe I would have identified as trans. I don't know. Could be. I can see the possibilities.

I am masculine of center. I present as butch. I like to wear the clothes I wear and to dress the way I do. I'm comfortable. It makes me feel strong. We're a dying breed, us butches are. In one sense, I embrace that label as it connects me to other masculine-of-center women in my circle that I see. We're few and far between anymore. There's not as many butches in the younger generation.

My gender is fluid.

I'm gender fluid. I'm Indigiqueer.

And when I say fluid, I feel like I don't fit a mold.

Identity eludes me. Am I two-spirit? Yes, kind of. That's why I identify as Indigiqueer. I'm Native queer. I am in the in-between. I'm in flux. I'm Joan.

STORMMIGUEL FLOREZ: I am not so attached to being masculine. I'm not so attached to being thought of as a man, or presenting masculine. I do have facial hair. I have long hair, now I put it up. I wear sarongs sometimes, I wear muumuus—I can be very feminine and embrace that. I've been trying to wear brighter colors, and that feels really good. I like to femme it up. I used to wear earrings, but my ears don't like them so much. But I have a coral necklace that was my mother's that I love wearing.

So yes, there are ways that I like to adorn myself now that are considered to be feminine, and I love that. I love to get to explore because I am based in the body that I want to be in, the gendered body that I want to be in. Testosterone is the thing that does that for me.

I respect everybody's gender presentation and gender identity and just gender, period. Because there are as many different genders as there are humans, right? We all do this in our own way.

ANDRÉS OZZUNA: I learned that I could create my own masculinity. That was an important thing for me to realize. Because I couldn't act like something I wasn't, do things that—I don't know—that bros do, or whatever. It doesn't come naturally, that's not the way I am, so I can do something else. It's about giving myself permission to create. It's about saying, "Well, I can be the man I want to be. I don't have to be the man who was socialized as male."

I think we can listen to ourselves. And ask, "How do I want to treat society? And how do I want society to treat me?" And create what we want. As a man, I still want to be kind, I want to be mindful, I want to be this and that. Your gender doesn't have to get in the way of how you want to be with others, with the world, with your family, with anyone.

We receive the message that if you're a woman, you have to do X, Y, and Z. If you're a man, you have to do that and that. But what if no matter what we are, we create what we want to be? Create the world the way we believe it should be?

TUPILI LEA ARELLANO: I shape-shift without having to change my clothes. I know how to shape-shift, and I can dive into the masculine.

CHINO SCOTT-CHUNG: Oh, it's funny, you just don't know what life is going to bring you. Here I am, an Asian, transmasculine guy who has all these experiences of being a little girl, being a lesbian, just all my different identities and personas. My whole life, I have studied what it means to be masculine. I have watched other men; I have learned how to be in relationship with other men. I have tried to figure out what masculinity means to me. I've studied what it means, and how to be a man. I'm still coming to learn what it means for me to be a man in this world.

It's weird. For example, I went to Reno for one of my birthdays, and I was at a poker table with this guy, a big guy. And we just really bonded. Here I am, five-six, not a big guy at all, and this guy is like six-two or something, an ex-linebacker for a football team, but this really sweet guy, a white guy. When it was time for me to leave, as I got up, he got up, and he just showed me this kind of respect that I never imagined another guy, especially this big linebacker guy, would show me. He said, "I really enjoyed getting to know you, and I hope we can keep in touch."

I remember being amazed that this big linebacker guy would be so bonded with me as another guy, and just show me this kind of respect I never thought I would have. And that's the thing that amazes me the most, these big guys, who I think are the ultimate form of masculinity, are showing me this kind of respect as another man, a little Asian man. I never thought that was possible. I never thought that I would have or be able to form these kinds of relationships.

But the other thing about that, though: I will never be able to get any closer to these guys. I imagine that they do not think I'm trans. I would have to come out to them as trans. I can never get beyond that kind of relationship with them. I imagine when I do come out as trans, that will change everything, our whole relationship. And we probably won't have one after that. That's what I imagine.

FRESH "LEV" WHITE: I was born and labeled female at birth, in this body, and I honor and embrace masculine energy. I don't know where it comes from. It's just part of who I am. And so, that's me.

YOSEÑIO LEWIS: What I love the most about my masculinity is that it has not been so infused with the way I was taught that there's no room for change. I love that there can be flexibility in both my masculinity and my femininity, that I don't have to dissuade myself from acknowledging either of them. And I don't have to dissuade others. I don't have to hold on to the prejudice that I carried with me from childhood that said, "Well, if a guy wears a dress, then he's sick, and he's probably a molester." That's what I was taught, by men in dresses every Sunday. I'm taught by men in dresses that men in dresses is a bad thing!

I can be the man who will cry at the drop of a hat, and is not ashamed of it, is proud of the fact that I am so aware and in touch with my feelings, supposedly a feminine trait. Show me some Hallmark card, show me some silly commercial of babies walking for the first time, I am all over it with the tears. And I'm no longer ashamed of that. If that is a feminine trait, then thank God I am aware of my feminine traits, and that I accept them, because that is what makes me human.

I am the guy who will say, "My favorite color is pink." It always has been. It's a soothing color. You see pink, and you just want to get wrapped up in it. It feels safe. It feels like going home.

"Well, what the hell, man, you're supposed to like black or red or blue, blue-blue-blue—"

I love blue! I love it. But pink is my favorite. That causes so much consternation for people who have their silo built for them, and they've lived in it forever, and they don't even see the walls. They don't see the borders. That's just how it is. You can choose to stay in that silo, but you can't choose to pretend like the rest of the world doesn't exist, because we do. If you don't like a certain way of being, then don't be that way. But don't deny it to somebody else.

VIVIAN VARELA: I am choosing not to identify as transgender. Because I do not have a feeling of—what is that word? Dysphoria, or dis-connect? I don't feel a disconnect with my body. I am satisfied with being in the body of a woman. I'm happy with my body and how it functions with my libido, and how that works. I'm grateful that it still does. You know what? It's still alive and well. Unless there's some kind of trauma, the sexual desire part of being human does not die until you die. That part of you will always exist and be active as long as you are being loved, cherished, and cared for.

CRYSTAL MASON: I was never really comfortable, actually, thinking of myself as a lesbian. That's for one. Then I saw myself as a dyke for a long time, and I still see myself as that. For years, I've identified as a dyke—as butch—but mostly also genderqueer, and that was before *nonbinary* came out.

At the end of the day, I carry all my identities with me. I don't leave them behind. All of that—the dyke, the butch—all of that is still part of me and can come up at any moment if I'm just being myself and being expansive.

That's also one of the things—I like that term: *gender expansive.*

C. NJOUBE DUGAS: I identify as nonbinary. I do identify on the trans spectrum. I identify as a woman. I don't necessarily identify with a term because, again, I think we all hold both. We hold both masculine and feminine, we hold a piece of our father and a piece of our mother, right?

I'm kind of complicated.

I'm all of it.

TUPILI LEA ARELLANO: I try to explain to people who don't understand trans. I say, "You know what? This is about your freedom. The nonbinary people, they're the leaders of justice and freedom for us queer people. They are the leaders because they are refusing to step into one of those two choices of pink or blue. Nonbinary people and trans people are leading the fight for freedom for all peoples, from the prisons of gender."

C. NJOUBE DUGAS: Identifying as nonbinary means I get to do and be and act any damn way I want, and you could love it or not, period. There's a freedom in that. I don't have to define anything, you know what I mean? I don't wear dresses, but if I felt like it, ha, that's my business.

It just doesn't feel like I'm in a box.

Even though it has a name. There's a name just so people can bite into something.

I feel like if it was a box, every side of the box is laying down on the floor, you know what I mean?

So this is me.

There are going to be people who love me for me and there are going to be obviously people who have a problem with me. But actually, they don't really have a problem with me. They have a problem with something inside of them that they really need to look at, and that's the deal. So it gives me an opportunity to just say, "Okay, well, am I going to allow that to affect me today or am I just going to say a silent little prayer and just keep it moving? And I hope you get well, I hope you get better, I hope you get *free*. I hope you get free from the bullshit that somebody taught you."

CRYSTAL MASON: At sixty-one, I'm still thinking about my gender, still questioning things that I've accepted and ideas and thoughts that maybe I've put aside, like the gender binary.

I mean, I grew up with that, too. But then, when you're open to new things, and you're thinking about things, you start to realize that, like everything else, gender is created.

Then my feeling is: anything that is created can be 1) torn down, and 2) rebuilt.

I feel like I'm this project where sometimes I tear a certain piece down, or off, to build something else back new.

STORMMIGUEL FLOREZ: Being trans, to me, is just an awesome thing. I love being trans. That's my gender really: I'm trans. And if I could come back and choose how I came back, I would be trans for sure. I'd never wish that I was born in any kind of cis way.

I love how I am in the world, and who I am.

I love my body.

I love my gender.

I love being queer. Yes.

C. NJOUBE DUGAS: I'm remembering what it was like being on my Schwinn. As a kid, I had the baddest Schwinn in the neighborhood: banana seat and the handlebars and the little horn. And just jumping on that bike and whipping off my shirt and being free.

It's all about child's play. It's about freedom. We come here like that, and then this society pushes us and pulls us and puts us in this box, and we're all boxed up. It's about crawling out of a box to know you're in another box, to crawl out of that box to know, oh shit, you're still in a box, but you're getting closer.

So the bottom line is getting free.

I just want everybody to just get free.

＊ ＊

FOURTEEN

Thoughts for Younger Generations

FRESH "LEV" WHITE: What I want younger generations to know: we're thinking of them. We know that they're coming. We are all, in our own ways, making way for them.

CRYSTAL MASON: Part of me feels like the job of my generation is to create the conditions where our young gender-nonconforming kids of color can live their best lives, whatever their lives may be.

I want them to be able to live the lives they imagine for themselves.

It's part of our job as elders to believe in movement and change.

NICKY CALMA: I'm so happy to see kids who realize they're trans, because that didn't happen before. Things were different before. It was more challenging.

KB BOYCE: What strikes me the most is seeing the change that has come about in acceptance and support, especially of trans kids, you know? Taking your kids seriously if they say something. Not laughing at them, but saying, "Okay. I get it. You feel different, let's explore that, let's help you figure this out." That change means the world to me.

For example: for one of the sold-out performances of *The Red Shades*, where I was an onstage musician, someone I know brought their preteen kid who identifies as trans. That kid brought four of their friends, all of whom identify on the trans spectrum. And they came to this trans superhero rock opera. They loved it. They took pictures of themselves afterwards with cast members, doing the little heart sign with their hands. They ran around and got all of our autographs. And I was just in heaven. I wish I could have had that, sure, as a kid, but that's fine: I'm able to be here now, and see that change, see them getting this acceptance. That change means the world. It's super important. I'm just happy that I'm still here, seeing it. Because I mean, I've been around for a long time, and it was not like that back in the day. Nowhere near it. It's amazing.

As they become adults, they're going to be so comfortable with themselves. That's the change that's coming, you know? The change is already happening.

FRESH "LEV" WHITE: Now people are coming out so early. And so, I want to give thanks to all of our transestors, and our trans elders, and trans people who are making space, and all the parents that are more open and loving. What inspires me is that these young people get to walk closer to their divine selves. They get to walk more authentically. While there's still going to be suffering, there's this possibility of them taking more space, of creating more loving space for others as well.

ANDRÉS OZZUNA: It's good to share stories. I don't know that I offer things to younger generations as much as they do to me. I think they really offer me a lot more—I've learned so much from them.

Our generation can offer history. These young folks are super trans, while super young. Well—there's a history of people who didn't live that way, who didn't have the joy of realizing they were trans. If you listen to those stories, you might find something beautiful.

I love seeing these young folks and saying, "How beautiful, that they are so young and can do what they want to do." I have an employee who's twenty-six years old and is about to get top surgery.

I watch him move through the world, and I go, "How wonderful, the freedom he has." I love it. I love it. Then I tell him some of my stories and he goes, "Woah!"

He's on testosterone. He's got the whole world before him. It's wonderful.

STORMMIGUEL FLOREZ: When people ask me things like, "What advice do you give to young people?" I'm like, "I don't have advice for young people, I just want to hear what I can learn from them." Because the things that young people are thinking about are very enlightening to me. I expand and stretch my way of thinking, and that's really important.

JOAN BENOIT: The younger generation has a grasp on gender identity in a way that my generation never did. But in a way that our ancestors fully embraced.

It's really quite amazing to me. I feel like I have a lot to learn from these young people.

Oh my gosh, these young people! It's not just with the language and ability to ask what somebody's gender is. Their view of the world is amazing. They have more of a sensibility of the world than we did. I think they also know more about the perils of the world. Whether it's the seven-year-olds asking me what my pronouns are, or the people hopping in one of our vans at work and heading to Sacramento to work for policy change. They're more engaged. I have so much hope for these young people.

NICKY CALMA: When I was young, I didn't have any role models. I don't want to be a role model. I just want the young ones, the new folks coming in, to see that we can succeed. We can do something. We can be productive. We can be meaningful. We can be at that table for decision-making. We can.

CRYSTAL MASON: There's been several walkouts in high schools across the country—mostly straight kids, in support of their trans and queer classmates. That gives me hope. There are just more conversations. Social media is a shit place, but it also fosters conversations.

One of the good things I hope can come of this is a lessening of shame. Because shame is really the killer. I'm hoping that young, gender-nonconforming people of color see themselves included, because so often, in the mainstream, when people think about gender-nonconforming people, it's usually a slim white person. I'm hoping that gender-nonconforming young people of color understand that they are part of—and also the creators of—possibilities.

You don't have to be asked to come to the party.

You are the party.

I'm hoping you feel that.

NELSON D'ALERTA PÉREZ: Live with dignity. And without fear. You've got to lose your fear. Fear will not help you endure. Nor will lack of information. Inform yourself. Educate yourself, so you can have the support you need to create your life, with dignity and respect. That's what I'd say.

Dignity, lots of dignity. Lots of respect for your own self.

ADELA VÁZQUEZ: Being yourself is best. You don't have to lie. You don't have to pretend. You can be a beautiful transgender person. Being a transgender person, you can empower yourself—you are who you are. You can be a beautiful Latina transgender that came from the middle of the fucking jungle, and you are beautiful. That beauty is not just skin; it comes from within. When you're beautiful inside, that's going to show. Don't lie to yourself. There's no need. There's always somebody that's going to listen to you, there's always somebody that's going to say, "Come here." There are good people in life and there are bad people—but there are good people. Think about that, always.

I want young people to go to school, regardless of your gender or whatever. It's very important to read. All those people that went before us and that went through shit, they did it for a reason. They did it for us to be happy.

Work with what you have. Sometimes you have very little, sometimes you have a lot. But we all have a story, we all have something to say. We have a story to tell. Think about that.

LANDA LAKES: There will always come a point where you have to decide what road you're going down. We all have a road to walk, and nobody else is on that road with us. We have to walk that road. Sometimes it's going to be bumpy, sometimes it's going to be hard, and sometimes, you're not going to see where the path is leading ahead of you, so you just have to keep going.

My mother gave me some advice many years ago that resonated with me my whole life. She told me, "You can't live your whole life pleasing everybody else. You have to do what's right for you."

She probably meant something completely different, but I thought, "You know what? I can be as flamboyant as I want. I'm going to be outside the box. I can be who I am." That stuck with me throughout my life.

I would give younger queer and trans people the same advice. I would say, "Don't wait until the autumn of your years before you realize that pleasing everybody else isn't going to please you."

DONNA PERSONNA: Don't get caught up in approval, "Does that one like me, are they okay with what they see?" Because when you do that, you're giving them some power over you.

Approve of yourself, approve of yourself. I would encourage you to have your power come from you. How did they find out what's right for you? And what happens when they say you're okay? And if no one ever says you're okay, then you're never going to be okay? That's not for me. I know I'm okay, I'm more than okay, I'm fabulous.

I'm going to ask you to love yourself.

I don't know what you're going through, but: honey, love yourself, everybody else is wrong.

CHINO SCOTT-CHUNG: I think about all the angst, and all the years I spent worrying about if people would accept me, being afraid that I wasn't trans enough. When I first started talking about that in trans communities, these guys were like, "We accept you." Of course they did. These guys hadn't ever not accepted me for who I am, who I perceive myself to be.

It's like: don't worry about it. Be who you are. Especially now, when we're talking about gender fluidity. No matter what your gender expression is, whether it's one thing now, a different thing tomorrow, or a different thing ten years from now—like me, I've transitioned and changed, my identities have changed massively over the years—let it change. Let it be who you are now and who you might be tomorrow. In all your glory and glorious gender expressions, be yourself. Don't worry about it like I did.

Or if you do, just remember what I shared about Christopher saying "call me 'he,'" as one of those first trailblazers. You don't know. You might be—and you will be—one of those trailblazers when you are yourself in all your expressions of who you are.

MS BILLIE COOPER: If you don't have the tools within you to come out or to speak about being your authentic self, or you don't understand what you're going through—never give up. Just keep pushing. Keep moving it forward. Keep asking questions, keep being a good person, search people out. Go see a psychiatrist or therapist if you have to. Talk to family members or friends or acquaintances. Never give up; never, ever give up. Because everyone deserves a chance. Everyone deserves to be all they can be and to live their authentic life. To be their authentic self.

Talk to trusted support, pull it together, and never let anyone tell you what you can't do. We can do anything and we can be anything we want to be.

SHARYN GRAYSON: First of all, you have to stand firm in your—I could say femininity, for younger trans women, but that's not all it is. You have to stand firm in who you are, in yourself. You have to understand who you are, the value in who you are. You have to set goals for yourself. They're not going to be easy, necessarily, but they're achievable.

Value yourself. Make sure you know who you are. Don't allow anybody else to interpret to you, or to make you believe that you're anyone else. I mean, that's all I could offer. That's all I could offer.

TUPILI LEA ARELLANO: I want young people, people of color, to know we're much more powerful than what we believe. We've been talked out of our medicines and our powers. That all has to change.

C. NJOUBE DUGAS: If you don't have a chosen family, understand no matter what you feel inside, they have already chosen you. All you have to do is just walk up and introduce yourself and say hi.

It's so important to have people who experience the same things you do, or with whom you're free to talk. You're free to go over to their house and put on makeup, or put on a suit and tie, or learn how to tie a tie. It's so important to have fun with that, and not feel uncomfortable or feel like you'll get judged.

In our community, being isolated or feeling alone can be really dangerous. No one wants to see you alone. There's a family out there for you. Just go fly. Go somewhere, sit in that group, and they'll accept you. We just do.

Coming out, now, there's more resources. Parents are more open. You can find people that are there to lift you up. That's also people there to tear you down—so find your people.

You'll find your folks. You will.

Never, never feel you're alone.

VIVIAN VARELA: Find people who love you for the unique individual that you are. Hopefully you have the privilege and honor of having at least one friend. At least one friend who will listen to you. Find someone. If you have to start with therapy so that you can get back on track, okay, do it. Do not isolate. And don't make yourself try to fit in. You just have to be yourself. Even if it means you only have one great friend. Because you're not going with the crowd. You have to be yourself all the way, all the way.

CRYSTAL MASON: One of the things we know is that for trans and gender-nonconforming kids, all they need is one supportive person in their life. Just one.

JOAN BENOIT: If you want to make a family, a queer family, find people that you love and make a commitment to be there for them. Make sure that it's given back. And that's it. That's all it takes.

   If they're the people that you love and who love you, you don't even have to be romantically involved with them to be a family. That's something that sometimes comes and goes. Romantic love isn't always a permanent love. I think the queer community has shown that. Lesbians, especially, are extremely adept at that. "These are people that we've made a commitment to, and even if we're not in a romantic relationship with them anymore, that doesn't make them any less family. It just means that the relationship has changed."

KB BOYCE: Life is hard. Adulting is hard. All the things are hard. It's hard to stay positive, but I feel like that is the key. Find things that bring you joy, and keep that positivity up so that you can function and move things forward.

VIVIAN VARELA: Know and see that we, in our own individual ways, have been in battle. And the battle is for our own integrity. We had to stand our ground.

I am unique. I am an individual. Even my queerness is expressed uniquely. There is no one like me. There is no one like you.

The key point is to maintain that integrity, have that tenacity of spirit as you go through life. Tenacity: someone says, "You can't do that." Well, yes you can. You find a way.

TINA VALENTÍN AGUIRRE: I'm sorry that you're still having to deal with so many fucked up things, because humans are flawed. And none of this—the horrible parts, how there's rape, murder, oppression—is going to go away. They're a part of our DNA, the same way that hope, and love, and beauty are a part of our DNA.

So what I'd say is, first: I'm sorry.

And: you're welcome.

Like, this is what we are. I hope that you can take something away from this.

BAMBY SALCEDO: Something we need to understand is that it hasn't been easy to arrive where we are. That others have fought for us to have the little we have today. That today, we have many things that many of our sisters—or we ourselves—did not have.

DONNA PERSONNA: I want you to know that you are standing on the shoulders of those that came before you. We took the "arrows of outrageous fortune," Shakespeare's words, we took the hits, and if you're enjoying anything today, it's because of what happened before. Learn your history if you can. Don't shy away, "Oh, that's not relatable, that doesn't resonate for me because it was so long ago." No: that's who you are. And if you can, say thank you to those people.

TUPILI LEA ARELLANO: We are valuable living, walking, talking archives of how we won the privileges that younger generations are enjoying now. It didn't fall out of the sky. Some of us want to be seen, and we want to be respected and honored for what we've done and what we've

given. Please know your history and your herstories, the things that
we have done. It's recorded, there's so much available.

NELSON D'ALERTA PÉREZ: I believe that everything is like a staircase. If
we hadn't been insistent, what's happening now wouldn't exist. So it's
important for people to be aware of everything we went through, all
the pain people experienced.

ADELA VÁZQUEZ: Old people have the key to the future. It's so refreshing
to talk to old people, and you learn so much if you just listen. They
have a wonderful life. They have a beautiful, beautiful way to address
things. And they already learned the crap.

We opened the door. We were once young, and we dreamed of the
future. Some of us got there and some of us never got to meet it. There
were a lot of transgender people who died along the way.

C. NJOUBE DUGAS: This is a Black thing: I'm just going to say it. There are
people in the Black community that have been around for so long,
they just cannot seem to get it straight. Be gentle on them. Really,
when someone hits sixty and they're told, "Please don't call me 'she' or
don't call me 'he' anymore, call me 'they/them,'" they're going to mess
up! But you gotta be gentle with them, you gotta just keep reminding
them in a kind and loving way. They really want to try. But when we
attack them, they become more resistant, right?

Pronouns are really important, and I think it's even more important that people respect them. I use they/them. Most people don't
have a problem. The older population does. Sixty plus, seventies, and
I don't even mess with people eighty and up. They're used to saying,
"Okay, Mama, child, girl."

I'm like, "Okay, Mama, right."

It does feel weird, it just doesn't land right. It used to piss me off;
I would internalize it and be burning up inside. But I also have to be
gracious. Some people may never get there, right? I never thought I'd

see a Black president, but I did. So things take time. People have been acculturated into this system. I try to leave space for that.

FRESH "LEV" WHITE: On misgendering, I just want to offer that your pain is valid, and you deserve love and compassion from your friends. The people who can't be there for you, take a break from them. You can always go back.

JOAN BENOIT: To be a leader, you have to listen. And you have to listen to voices other than your own. Or listen to voices that are unlike your own. So you have to take different perspectives, and let people have their voice.

YOSEÑIO LEWIS: There are things that you have to offer. There are people waiting for you and your counsel and your love, your hug, your brand of femininity and your brand of masculinity. You were given that gift for a reason.

That's how I became at peace with my body. If I keep looking for perfection, I'm never going to get there. But if I accept this body, as it is, this body is a temple.

Not everybody fits in the cookie cutter, and not everybody needs to. There's room for everyone. You'll never know all the colors of the rainbow, because the shades are infinite. As soon as you move a little more to the yellow and a little more to the green, you have a new color. There's always a new color.

You are you. And the world needs you, because there's no one else like you. What you have to offer is what's going to bring us to the paradise we keep being told we're going to. So you have to stay with us, and you have to give us that gift. Not to the depletion of you, but enough so that we are infected with that joy, that passion. And then we go out and do for others.

TINA VALENTÍN AGUIRRE: It's scary to put yourself out there. And it's worth it. There are going to be times that are fucked up, and sad, and horrible, but there are also going to be so many times that are fabulous and grand. Beautiful. Worth it.

C. NJOUBE DUGAS: You got your whole life ahead of you. Have fun today, just for today. You don't have to worry about where you're going to be in ten years, da, da, da, da. Deal with what you got right now, today, and live it. Have fun. Follow it. Enjoy your life. This is your playground, believe it or not. Don't let society tell you it's something else. This is your play time.

Understand that people are going to tell you "no," and people are going to say negative things about you, but I want you to pretend that you're holding up a mirror and they're actually just saying it to themselves. They see a light in you, and they want to attack it. That's because you're having fun, you're free.

Stay free, stay free. You make your own reality. Do what your heart tells you to do, and you're going to be good.

Experience everything that you want that is good, that feels right to your spirit.

And whenever it feels good to your spirit, help people. Yes.

YOSEÑIO LEWIS: The journey is always going to be amazing and scary, and revealing. And the journey never ends. It doesn't end until you take your last breath. So there's always a chance to learn something new. There's always a chance to learn a new way to be in connection with someone. There's always another opportunity.

FRESH "LEV" WHITE: Expect the best from humans, and be prepared to hold yourself when they don't show up. Play with the Earth, touch the Earth, know that this planet is all here for you. It's here to help heal and grow you when you can't find anything else.

And maybe as importantly: each inhale tells you that you are worthy. Each inhale is life coming into you, saying that you are enough. No matter what is going on, you get to begin again every time, with every breath.

Know that that's part of what it means for the divine to live within you, and for you to become that.

JOAN BENOIT: To the younger generation: trust the universe. Trust it. Good things come out of everything. I really believe that. You just got to have patience and trust in yourself. Tread lightly and try to do no harm. And love the people around you as hard as you can. It's the best we can do.

MS BILLIE COOPER: I want to be remembered as an ancestor. I hope I live a hundred years. But those three little dots between your birth date and your death, that's our whole life right there, those three little dots. So much is encompassed in those dots. I just want to be remembered as a loving, caring soul, always a shining light to someone in distress, someone looking for shelter in a storm, because I had been there many, many times, and someone always guided me to the lighthouse.

Just think of me as an angel, you know, a guiding force.

KB BOYCE: No matter how terrifying something seems, if something in you says, "No, you need to be doing this," you've just got to do it.

Just go. Just go. Just keep going, no matter what. That's where I feel like the ancestors have been there for me—just going, "You know what, child?"

Do this thing.

You just do that.

We've got you.

You are going to be okay.

Just do it.

That's what has driven me.

I hope that folks, especially youth, can find the things that give them that bravery, that strength—like punk rock did for me—so that they can move forward and just say, "To hell with it. I need to do this."

Because we need the youth to do that.

We need you to be brave and, no matter what, just do it. Do it. And create that next wave for the ones who come after you.

SHARYN GRAYSON: You can be who you want to be, and you can be happy. Don't accept anything less. You are entitled to it, just like everybody else. Be you. Be you. And enjoy.

Understand this is such a precious gift—life. Live it. Live it in a way that you hope to leave something for the others who come behind you. That's it.

KB BOYCE: We are the dreams of our ancestors. Yeah.

* *

FIFTEEN

Visions for the Future

ADELA VÁZQUEZ: The future is bright if we want it to be.

STORMMIGUEL FLOREZ: I have hope. I feel like people are really pushing to uplift trans people. And also, to look at the ways that they're not being inclusive, who's in power and who's not in power. Which I'm so happy about.

TINA VALENTÍN AGUIRRE: Much of the world has actually caught up to me and us as people, and it's an amazing thing.

NICKY CALMA: We're everywhere.

JOAN BENOIT: All the right-wing stuff that's happening throughout the world—it's happening in a bunch of countries—I think that's their last hurrah. They're hanging onto that last little straw that they've got. They know they're going. They know they're a dying breed. That's why they're being as charged and as violent as they are.

ADELA VÁZQUEZ: Look at where we're at. You think the queers at large are going to allow people to come and oppress them again? No. No, child. There's going to be somebody who's going to say, "Fuck that. Fuck off. Get off my dress! I don't want you to oppress me."

It happened before, back in the seventies—we were pioneers in many ways. We learned how to fight AIDS, that was very important.

And we didn't know half of what we know now.

JOAN BENOIT: We're not going to go backwards. There's no putting it back in the closet. The closet's wide open now. The door's been removed from the hinges, there's no going back. None of us will stand for it. I think we're going to take it so much further than what we can even imagine. I think we can make the progress that I dream of.

We laid the foundation for a lot of this work. You can take the work that we did and move it forward, but you can't deny what happened during our lifetime, the gains we saw. From when I came out in high school in the early eighties, and was denied, and disowned, and treated like a second-class citizen, like I didn't even count for nothing, to where we are now as queer people.

Imagine what can happen in the next one hundred years.

BAMBY SALCEDO: We need to understand, too, that we shouldn't be complacent. We're not yet in the place in society where we should be. We should have economic power, political power. We should be elevated in a more significant way, in society. We haven't done that yet. So we have to keep doing it. We have to keep fighting. We have to keep demanding what is rightfully ours.

We have the divine intervention for us to exist. It's our right to be here. It's our right to navigate the world. It's our right to live dignified lives. But that's not going to happen if we just sit and do nothing about it. We need to be involved. We need to participate. We need to learn. We need to grow. And we need to act.

TINA VALENTÍN AGUIRRE: Politically, we have a lot of mobilization to do. Trans people are being targeted by laws on hyperlocal, then state, and then federal levels, and internationally. It's clear that we are used to raise money by conservatives. We are used as bogeypeople, scary figures, scary monsters.

SHARYN GRAYSON: You hear all the horror stories about, "I don't want my daughter in a bathroom with someone of trans experience." When it

comes to the trans community, we are some of the most giving people. We are not out to harm anybody. It is our nature because of the
oppression that a lot of us have suffered, the circumstances of being
separated from our families—all of those things make you more
emotionally accepting. So, this concept that trans and gender-
nonconforming people are these horrible creatures, that's not true. I
wish that more people would sit down and get to know us. Talk to us.
Just have a conversation.

TINA VALENTÍN AGUIRRE: Drag queens are now even being targeted,
drag queen story time, and I think, "Oh, how ridiculous is that?" In
the seventies, there used to be clowns who were hired for parties.
Essentially, it's the same thing. I know some drag queens may not
like that, but some will acknowledge that there is an aspect of it that's
entertaining. What's presented in drag queen story hour is not the
most subversive form of drag. And all I could think is, oh, you're
going to fight against that? You're fighting against joy. Let's do this,
then. Like, if you try to outlaw a woman's right to her own body, or a
person's reproductive rights, you're trying to outlaw joy.

The future needs to have many more trans, queer people of color
in leadership. So many of us have had to step up. And the future, I
think, will be better. It will come out of strife, though. I think what a
lot of the right does not understand is the more that you try to cod-
ify this, you try to erase us through law, the more that we're going to
realize, oh, then we need to be legislators. We need to be judges. We
need to be throughout society.

MS BILLIE COLLINS: Equality across the board. Housing, jobs, financial
stability, loving and caring families to trans people. To see more trans
people run for political office, to see a trans mayor or governor, to
see a transgender president, trans people held at a higher level in the
world. To see more trans parents, more trans children coming out to
their parents. To see trans people respected more.

NICKY CALMA: Like, if the president of the Walt Disney company is transgender—you know? That would be great.

I would love to see talented trans folks out there to take the lead, to take control of things, so they can contribute, make it better. That's my dream.

NELSON D'ALERTA PÉREZ: Transgender people still have problems: we're still getting killed, nobody supports us. It's still taboo. People look at you strangely, don't want to walk with you.

NICKY CALMA: Trans women are still impacted highest by HIV. Because of what we're experiencing around discrimination, violence, and just plain ignorance of people. There's still a lot of learning to do for other folks who do not understand.

ADELA VÁZQUEZ: What I don't understand, actually, about life in my time, is how come people are not free? I mean, if we understand all this stuff, how can we not stop war and shit like that? Colonialism, which is pretty much the root of all wars, is way out of fashion. It's like, please, get with the program! You know what I'm saying?

MS BILLIE COOPER: We as people, we have to dispel transphobic hate, transphobic language, transphobic speech, transphobic meanness. We have to be a more caring and compassionate community, to each and every person.

BAMBY SALCEDO: Things are not going to come to us. We need to go and get them. And it is up to this new generation to ensure that they get that, if that's what they really want.

DONNA PERSONNA: Keep working, keep working at it, and call it out when it isn't offered to you.

ANDRÉS OZZUNA: In Oakland, where I live, the future is here. The ideas that come forward here end up becoming globalized. Ideas about nonbinary and trans identities. Different concepts for a more integrated society in every sense. Here, we are in the Mecca of the future. And it keeps expanding, because now, with Instagram, what happens here today is, let's say, in Buenos Aires tomorrow.

Younger people have these new concepts that older adults maybe don't want to hear, or resist. But they're incredibly interesting, and it's important to listen, so we can overcome the homogenous ideas of society we had before.

The future is right here, with the young people. They've got the spark. It's good to listen to them.

TINA VALENTÍN AGUIRRE: The best possible future for us as queer and trans people—I think—is happening now. This is for us, and it's now. It's not the future. Fuck that. I've always, always pushed back against that, the idea that my time is in the future. No. My time has always been now.

And, in this context, I'm not alone. Not only am I not alone, there are younger people who are, like, "Ah, you're here. We've been looking for you. We needed your story. Let's have this conversation. Let's engage."

So, for me, the future is now. What is happening right now is new iterations of great art, and community, and coming together. We don't have everything that we need. We don't have all the spaces that we need. But we're making them. We're finding what we need. And part of that is also us building a resilience, to cultivate hope and love. I'm happy about where we're at right now.

NELSON D'ALERTA PÉREZ: A lot of freedom for people to be the way they are, for there to be liberation of that kind: that would be marvelous. It would be: wow. May it be so. I haven't lost faith. We've advanced so much. So very much. We have small setbacks, but we keep advancing. I'm inspired by what I see. I see: sí se puede—"it can be done."

There have been many changes. And there will be many more.

ADELA VÁZQUEZ: My biggest dream in life? Freedom. Freedom, to be free. Whatever you want to do with your life, it's your life. That's the only thing you have that is yours.

DONNA PERSONNA: We live in a capitalistic society. It's not your fault, it's not my fault, but it leads to never being satisfied. So me, personally, I found a way to be satisfied, and that's by giving what I have.

Take any opportunity to think outside of yourself, that's what I would invite you to do. I don't know if this is easy or possible, but in your lifetime, give more than you take. Check that out. Everybody I know is on the take, and you know what? It leaves me empty. I personally have found the ultimate joy in giving. So that's what I would say: in this life, give more than you take. Try that.

MS BILLIE COOPER: We have moved forward. We have made steps to move us forward, to be more in tune with the world. But we have so, so much that we still have to get right. There are still disparities; racism, transphobic issues, people treating us like crap. You know, we're still not accepted by everybody. Everybody will not be on the transgender bandwagon; I understand that. But treat us with respect. That goes a long way. Because you want to be treated with respect, too. So, you know, in order to get respect, you have to give it.

SHARYN GRAYSON: Some of the things that I hope for the future: acceptance and equity. Acceptance would encompass so much. And equity, I think that encompasses everything else.

I hope that the younger population begins to understand the importance in being visible, in being educated, and not only in school, but educated to life, which includes politics, economics, all of that. I hope that we have a smarter trans community, a smarter trans generation. People who can think outside the box, and who are not afraid to speak out.

MS BILLIE COOPER: I just hope one day the world will be more trans sympathetic.

JOAN BENOIT: God, having no fear would be the ideal. This is why I'm in Oakland, why I live where I live. I leave this bubble and there is genuine fear out there. Especially in this political climate. In a way that wasn't there before Trump. Before, if somebody was like, glaring at you at an airport, you could look at them, and they would look away. They don't look away anymore. They're not embarrassed by their feelings. They are emboldened to act on them. And it's terrifying.

You shouldn't have to fear for who you are and how you present. People are just people and they should be taken for what they do, what they give to community, not what they look like.

C. NJOUBE DUGAS: Be you no matter what. Walk through the fear. You got to walk through the fear. Understand what fear feels like in your body. Don't let fear rule you, don't let it guide you, don't let it stop you.

ANDRÉS OZZUNA: I hope people can be themselves, in the way they want to be.

JOAN BENOIT: That we take people as people. That's what I want for everybody. That's what makes a community. We're taking what people have to offer, and not shitting on them because they look a certain way.

We all are entitled to the same things. We're all entitled to love, we're all entitled to housing, and water, and food. All of those things that keep us alive. That's our entitlement. It's not an ask. It's required and it should be given to everybody. So yes, I think things are changing in that way. I think we're going back to the old ways. I mean, look at the way Indigenous people are held up and prioritized now. And it's not just our caretaking of the Earth. I think it's the caretaking of our communities, and ourselves, and holding everybody accountable. Holding everybody as sacred.

FRESH "LEV" WHITE: I believe that trans people, and particularly trans youth, are bringing us closer to our human experience. The last I looked, there were 263 pronouns. People, we're just trying to find ourselves, trying to get to that place where we get to say and know who we are.

And I believe that, one day, those will all disappear, that it'll just be the name that you want to be called, or the gender that you want to be called. And we're just accepting. We're accepting of this gift that was given. Trans people have been here since the beginning of time. It's part of creation.

YOSEÑIO LEWIS: There's a variety of ways we can all work toward ending racism and transphobia. There's always a multi-pronged approach. There are different ways to address an issue. Your way is not the only way, but it is a way. We can all cause change, even if we only focus on a sliver of what needs to be done.

NICKY CALMA: I think it's going to be a continuous process. I do like the direction of how things are going. I think we all just have to work together. My hopes are always going to be positive, for the good of everybody, for the good of things.

FRESH "LEV" WHITE: There are more people in this world, I think, that want to be loving, caring, be free, be safe, and to have that for others, than there are not. Otherwise, we wouldn't be here. A hundred, two hundred, three hundred years ago, it was an ugly scene in most places. We've gotten here because people have envisioned something else for us. They have envisioned something else for the world, and we are part of that vision.

It's our responsibility to envision what we want to see, the world that we want to see. That we can all do our internal healing, look at our suffering, do the work to begin healing it. And at the same time, spending time looking at what we love, and what we want more of, right? The garden grows by looking at it, right? So, this flower looks great, what flower would look good next to that flower? What's the world that we want to live in? What do we want to create? How do we want to do that? Who could we call on to help? And whom can we help in the process?

KB BOYCE: I envision a future where trans people, or people of color, all of us can just feel supported in being ourselves. I like to think that I'm seeing positive forward momentum. What I see for the future is more strength, and more freedom to be who it is that you are on this planet to be, with the support that we need to be happy, functioning human beings.

I dream of a world where gender is not this huge thing. Like, why can't we all just be human beings? All of my life, I have simply wanted to be myself. That's all I ever asked for. And I'm hoping that in the future, that is what's going to happen.

It's slow. It's slow going. But here we are, watching this ride, watching it unfold. You can either just sit there and let it go by, or you can jump in and go, "Wow, this is amazing!"

BAMBY SALCEDO: My hope is that you understand that you do have power, and not just individual power, but also collective power. We need to be able to exercise our power. We need to be able to change the structures that have marginalized us for many, many years.

I believe that it could happen. Even if I don't get to see that, I believe that it will happen. My hope is what keeps me alive.

YOSEÑIO LEWIS: People just want to be acknowledged. They want to feel safe, and they want to feel like they're part of something.

FRESH "LEV" WHITE: That's the vision: human liberation.

JOAN BENOIT: Safety for everyone.

C. NJOUBE DUGAS: Just freaking stay free.

TINA VALENTÍN AGUIRRE: Fuck shit up. Fuck shit up! Do something that fucks everything up, and then, make something grand.

DONNA PERSONNA: Do magnificent things.

TINA VALENTÍN AGUIRRE: I think we have an obligation—I have an obligation—to put something that's wondrous into the world. It doesn't matter that it's short term. I need to be a part of bringing this magic alive.
    So can you.

NELSON D'ALERTA PÉREZ: There is space for everybody in this world. Fight for it. It's right there. All you have to do is claim it.

ABOUT THE NARRATORS

* * * * * * * * * * * * * * * * * *

ADELA VÁZQUEZ was a longtime transgender rights activist and drag performer. Born in Camagüey, Cuba, she came to the United States in 1980 as part of the Marial Boatlift, also known as the Marielitos, and lived in Los Angeles, Tennessee, and other places before settling in San Francisco. There, she became part of the queer community, began performing in drag, and was crowned Miss Gay Latina in 1992. At that time, she began working at Proyecto ContraSIDA por Vida, a groundbreaking organization serving the Latino community around AIDS, providing outreach and lifesaving community education to her fellow trans Latinas. Vázquez's life and contributions have been documented in films, scholarly texts, and a graphic novel. She also provided extensive mentorship as a mother, taking generations of younger queer people under her wing over the years. Adela passed away unexpectedly on October 11, 2024, in the loving arms of fellow narrator Nelson D'Alerta Pérez.

ANDRÉS OZZUNA is a trans Latinx immigrant business owner, baker, and tango dancer. He grew up in a working-class family in the outskirts of Buenos Aires, Argentina, and migrated to the San Francisco Bay Area at the age of twenty-eight, without speaking the language and in search of a place where he could live freely as a queer person. Ozzuna is the founder and owner of Wooden Table Baking Company, a thriving

business making alfajores—traditional Argentinean cookies—along with other pastries and confections. He is also a respected, cherished figure, teacher, and community builder in the Bay Area queer tango scene, where he has found himself able to experience self-expression, healing, affirmation, and a connection to his cultural roots.

BAMBY SALCEDO is a transgender icon and community leader, who founded and currently leads the TransLatina Coalition. She was born in Guadalajara, Mexico, and arrived in the US at the age of sixteen. Ms. Salcedo overcame many years of poverty, sex work, abuse, drug use, and incarceration to ultimately find community with trans women and to become a core leader of the movement for justice for transwomen in general, and for trans Latina immigrant women in particular. She has been featured in the documentary *TransVisible: Bamby Salcedo's Story*, and the HBO documentary

The Trans List, and has received the James Earl Hardy Legends Award, Lambda Legal's West Coast Liberty Award, the City of West Hollywood's Women in Leadership Award, and numerous other honors.

C. NJOUBE DUGAS is a nonbinary Black activist and community presence. They work as a financial coach and trainer with a focus on empowering entrepreneurs in Black communities and other communities of color. Born and raised in San Francisco, they witnessed various eras of queer culture in both their birth city and in Sacramento, California, where they lived for ten years.

CHINO SCOTT-CHUNG is a trans man of Chinese and Mexican origins who has been deeply engaged in API queer communities since his arrival in the San Francisco Bay Area in 1986. Assigned female at birth, he was born and raised in Denver, Colorado, and went from high school to the Army, where he came out as a lesbian. Among other things, Scott-Chung was deeply involved with the founding and community work of APLN, the Asian Pacific Lesbian Network; was part of a vanguard of Asian transmasculine people transitioning from the early 1990s on; has raised a daughter as a trans parent; and, after the tragic death by suicide of his best friend Christopher Lee, honored his memory by transforming California State law to honor trans people's true genders on their death certificates.

CRYSTAL MASON is a Black gender-queer activist, artist, coach, and community leader. Born and raised in Richmond, Virginia, they arrived in the San Francisco Bay Area in 1989. Their activism has included organizing with Act Up, founding and running the groundbreaking Luna Sea Women's Performance Space, and cofounding the organization Queering Dreams, where they currently work.

DONNA PERSONNA is an activist, artist, drag performer, and community leader. Raised in San Jose, California, in a Mexican American family, Personna migrated to San Francisco as a young person and took part in various communities from the mid 1960s onward, including the gay, transgender, and hippie communities. She spent a great of deal of time at Compton's Cafeteria, the transgender haven in the Tenderloin District that became the site of the first recorded LGBTQ+ rights riot in the US. Since becoming a drag performer and starting to live openly as a woman at the age of fifty-eight, Personna has become a tireless speaker and advocate for transgender rights, serving on the boards of the Trans March and the Trans Day of Remembrance, and as Grand Marshall of the San Francisco Pride Parade. She is the subject of the feature documentary *Donna*.

FRESH "LEV" White (he/they/love) is a love and compassion activist, coach, diversity trainer, and mindfulness and meditation teacher. As a Black transgender man, he has led extensive workshops for those who wish to be allies to trans and LGBTQ+ people. He was also a groundbreaking drag king, performing as early as the mid 1980s, through the late 1990s, including under the name Barry White. As a community leader, White has been and continues to be a tireless voice for compassion, racial and gender justice, and many forms of liberation.

JOAN BENOIT is a Native woman who embraces indigiqueer, two-spirit, butch, and lesbian identities. A long-time activist, she has worked with various organizations, including the Native American AIDS Project (NAAP), and has been the recipient of a Circle of Honor Award, which recognizes the lifetime achievements of American Indians who have enriched the lives of others. She has also served as a Grand Marshall of the 2008 San Francisco Pride Parade. Born and raised in Michigan, Benoit has made her home for decades in Oakland, California, where she lives with her wife and their seven-year-old son.

KB BOYCE is a Black transmasculine musician, artist, and activist whose career spans four decades and many genres. Born and raised in Brooklyn, NY, raised in a matriarchal Black nationalist household, they became a member of the groundbreaking punk band Nasty Facts in 1978, at the age of fifteen. Since then, they have recorded and performed in a range of genres, including becoming the Drag King of the Blues in the persona of King TuffNStuff. They have also worked as a sound engineer, including in post-production for the film *Vulveeta*. They are the cofounder of Queer Rebels, a people-of-color arts company that connects generations and supports visionary arts for the future.

LANDA LAKES, aka Miko Thomas, is a prominent and celebrated drag performer, two-spirit community leader, and activist for queer, trans, and Indigenous rights. A person of Chickasaw heritage raised on Indian land in Oklahoma, they connected with the femininity in their gender from an early age, and were involved in campus activism at Oklahoma University with the GLA (Gay and Lesbian Alliance).

Once in San Francisco, they became involved with Bay Area American Indian Two Spirits (BAAITS), and cofounded the first ever two-spirit Pow Wows, which have grown to an attendance in the thousands. They also founded the first known all-Native drag group, the Brush Arbor Gurlz. In their drag persona of Landa Lakes, they have created a vast range of performances, often embodying political content, and have served as inspiration for younger generations of Indigenous and BIPOC drag artists.

MS BILLIE COOPER is a Black trans woman, as well as a civil rights activist, advocate, and community leader. She was born in Philadelphia, and grew up navigating her gender as a person assigned male at birth in a working-class Black community. She then served in the US military before migrating to the San Francisco Bay Area. Cooper has spent four decades living and working in San Francisco's Tenderloin District, and was diagnosed with HIV in 1985. Years later she would found a program at the San Francisco AIDS foundation called TransLife, as part of ensuring services for trans populations. In 2022, Ms. Billie Cooper ran for office in San Francisco, in a bid to become the first Black trans woman to serve as a District Supervisor in that historically LGBTQ+ city.

NELSON D'ALERTA PÉREZ is a longtime drag performer, artist, cosmetologist, and transgender woman living in San Francisco, California. She has also been known widely in both Cuba and the US by her drag name, Catherine White. She was born in Isla de Pinos, Cuba. At the age of eighteen, she left home for Havana, where she created an underground drag

cabaret in defiance of the laws against private businesses, cross-dressing, and homosexuality. In that cabaret, she performed as Catherine White to packed houses, gaining significant fame within the unsanctioned gay community. She was frequently arrested and at one point tortured for this work. She left for the United States in 1980 and arrived in San Francisco soon thereafter, where she became involved with queer and trans communities, continued to perform in drag shows, pursued a career in cosmetology, and wove an enduring chosen family.

NICKY CALMA, also known as Tita Aida, is a longtime AIDS/HIV awareness activist, and advocate for trans rights as well as Asian transgender rights in particular. Born in the Philippines in 1967, she was assigned male at birth and raised in a Catholic family. She left for the United States in 1989, and became involved with the LGBTQ+ community in San Francisco, where she became an activist in the movement around AIDS, working with Asian AIDS Project and developing the onstage persona of Tita Aida, who entertained while offering health and sex education in queer Asian spaces. A tireless and widely beloved community leader and icon, Calma is currently Managing Director at San Francisco Community Health Center.

SHARYN GRAYSON is a Black transgender woman, and a longtime tireless activist for transgender rights. Born in 1949 in Dallas, Texas, she migrated first to Los Angeles, and then to the San Francisco Bay Area. She transitioned and began living as a woman at the start of the 1970s, and has spent many decades as a tireless advocate and activist for trans rights. At the height of the AIDS crisis, she was deeply engaged in the movement to save and protect Black trans women's lives. In recent years, she briefly moved to Little Rock, Arkansas, then returned to the Bay Area. She is currently the executive director of the TGI Justice Project, which supports trans, gender-variant, and intersex people both inside and outside of prisons in the journey toward survival and freedom.

STORMMIGUEL FLOREZ is a Mexican American trans man as well as a musician, performer, and documentary filmmaker. Born in 1970, he was raised in Albuquerque, New Mexico, where he witnessed and participated in gay and queer communities in the eighties and nineties before migrating to the San Francisco Bay Area and forming part of that region's vibrant queer culture. StormMiguel came out as a trans man in the early 2000s after living as butch for many years, and was a trailblazer in the documentation of his transition and in the fomenting of transmasculine culture and creative expression.

TINA VALENTÍN AGUIRRE is a Chicanx genderqueer and trans artist, activist, and cherished leader in San Francisco. In the eighties and nineties, they played key roles in the groundbreaking queer Latinx organizing work of Community United in Responding to AIDS/SIDA

(CURAS) and Proyecto ContraSIDA por Vida. They have served as chair of the board of the GLBT Historical Society, and are currently district manager for the Castro LGBTQ Cultural District. They have also worked on many creative projects, including the documentary *¡Viva 16!*, which documents the LGBTQ+ Latinx community of 16th Street, in the Mission District of San Francisco, and the opera *Juana*, based on the life of Sor Juana Inés de la Cruz.

TUPILI LEA ARELLANO is an indigenous Chicanx elder on the trans spectrum, a two-spirit person, and self-identified butch dyke. They are a longtime artist, community weaver, social justice activist, and practitioner of sacred medicine work. They grew up in Silver City, New Mexico, and Tucson, Arizona, then migrated to Oakland, California, in 1981 and became a core member of the San Francisco Bay Area's rich lesbian-of-color communities. Their art includes the publication of poetry chapbooks, painting, and performances as La Chola Priest, a persona in which they delivered sermons on the sacred goodness of queer people onstage or passing as a cis male priest in public spaces. Now, in retirement, Arellano has relocated back to their hometown of Tucson, where they continue to advocate for racial, gender, and economic justice in their daily life.

VIVIAN VARELA is a nonbinary, two-spirit, lesbian elder of Mexican American origins living in Garden Grove, California. Assigned female at birth, he uses the pronouns *she/her* and *he/him*. Varela spent his early years as a missionary with a group called Christians in Action and grappling with the reality of his gender and queer desires, before coming out at the age of twenty-six. After this, she moved to the San Francisco Bay Area and became involved with the lesbian of color communities there. Varela identified as a lesbian and as masculine for most of her life, and embraced the identities of nonbinary and two-spirit at the age of sixty-five.

YOSEÑO LEWIS is a longtime activist, educator, writer, and advocate for queer and trans rights. Born in Rhode Island in 1959, he grew up in a Black Panamanian immigrant family in an environment where there were few Central American or Black Latinx folks, and learned early on to negotiate the gaps between personal identity and the projections of others. He became an activist at the age of thirteen, and migrated to California after high school, first to San Diego and later to the San Francisco Bay Area, where he participated in movements for queer and trans rights, racial justice, and sex justice. He has served on the National Advisory Board for the Center of Excellence for Transgender Health, on the boards of Unid@s and the National LGBTQ Task Force, and has been featured in documentaries including *Transgender Revolution* (1998) and *Diagnosing Difference* (2009).

RESOURCES

✳ ✳ ✳ ✳ ✳ ✳ ✳ ✳ ✳

THE TREVOR PROJECT

Resources, community, crisis intervention, and lifeline support for LGBTQ+ youth: 24/7 Lifeline: 866-4-U-TREVOR ([866] 488-7386).

There is also text-based support, peer support in online spaces, and more online: thetrevorproject.org.

TRANS LIFELINE

A grassroots hotline offering direct emotional and financial support to trans people in crisis—for the trans community, by the trans community: (877) 565-8860. Their web site is www.translifeline.org.

GLAAD RESOURCE PAGES

GLAAD maintains a continuously updated list of trans organizations serving specific communities, as well as links to further resources and information: glaad.org/transgender/resources. GLAAD's list of LGBTQ+ resources is at www.glaad.org/resourcelist.

FULL ORAL HISTORY ARCHIVES FOR *I SEE MY LIGHT SHINING*

The interviews featured in this book form part of the Baldwin-Emerson Elders Project *I See My Light Shining*, which captures and celebrates the untold stories of BIPOC elders who have witnessed and shaped monumental change in American public life. The full audio recordings, as well as accompanying historical photographs, are housed at the Center for Oral History at Columbia University, and are available to the public online.

To listen to full audio interviews with this book's narrators, and to explore their photographic archives, please visit www.eldersproject.incite. columbia.edu/collections/caro-de-robertis.

ACKNOWLEDGMENTS

✳ ✳ ✳ ✳ ✳ ✳ ✳ ✳ ✳ ✳ ✳ ✳ ✳ ✳ ✳ ✳

EVERY PUBLISHED BOOK is carried—lifted—by many hands.

I am supremely grateful:

To Michelle Brower, agent extraordinaire, for her talent, vision, and tireless belief in the work. And to Allison Malecha, Elizabeth Pratt, Natalie Edwards, and the rest of the team at Trellis Literary Management, for their essential contributions to this and so many books.

To Madeline Jones, incomparable editor, for helping shape this book into a stronger version of itself, for saying "Yes" to the adventure, and for supporting these trans- and gender-nonconforming BIPOC voices in the most nuanced, beautiful way. I'm also deeply grateful to the whole team at Algonquin, including Jovanna Brinck, Sally Kim, Michael Barrs, Marisol Salaman, Christopher Moisan, Brenna Franzitta, Brunson Hoole, Steve Godwin, Michael McKenzie, Nadxieli Nieto, and Betsy Gleick. Thank you all for helping create, and create space for, this book.

To Jacqueline Woodson, for the visionary *I See My Light Shining* oral history project that launched this journey, for inviting me to become a Baldwin-Emerson Fellow, and for being at once both an intellectual giant and a constant champion of literary inclusion and transformation. You are a light and inspiration; thank you. My thanks as well to the Center for Oral History Research at Columbia University, for the excellent oral history training, and for housing these voices in their online archive; to Baldwin for the Arts and the Emerson Collective for their generous collaboration with this project; and to my fellow fellows for their company along the way.

To the friends, writers, and beloved chosen familia who supported me in myriad ways while I was researching and writing this book—thank you. It means everything. Gratitude in particular to Lars Horn, Jaquira Díaz, Angie Cruz, Aya de Leon, Achy Obejas, Cristina García, Tijanna O. Eaton, Chip Livingston, Julián Delgado Lopera, Ceci De Robertis, Alex Cohen, Margaret Benson Thompson, Tasha Wilson, and Shanna Lo Presti. To my students and colleagues at San Francisco State University, where I teach: thank you for the literary community, and the many enriching conversations. And, of course, to my children, Rafael and Luciana: you are my heart and spark; you teach me every day; you fuel me to keep working toward a better future for everyone. Los adoro, siempre.

To the narrators of this book: thank you for taking this journey with me, and for so generously sharing your voices with the world. I could not be more honored and grateful to be allowed to witness and gather your stories. And a particularly deep bow to the one and only Adela Vázquez, who passed away unexpectedly on October 11, 2024, in the loving arms of Nelson D'Alerta Pérez, her housemate, chosen family sister, and fellow narrator. Adela, you are grieved, and missed; your voice, and the iconic life you lived, will be with us always.

To all trans, nonbinary, genderqueer, and two-spirit people of color—past, present, and future—this book is intended as a tribute to you, each of you. I salute and thank you.

And to trans, nonbinary, genderqueer, and two-spirit youth: I hope you can feel the love and joyful embrace that's here for you, in these pages. Thank you for being here and for being your whole self. This book is yours, as is the world.